Corsairs

of Malta and Barbary

Corsairs

of Malta and Barbary

PETER EARLE

SIDGWICK & JACKSON

LONDON

961.02
Ea 75c
70-3534

SBN 283 98093 1

Made and printed in Great Britain by
The Garden City Press Limited
Letchworth, Hertfordshire

for Sidgwick and Jackson Limited
1 Tavistock Chambers, Bloomsbury Way
London, W.C.1

ACKNOWLEDGEMENTS

Most of the section on the Maltese corsairs is based on original research in Malta and I would like to thank all those who have made my work there so pleasant; in particular Avv. S. R. Borg Cardona without whose very generous assistance and vast knowledge of the corsairs I could never have found out what I did in the time available; Father Michael Psadni, Dr Mario Borg Olivier and Mr Godfrey Wettinger, my fellow researchers in Malta's splendid and still largely unexplored archives; Mr Joseph Galea of the Royal Malta Library; Notary Victor Miller of the Notarial Archives; Mr John Bonnici of the Archives of the Superior Courts of Justice, and Father John Azzopardi of the Archives of the Maltese Inquisitor.

My greatest debt in the rest of the book is clearly to my colleague, John Gillingham, who translated for me the story of the Gaoler-Captain (chapter 12).

I would like to thank Messrs. Jonathan Cape for permission to quote at length from *The Life of Captain Alonso de Contreras* in Chapter 10; the Trustees of the British Museum for permission to reproduce the illustrations on pp. 25, 29, 33, 51, 57, 77, 83, 103, 113, 139, 163, 203 and 205; the Trustees and Director of the National Maritime Museum, Greenwich for permission to reproduce the illustrations on pp. 65, 151, 155, 161, 215, 225 241 247, and 255; the Curator of the National Museum, Malta for permission to reproduce the illustrations on pp. 143 and 147; and the Librarian of the Royal Malta Library for permission to reproduce the illustration on p. 135.

PETER EARLE

CONTENTS

Part Four: FIVE CORSAIRS

Part Five: EPILOGUE

LIST OF ILLUSTRATIONS

PREFACE

This book is a comparative study of the two parts of a very strange institution which flourished in the Mediterranean for several centuries. One part, the Barbary corsairs, is quite well known to both the historian and the general reader. These were Moslem corsairs who, from their bases in North Africa, made a living by raiding the ships and the coastline of Christian Europe. They sold the ships and cargoes that they captured in their home ports, and enslaved their prisoners. Pious horror has been expressed by generations of Christian writers at the long-continued existence of these raiders. What very few writers have said is that the Barbary corsairs were exactly paralleled by a similar Christian institution. Operating from their bases in Malta and Italy the Christian corsairs raided the ships and coastline of the Moslem Mediterranean, and they too sold their captives into slavery. Both Moslem and Christian corsairs treated their profession as a business, a business which they organized very efficiently.

Drawing on an abundance of original material and contemporary accounts this book sets out to describe and analyse in detail the organization and methods of operation of the corsairs. Much attention is also paid to the ways in which the corsairs disposed of their booty, to the life of the slaves and the means by which some of the latter eventually returned to their homes.

The book is divided into five parts. The first part is an introduction intended to set the scene for the more detailed description of the corsairs which follows. Part Two discusses the Barbary corsairs, and Part Three the Maltese corsairs. In Part Four attention is focused on the particular rather than the general, and an account is given of the activities of five rather different corsairs. Finally, in the last part, a brief description of the last years of the corsairs is given.

PART ONE

Introduction

CHAPTER 1

The Holy War in the Mediterranean

'Captain,' said the Agha, wiping his moustache, 'if our Mahomet
and your Christ had drunk raki and clinked glasses like us two,
they'd have become friends, and they wouldn't be spoiling to
scratch each other's eyes out . . . Through not drinking, they've
rolled the world in blood.'

NIKOS KAZANTZAKIS, *Christ Recrucified*

By the period in which this book is set, Mahomet and Christ
had been scratching each other's eyes out for a millennium.
After so long a struggle there were signs that their followers
were weary; cynicism and greed had replaced religious
enthusiasm as the basis of much of their antagonism, but there
was still little evidence that the bottle had superseded the sword
as the normal means of communication between the adherents
of the two religions. In this book we shall be looking at yet
another episode in the Holy War, in that eternal war between
the followers of these two Faiths. In this period the war is not
the large-scale war which forms the normal subject-matter of
history books. The participants in any one action are numbered
in hundreds, not thousands. There are few great generals and
few great events. The war is fought almost entirely at sea or
within a few miles of the coast. It is the war of the corsairs.

Unlike normal wars the war of the corsairs had neither
beginning nor end. It was an *eternal* war. Every year in the
seventeenth and eighteenth centuries both Christians and

3

Moslems set sail to fight the war, and no one ever thought of peace. When the war of the corsairs did eventually stop, it was outsiders who stopped it, not the corsairs. For centuries the normal occupation of thousands of men in the Mediterranean was to set sail from their home ports in order to attack the shipping or the coastal regions of the area. Their victims were slaughtered or sold into slavery, their goods plundered and sold as prizes. The definition of the corsairs' enemies was that they worshipped a different God. Ships trading in the Mediterranean and the population of the coastal littoral never knew peace. No ship's captain setting off on a peaceful commercial voyage ever knew whether he would reach his destination. Any voyage might end with his ship captured, his cargo plundered, and he himself, his passengers, and his crew sold into slavery. No villager going to bed at night could be sure to wake up a free man the next morning. A writer could warn travellers not to walk on the sea-shore, lest they be picked up by a frigate and given 'a slavish breakfast'.[1] For the corsairs were just as ready to plunder ashore as they were to plunder ships at sea. The Mediterranean tried to defend itself against the corsairs. Towers were built to watch for their arrival, so that villagers could flee to safety. Merchant ships were armed and sailed in convoy. Travellers' tempers grew short at 'the almost daily whistle which gave the order to clear the ship for action, when the passengers had to muster in the waist or on the deck with their muskets and bandoliers'.[2] Ships travelled without lights at night and wore black sails. But the corsairs still made prizes. Eventually much of the Mediterranean littoral was abandoned as a result of the threat from the sea, but trade had to go on. Without it the civilization of the Mediterranean would have come to an end.

Who were these corsairs? A corsair (or privateer) is a private individual granted a licence by his sovereign to fit out a ship to attack his sovereign's enemies. The prizes which he takes, if judged lawful by the courts of his country, are his to dispose of as he sees fit, subject normally to a share being paid to his sovereign. Legally, therefore, privateering was clearly distinguished from piracy by the fact that the privateer (or corsair) had a licence to attack specified ships or people. But normally the corsair's licence was good only in war time. In the Mediterranean, however, human ingenuity had solved the problem of such arbitrary interruption of what was a very profitable business. For while political wars, though common-place, were intermittent, there was one war that was eternal. And that was the Holy War.

Originally the Holy War had been a war on the grand scale. Islam had set out to conquer Christendom, and Christendom had fought back. The massive conquests of the Arabs had been countered by the Crusades and the Reconquista in Spain. In the fifteenth and sixteenth centuries a new impetus had been given to Moslem expansion by the conquests of the Ottoman Turks. But by the end of the sixteenth century the Holy War in the Mediterranean had reached a position of stalemate. After centuries of Jihad and Crusade, of Moslem conquest and Christian reconquest, the lands around the sea were now fairly evenly divided between the two religions. With insigni-ficant exceptions the whole of North Africa and the Middle East was Moslem. The remainder of the eastern Mediterranean, which had been overrun by the Ottoman Turks, was split between the two religions. Much of Anatolia had been settled by the advancing Turks and was Moslem, but there were large Greek Christian minorities. Most of mainland Greece and the archipelago was Christian, with some Turkish minorities in the north and in the towns and ports. The most confused area was modern Yugoslavia and Albania where Turkish settlers and Christian communities which had apostasized in the fifteenth century lived side by side with Christians.

But the great period of Turkish expansion into Europe was over by the end of the sixteenth century. On land the failure of the siege of Vienna in 1529, on sea the failure of the siege of Malta in 1565 and the defeat of the Turkish fleet at the battle of Lepanto in 1571 marked the limits of the Turkish threat. The Turks were successful in various mopping-up operations after this date, but their one attempt at a real invasion of Europe was a disaster. The victory of the Polish King, John Sobieski, outside Vienna in 1683 was a turning-point in history. As Kara Mustafa's defeated army fled back down the Great Hungarian Plain, the tide of Islam was turned for ever, and that process which was to make Turkey the 'sick man of Europe' in the nineteenth century had begun. But the process was slow, and apart from the short-term conquest of southern Greece by the Venetians in the war that followed the raising of the Siege of Vienna, the Turks did not lose any territory in the Mediterranean until the end of the eighteenth century. Southern Greece was soon reconquered, and despite the loss of frontier provinces to the Austrians and Russians, the Turks remained one of the great powers in European politics.

The end of Ottoman expansion was not however paralleled by the development of mutual tolerance and understanding between the Christian and Moslem parts of the Mediterranean. The two worlds, though connected by trade, remained apart. The Turk as the nearest representative of Islam and as the invader of Europe remained a monster in European literature and folklore.* The very word 'Turk' in English was an epithet meaning barbarous, savage and cruel – qualities which had for centuries been attributed to the Turks. Ridiculous distortions of the Moslem religion and Turkish culture were normal in any description of the Levant or North Africa. Nor was Moslem knowledge of Christendom much better. The fact that it was Islam which had advanced, Islam which made converts, and Islam who ruled Christian minorities probably meant that Moslem knowledge of the realities of Christianity, at least Orthodox Christianity, was better than Christian knowledge of Islam. But Moslem knowledge of the Land of the Franks, western Europe, must have been very limited. For there was no stream of Moslem travellers, seamen, and merchants going to western Europe to match the flow from western Europe to Islam. In the early sixteenth century it had looked as though the Turks might emulate that commercial conquest of the Mediterranean that had followed the Arab invasions of the seventh and eighth centuries.[3] But it was not to be. Slowly, but inexorably, the Christians conquered the major

---

* An example of the almost automatic acceptance of mutual dislike between Christian and Turk can be found in, of all places, a mathematical textbook. The French mathematician, Bachet, in his textbook *Problèmes*, published in Lyons in 1624, uses the following example as one of his problems:

A ship, carrying as passengers fifteen Turks and fifteen Christians, encountered a storm. The pilot declared that, in order to save the ship and crew, one-half of the passengers must be thrown into the sea. To choose the victims the passengers were arranged in a circle and it was agreed that every ninth man should be cast overboard, reckoning from a certain point. It is desired to find an arrangement by which all the Christians should be saved![4]

trade-routes, and by the late seventeenth century practically all trade between Islam and Christendom was carried in Christian ships, even though this might well be on behalf of Moslem merchants. On the longer routes the Christians tended more and more to be the citizens of the powerful states of western Europe, England, France, and Holland. Even on the shorter routes these newcomers were cutting into the preserves of the old maritime powers of the Mediterranean such as the Italians and the Catalans. The only routes on which Moslem ships carried Moslem goods were those linking ports within Islam, and even here the competition was growing as English and French shipping combined coastwise shipping with trade to Marseilles or out of the Mediterranean, and as the Greeks became more and more formidable competitors in the coastal trade of the Levant. And so not many Moslems visited western Europe, except as slaves, though many of their Jewish, Armenian, and Greek subjects did.

While the end of Ottoman expansion did not lead to greater understanding, neither did it lead to the end of the Holy War. During the long struggle between Moslem and Christian in the Middle Ages and the sixteenth century, privateers had been licensed to attack the enemies of their Faith, just as Englishmen had been licensed to attack Frenchmen during the Anglo-French Wars. But since the participants in the Holy War rarely made peace with each other, since in fact the war was eternal, privateers could continue to be licensed even though large-scale war between Christians and Moslems was only occasional. Such licences were to continue the existence of the Holy War right down to the seizure of Algiers by the French in 1830. Only then did continuous privateering cease in the Mediterranean, and only then was it possible for commercial shipping to go about its business in peace.

The most celebrated exponents of this latter-day Holy War are the Barbary corsairs. The word 'Barbary' in this instance poses a problem of definition since pirates and corsairs from both the Atlantic and Mediterranean coasts of North Africa are described as 'Barbary' in western European sources. In this book, however, the term Barbary corsairs will be used to describe only those corsairs who operated from the three Turkish North African regencies of Tunis, Tripoli, and Algiers.

The Barbary corsairs were ships fitted out by the rulers or private individuals in these regencies to attack Christian shipping. During the sixteenth century Barbary corsairs attacked and captured Christian shipping indiscriminately. By the same token they were considered as enemies by all Christian powers. In the seventeenth century, however, the position changed. By 1629 the English prize courts were debating whether Turkish and Algerine ships should be treated as pirates or as public ships of a sovereign power.[5] In the second half of the century England, France, and Holland all sent punitive expeditions against the regencies. The result was that the Barbary corsairs entered into treaty relationships with the western European naval powers, agreeing not to attack their shipping in return for presents or the payment of tribute. Although such agreements were often broken by both sides, they meant that in the eighteenth century there was a considerable limitation of the potential victims of the Barbary corsairs. Ships from Algiers, Tunis, and Tripoli were not the only Moslem ships to be licensed to attack Christian shipping. Ships from the ports of the Empire of Morocco and also from the Ottoman ports in the Adriatic were added to the numbers of the Moslem predators, but for the Mediterranean itself, as opposed to the Atlantic, the Barbary corsairs were by far the most important.

The Barbary corsairs are an institution well known to the western European. Indeed they form part of his folklore. Just as the myth of the barbarous Turk exists, so does the inherited fear of the Barbary corsair, of wild-looking men with turbans and long knives who may appear out of the mist and drag innocent families away to a lifetime of slavery. Such fears have firm foundations. Corsairs from Barbary and Morocco did in fact raid the whole of the west European coast. What is intriguing, however, is that while Moslem corsairs are well known, and their brutality forms part of the legend of Turkish cruelty, the fact that they had exact Christian counterparts is known by few, even in Malta itself, the very headquarters of the Christian corsairs. And yet not only were Christians licensed year after year to attack Moslems, just as Moslems attacked Christians, but in the long run the Christians were the more successful of the two. From the general silence on this subject one might assume that Christian Europe has had a collective feeling of guilt about the activity of its corsairs for some two hundred years.

Not all Christian powers licensed corsairs to prey on Moslem shipping. For some who had strong political or commercial relations with Moslem powers, this would have made little sense. The French, English, and Dutch, for instance, with their colonies of merchants in the Levant would have been running a very strong risk of reprisals if they had been known to license corsairs to attack Moslems. Nor did the Venetians license corsairs except when the Venetian State was engaged in full-scale war with the Turks. But many of the other potentates of the Mediterranean were almost always at war with the Ottomans and with Barbary and continued to issue privateering licences for most of this period. Such were the King of Spain, the King of Sardinia, the Grand-Duke of Tuscany, the King of Spain's Viceroy in Sicily and the Prince of Monaco, but throughout the period the most regular issuer of licences for the corsair business was the Grand Master of the Order of the Knights of St John in Malta. So much did Malta dominate the Christian corsairs that the generic term for these in the Levant, wherever they originated from, was 'the Maltese corsairs'.

How were these corsairs organized and what did they do? Most of the rest of this book will be discussing the organization and methods of operation of the corsairs but the similarities in organization between Moslem and Christian corsairs were so great that it will be useful to make a few introductory points at this stage. Both in Malta and in Barbary there were two main types of organization of the corsair business. Firstly the rulers of both territories fitted out ships themselves. These were the equivalents of the regular navies of other states. But they also licensed private individuals to fit out ships on their own account. For the privilege of doing this they had to pay a share of their prizes to their rulers, normally one-tenth in Malta and one-eighth in Barbary. Once fitted out, the organization of the ships in action was also similar in both places. Barbary ships cruised mainly in the western Mediterranean plundering Christian ships and Christian territories. Maltese ships made a cruise of the eastern Mediterranean or the Barbary coast plundering Moslem shipping and Moslem territories. Both Maltese and Barbary ships also made cruises searching for each other. The capture of a Barbary corsair by a Maltese ship was the greatest prize of all, and vice versa. Both the Moslem and the Christian ships sometimes operated individually and sometimes in fleets, but fleet operation was much commoner for the Barbary corsairs than it was for the Maltese.

The most important prizes for both parties were slaves and ships. It was only rarely that a cargo was of very great significance. In Islam and Christendom there were specialized facilities for the disposal of these prizes. There were great slave markets in Constantinople, Algiers, Malta, and Leghorn where corsairs knew they could always dispose of this most valuable cargo. And in these centres there were also facilities for arranging the ransom of slaves. A whole complex of middlemen and specialist redemptionist organizations had grown up to arrange for the return to their homes of the unfortunate slaves whom the corsairs had captured in the course of their depredations. For those whose private fortunes were not large enough to provide for ransom, cities and religious orders had organized special redemption funds to assist in this business. Often when slaves were redeemed they were paraded through the streets of their home lands in order to arouse the pity of their fellow-citizens for those who still remained in slavery. In this way it was hoped to swell the funds available for further redemption. Not all slaves were redeemed, however, for the demand for slaves in the Mediterranean was one of the strongest reasons for the continued success of the corsair business, and many slaves were too poor or too unlucky to have their ransom organized. The major source of demand for slaves came from the Mediterranean navies. Galleys powered by slaves formed the major component of the French, Spanish, Italian, and Turkish Mediterranean navies right down to the end of the seventeenth century and even later. The size of the French Mediterranean galley fleet was at its greatest in the last thirty years of the seventeenth century and French agents appeared regularly in the slave markets of Malta and Leghorn. Demand was in fact outstripping supply at this period and the French went to great lengths to try to cut costs. Despite the scruples of some, Russian and Greek Christians were bought and put to service in the French galleys. Experiments were also made with West African negroes and with Iroquois Indians. Both the latter were unsuccessful and the French finally relied for the bulk of their galley slaves on convicts, and, after the Revocation of the Edict of Nantes, on Huguenots. But the élite of the French galleys remained the Moslems of North Africa.[6] Other big buyers of galley slaves were the Barbary corsairs and the Knights of St John themselves. But the galleys were not the only source of employment for slaves. Many were also used in domestic, and occasionally in agricultural, work as well.

Both in Malta and in Barbary the proceeds from the sale of slaves, ships, and cargo were divided in a similar way. After the share belonging to the government had been deducted, certain payments were made to officials who helped to run the business and also to religious institutions whose prayers were expected to assist in the success of the chase. Then the rest of the booty was shared between the capitalists who had put up the money for the expedition, either the State or private individuals, and the officers and crews who actually manned the ships. In both Malta and Barbary these divisions were made after time-honoured custom, 'the custom of the corsairs'. A high percentage for the captain and the pilot, inflated shares for the other officers, a prize for the first man on board a ship which defended itself – the customs of both religions are virtually identical. Privateering, like trade, had various problems to face, and, as in the case of trade, the answers to these problems were likely to be similar. Both Moslem and Christian had to finance expeditions and naturally the capitalists required reward. Both needed to encourage their crews to fight hard, and hence the payment of shares to all and a reward for the brave. Both had to try to stop the crews from pocketing the booty, hence the institution of the share-out where every crew member had an interest in making sure that the total to be shared was as high as possible.

No estimate has ever been made of the effect of all these corsairs on trade in the Mediterranean. But in the seventeenth century at least the effect must have been very considerable. For it seems certain that altogether there must, in nearly every year, have been well over one hundred well-armed ships operating in the Mediterranean whose only justification for existence was not only to attack the commercial shipping of their religious enemies but also to make a profit from this activity. These numbers were to become considerably less in the eighteenth century, as a result of the treaties made by the Barbary corsairs with many European powers, and also because of a growing restriction of the activities of the Maltese and other Christian corsairs, as European powers began to think more in terms of trade than war with Islam. But even in this period the actual number of ships engaged in the corsair business and the prizes taken remained considerable.

Indeed sometimes it seems surprising that there was any scope for normal trade at all with so many corsairs active in the Mediterranean. One might have thought that the profusion of potential enemies would have killed the golden goose. But here we have to remember that it was virtually impossible for the countries peripheral to the Mediterranean to exist unless there was trade. Great cities and small islands depended for their very survival on the arrival of foodstuffs from areas with more land and less people. Urban populations depended on raw materials to feed the industries that provided them with a living. Baroque courts needed luxuries to satisfy their taste for conspicuous consumption. And before the advent of the railway it was virtually impossible for all these goods to arrive unless they went part of the way at least by sea. This was particularly true of the trade in food, the price of which would have been prohibitive if it had had to travel all the way by land. And yet it was this particular trade which was the most vital of all. In other words the Mediterranean world, with its great cities and its multitude of small islands, just could not exist without a very extensive sea-borne trade. A paradise for the corsair!

The general acceptance of the situation is shown well by the cynicism of the organization. To a merchant or a sea-captain capture was just one of the many factors that had to be taken into consideration when estimating costs. Naturally he would take out insurance, equally naturally at high rates. But as a merchant he would not expect to be a slave long. Since privateering was a business, the privateer had no interest in feeding a merchant, poor as a slave but rich as a merchant, purely for the glory of God. And so in Malta we find alongside the letters patent licensing the corsair captains to fit out to attack Moslem shipping, safe conducts for Islamic merchants to return home after capture to raise money to ransom themselves and the hostages left behind as sureties for their good behaviour, and there existed similar institutions in Barbary.

It may be asked why powerful maritime nations should allow trade to be continuously disrupted by corsairs. There seems little doubt that the English, French, and Dutch, either singly or together, could have swept the Mediterranean free of corsairs, and indeed of pirates. An English ship of the line, for instance, was so powerful that no corsair or combination of corsairs could stand up to its attack. But here we come up against the cynicism which is such a marked feature of corsair activity in the Mediterranean. For, far from being a real handicap to their activities, the corsairs actually assisted the new maritime powers in building up a dominant position in the Mediterranean. The English, for instance, confined their operations against the corsairs to a few, fairly successful, attacks on the Barbary coast. Once the Barbary corsairs were aware of the strength of British sea-power, they were glad to come to terms and enter into treaty relations. The result was greatly to assist the expansion of British commerce in the Mediterranean. Free for the most part from the danger of attacks by the most powerful Moslem corsairs in the region, the British merchantmen also benefited from the attacks of Christian corsairs on Moslem shipping. Both Moslem and Christian corsairs thus assisted the British by removing to a very considerable extent the threat of major competition in the carrying trade. British ships were also able to dispense with much of the great complement of men and arms that they had formerly carried to defend themselves, thus reducing their costs and their freights.[7]

French policy was different, and possibly even more cynical. In the early part of the seventeenth century French merchant ships were built for speed, so that they could get away from the Barbary corsairs. Later the French, like the British, attacked the ports of Barbary and eventually managed to extract privileges and protection from attack. They were also in constant treaty relations with the Turks. So far a similar policy to the British. But the French were also the biggest financiers of corsair activity against the Moslems. Throughout the seventeenth century we find that French capitalists and French captains are the biggest single support of the Maltese corsairs. Thus, while French government policy was nominally one of friendship with the Turks, French individuals, often with the secret connivance of their government, were the greatest enemies of Turkish commerce. In 1729, for instance, the French Minister of Marine sent funds to Malta to finance the fitting-out of two corsair ships but emphasized 'that the business must be carried out without it seeming that France had any part in it'. The French attitude towards Barbary was neatly summed up in an anonymous memorandum of the same year. 'We are certain that it is not in our interest that all the Barbary corsairs be destroyed, since then we would be on a par with all the Italians and the peoples of the North Sea.' On the other hand it was not felt wise to encourage the corsairs by selling them arms. In other words, what France wanted was 'just enough corsairs to eliminate our rivals, but not too many!'[8]

The result of such policies by the great Christian maritime powers was that, while they avoided the worst effects of Holy War privateering, all this turned on their less powerful competitors. Moslem corsairs concentrated their activity on the weaker Christian traders, e.g. Italians, Catalans, and Maltese, whilst Christian corsairs naturally attacked Moslems (and as we shall see later, Greeks). There is little doubt that such a policy greatly assisted the infiltration of western European commercial shipping into the coastal trades of the Mediterranean. Far better to pay the high freight rates demanded by the heavily armed and powerful English ships and arrive at one's destination, than tò pay the high insurance rates required to cover the risks of travelling on the ships of weaker nations.

While the strong thus benefited from the discomfiture of the weak they were also able to acquire the trade goods of the Mediterranean at low prices. For the goods seized by the corsairs on their way from Constantinople to Alexandria, or Barcelona to Marseilles, were sold at auction in the great prize markets of Algiers or Tunis, Malta or Leghorn. And who bought them? Why, those same English, French, or Dutch merchants who had sailed to the Mediterranean to buy just these goods in the normal run of commerce. And normally the price they paid was considerably less than the price that they would have had to pay in the port of origin. Privateering was thus just another system of exchange. And the danger of these goods being claimed at some time in the future by their former owners was brought to a minimum by the fact that in all the great prize ports there were specialists in the business of altering the marks on bales, so that they could not be identified by their original owners.

What sort of people were the corsairs? It should be emphasized that, in the conditions of the Mediterranean, the pursuit of corsair activity, the *corso*, could be a lifetime profession. The Italian word *corsale* describes a man who is a professional corsair. When asked to give his profession in court the corsair said *corsale*, just as he might have said butcher or baker. He entered the trade as a young man. With good fortune, progress to the upper reaches of the profession could be rapid, until eventually the ambition of every young corsair, to be a corsair captain, could be achieved. Now, with maybe the right to ten per cent of the booty, was the chance for fortune and glory, perhaps to become one of the almost legendary successful corsairs whose name alone could instil fear into the coastal populations of the Mediterranean. Once he had made good profits in the *corso*, the corsair might well branch out into other activities. Profits from the *corso* could be invested in commerce or property. Profits from the *corso* could be used to found a dynasty of merchants and corsairs, such as that of the Preziosi in Malta or the Djellouli in Tunis.[9] This career structure of the corsair should be compared with the English type of privateer, normally a merchant captain or nobleman who fitted out a ship for privateering in a period of war and would revert to his normal activity when peace returned.[10] Only in very long periods of general warfare did the possibility of such continuity of employment for a non-religious corsair exist.

One does not have to look very far for the motivation of the corsair. The Mediterranean was an area where the mass of the people lived in conditions of extreme poverty and the opportunities for escaping poverty were few. No such modern escapes as economic growth or mass emigration were available at the time. In a fairly static society the only way to climb out of poverty was to take the place of someone higher on the social scale or to take the wealth of someone better placed. The chances of improving oneself by sheer hard work were very slim.

That there were other states of existence besides poverty was apparent to even the most near-sighted of the poor. For amongst the great mass of the poor were the few rich – more magnificent than ever before in this age of the Baroque and the Rococo. And largely dependent on the rich were those people of middling wealth whose main function in this society was to serve the rich. Lawyers, merchants, bureaucrats, army officers and priests – these were the middle classes. There were then other standards of existence, not everyone was poor. This was certainly a challenge to the poor, though few recognized it, let alone acted on it. But for the ambitious poor much the most feasible way to become rich, even if only temporarily, was to become a successful gambler or a successful thief. Privateering was an institution which made both thieving and gambling respectable, and thus provided the poor man with an opportunity of getting a little richer, and the rich man with the opportunity of making a fortune.

Privateering was also of course an institution which served to enhance the glory of one's own God and to lead to the abasement of the God of one's rivals. Any institution which serves at one and the same time to make a person rich and to save his soul is never likely to suffer from a dearth of recruits. How important the religious motivation for the Holy War was is extremely difficult to say from our twentieth-century standpoint. Certainly one's instinctive cynicism is reinforced by much of the contemporary evidence. But then one is impressed by the enormous number of ordinary Christians who refused to apostasize, even though this might release them from slavery or even death. Perhaps it will be sufficient to close this chapter with a conversation from Chekhov's story *The Duel*:

'How do you say "God" in Tartar?' the deacon asked as he went into the lodge.

'Your God and my God are the same,' said Kerbalai, not understanding him. 'God is the same for all, only people are different. Some are Russians, some are Turks, some are English – all kinds of people, but God is one.'

'Very good. If all men worship the same God, then why do you Muslims look upon Christians as your eternal enemies?'

'Why are you angry?' asked Kerbalai, clasping his hands over his stomach. 'You are a priest, I am a Muslim – you say you want to eat, I give you food . . . Only the rich decide which is your God and which is mine, to the poor it is all the same. Eat, if you please.'

PART TWO

The Barbary Corsairs

CHAPTER 2

The Barbary Regencies

The three Turkish North African regencies of Algiers, Tunis, and Tripoli had been conquered for the Ottomans during the course of the sixteenth century.[1] Their conquerors were Moslem political adventurers and corsairs, whose names form a roll-call of the most celebrated figures in Turkish maritime history. The Barbarossa brothers, Dragut, Ochiali – extraordinary men, who for a whole century flouted the myth of Christian supremacy at sea. The acquisitions in North Africa were seen at first as forward bases from which to pursue the long naval war against Spain. But these adventurers soon went further than this, and achieved what many an ambitious Spaniard had dreamed of, the creation of a North African empire. Almost from the beginning the bases in Barbary had a dual purpose. From the harbours fleets of galleys were sent out to raid the commerce of Christendom; and from the towns armies of janissaries were despatched to subdue the Arab and Berber tribes. This duality was to last almost as long as Turkish Barbary. Its strength lay in the fact of a conquered hinterland. Where Spanish and Portuguese adventurers never controlled more than small sections of North African coastline, the most successful of the Turkish rulers controlled the land right up to where it met that second sea, the Sahara. Its weakness lay in the very duality of purpose. North African politics was dominated for centuries by the clash between two different sorts of military men – those who saw the main purpose of the

Barbary states as havens for corsairs, and those who believed in the expansion of Turkish power into the interior.

From the beginning Turkish Barbary had more autonomy than other provinces of the Ottoman Empire. The Sultan's authority rested in a Pasha appointed from Constantinople, and in the early years these Pashas were often the conquerors themselves, ambitious and powerful men, not likely to trouble themselves too much about the wishes of a superior so many miles away at the other end of the Mediterranean. The second generation were lesser men appointed for a triennial term of office, who had to struggle hard to maintain their authority in a turbulent environment. To help them keep order they relied entirely on a militia of janissaries, mainly recruited in the Levant. By the end of the sixteenth and the beginning of the seventeenth century it was the janissaries who were ruling, and not the appointed Pasha. Only in Tripoli, much closer to Constantinople than the other two regencies, did the Sultan through his Pasha retain much authority, and even here he was to lose it eventually. In Algiers and Tunis it was the elected head of the janissaries who held the real power, even though Pashas continued to be sent at regular intervals from Constantinople. Power rested in the Divan, a council consisting of the senior officers of the janissaries, and other military and naval elements in the state, and the real rulers, known as Beys and Deys, were elected through revolutions of the local Divan. Such revolutions were frequent, and the political history of Barbary in the seventeenth century is a dull chronicle of poisonings, stranglings, janissary revolts, and internecine strife, though occasionally a more powerful and successful leader was thrown up who could hold the state together for several years before succumbing in his turn to political intrigue. In the eighteenth century the government of both Tunis and Tripoli was much stabilized by the successful adoption of power by a local dynasty. But in Algiers the near anarchy of the seventeenth century was to last until the French invasion of 1830.

It is doubtful if the Sultan was over-troubled by the growing autonomy of Turkish Barbary. As long as the region remained Turkish it was an extremely valuable part of the Empire's defences, as well as a continuous thorn in the flesh of his

Algiers, 'that proud city, that retreat of the men who have made God bankrupt'.

Christian enemies. There was a very close parallel between Barbary in the west and Crim Tartary in the north. The Tartar horsemen accepted a rather loosely defined sovereignty from Constantinople just as the Barbary corsairs did. As the Venetian, Salvago, put it: 'the Sultan has two wings with which he flies very far. One is Barbary on the sea and the other Tartary on the land; both are insatiable birds of prey.'[2] And for the most part Tartar horsemen and Barbary corsairs accepted the obligations of Turkish sovereignty. Just as the Tartars played an important, if rather undisciplined, role in the campaign against Vienna in 1683, so did the Barbary corsairs send fleets to fight alongside the Turks in most of the naval wars of the seventeenth and eighteenth centuries. Not that they were always particularly keen on doing so. Ali Piccanino of Algiers, for instance, refused to join the Grand Vizier's fleet against Venice in 1643, seeing little profit in real warfare, and having little hope of indemnity for any losses.[3] It also depended on whom the Turks were fighting. Algiers showed little enthusiasm for joining the Ottomans against France after Napoleon's conquest of Egypt, since French reprisals were a much closer threat than any possibility of Turkish assistance if things went wrong.[4] Except when the Ottomans were actually at war with a Christian naval power, which for the most part means Venice during the period we are considering, Barbary and Turkey acted independently. States which were at peace with Turkey were not necessarily at peace with Barbary, and vice versa.

Apart from a formal acceptance of the Sultan as both a political and religious superior, there was only one other field in which Barbary had really close links with the Ottoman Empire. This was in the recruitment of janissaries. The original janissaries in the regencies had formed part of the conquering forces in the sixteenth century. But, once conquest had been made permanent, large numbers of janissaries were left in North Africa to maintain Turkish power. The existence of this permanent body of soldiers was so much the essence of Turkish rule, that the North African states themselves were often referred to as *Odjaks*, a word which means literally a body of janissaries. The Turks felt that their power rested on a racial superiority to the indigenous population, and so no native soldiers were ever enrolled in the janissaries, though they were enlisted as lightly-armed auxiliaries. Gaps in the ranks of the janissaries through death or retirement were filled almost entirely from two sources – Turks recruited in the Levant and Christian renegades.[5]

Service in North Africa was an extremely attractive proposition to a Levantine Turk. It offered the possibilities of quite remarkable social and political promotion for the very lowest ranks of society. Promotion rested almost entirely on age, and so a young janissary could expect eventually to become an officer, and if he was lucky a member of the Divan, the body who effectively ruled the state. As a member of such a social and political élite he could intermarry with the local Moorish aristocracy, and found one of those *coulougli** dynasties which played such an important part in the social and economic life of Barbary. Finally Barbary offered the possibilities of wealth. The recruiting officer in the Levant 'paints a magnificent picture of the fate that awaits them at Algiers, of the immense profits that the *corso* against Christians will give them'.[6] The Spanish writer, Haedo, remarked that the Turks rushed to Barbary to seek their fortunes like the Spaniards to Peru.[7]

Given these opportunities what sort of men became janissaries in Barbary? The Christian writers are almost unanimous on this subject. According to d'Arvieux the recruiting officers in the Levant 'pick up all the bandits, the rebels, the fugitives from creditors and justice, the uncontrollable young men whose parents wish to rid themselves of, in a word, all the excrement of the states of the Sultan'.[8] Salvago echoes d'Arvieux when he described Barbary as the 'cess-pool of the Ottoman Empire'.[9] These may be the views of prejudiced people, but it would probably have been unwise to inquire too deeply into the past of any seventeenth-century soldier, Moslem or Christian. What is certain is that there was never any difficulty in finding recruits. 'There was always someone in the ports of the Morea or the isles of the Archipelago, at Adalia, Cyprus or Cairo, waiting for their passage to Barbary.'[10] And from time to time

---

* *Coulougli*: the son of a janissary and a Moorish woman. In order to retain the purity of the janissary stock few *coulouglis* were recruited, but they played a very important social and economic role in Barbary. They also presented a potential opposition to pure janissary rule.

the Barbary states sent ships to collect them. Whatever Christians may have thought of the origins of the janissaries, most writers have a grudging admiration for the seasoned product. Extremely well-disciplined and brave they made a striking contrast to most European soldiers of the period, and it is noteworthy that the Knights of St John were ordered to attack the galleys of Tunis only if their numbers were equal or superior, indicating that even the finest soldiers in Christendom considered the Turkish janissaries to be their equal.[11]

The life of the Turkish soldier in Barbary, despite the discipline, seems to have been extremely pleasant. Lodged in elegant barracks, with fine courtyards and fountains, served by Christian slaves and regularly paid and fed, they lived a life of ease relative to the conditions current back in their homelands. Nor were they troubled by the finer points of the Moslem religion. 'For Tunis is a country of liberty', writes d'Arvieux. 'Religion bothers nobody there; one prays to God when one wants to, one fasts when one cannot do otherwise, one drinks wine when one has money, one gets drunk when one has drunk too much.'[12] Provision was also made for leave. Up to three years on half-pay could be granted to the soldier who wished to make the pilgrimage to Mecca or visit his relatives in the Levant. And if things went wrong, if for instance his pay was not paid regularly, then the Turkish soldier had his own solution. Revolt! The new ruler would almost certainly give the soldiers double pay as his first political move.

The Turk had acquired a remarkably well-adjusted character. Despite his ferocity in war, 'he had cultivated a fatalism which showed itself in an imperturbable tranquillity. In times of distress, fear or grief he could be soothed with opium, and when things went well with him he could spend all day sitting cross-legged on his divan, playing the tambour, smoking his pipe, and contemplating his garden.'[13] Coffee and tobacco were his dual solaces. In 1815 when the Algerine flagship was captured by the American navy, the crew was found 'quietly seated on the cabin floor, smoking their long pipes with their accustomed gravity'.[14]

The attractions and privileges of Barbary were open, not only to the Levantine Turk, but also to the Christian renegade. Christian renegades were treated better than any other non-

Close-up of Algiers. The size of the harbour was really quite small and could not hold the entire Algerian fleet when the city was at its strongest.

Turk in Barbary, and as members of the sect of *hamafi*, the sect of the Turkish ruling class, could enter the army and the highest posts in the government.[15] This being the case many Christians took advantage of the opportunities offered by Barbary for a successful and adventurous life. There were three types of renegade, those who had been enslaved as children and brought up in the Moslem faith, those enslaved as adults who had apostasized in captivity, and those who had come voluntarily to Barbary with the specific intention of 'turning Turk'. The first group, mainly Greeks and Albanians, was probably the largest, but in many ways it was the third group who played the most important role in Barbary society. Consisting mainly of western Europeans they represented some of the most wayward and footloose elements in European society. One major source was seamen who 'sought redress from numerous injustices in changing their allegiance or religion, sometimes whole crews at a time'.[16] Seamen were indeed a race without a country who, as a document of 1695 tells us, 'go where merchants and sovereigns pay the most'.[17] But not only seamen went to Barbary. Anyone with a grievance or with a thwarted ambition in the Christian Mediterranean might choose the path of apostasy. Nor need apostasy itself be too traumatic an experience. Where there was not much strict Moslem orthodoxy, there was an opportunity for such mystical elements as the Bektashi Dervishes to play an important part in religious life. Such dervishes taught 'that all religions were merely defective approximations to the truth, which lay in a private and ineffable vision of God'. In such circumstances a Christian could apostasize without expressly repudiating too much at once.[18]

Western European renegades played a vital role in Barbary society, by being the means of transmitting western military technology to a state which depended on military technology for its existence. The most dramatic example of this was the introduction of the fighting ship-of-war into the Barbary fleets by Christian renegades in the early seventeenth century, but throughout the history of the corsairs, Barbary relied on Christendom for the diffusion of techniques.[19] Another field in which Christian renegades played an important part was in commerce where they often retained links with their former business associates in Christendom. But most renegades were just absorbed in Barbary society – as janissaries, as corsairs, or simply as artisans. For the most part they seem to have assimilated well. For instance, Father Dan described the extraordinary number of nations represented amongst the Algerian janissaries and was amazed at their peaceful co-existence. 'They all live in a great harmony, and only very rarely quarrel with each other.'[20] A few Christian renegades acquired great power in Barbary, even becoming Bey or Dey. Most of these were successful corsairs. By the eighteenth century, however, it was much rarer for a former Christian to rise so high in Barbary, although it was still possible to live a satisfactory life there.

We have seen the important political and social role of the janissary in Barbary, but what did he do? There were three main types of duty: serving in the galleys or ships of the state, in garrisons, or in 'flying camps' to collect tribute from or subdue the Arab and Negro tribes in the interior. These duties by no means took up all the janissary's time and when he was not otherwise engaged he was free to increase his earnings by other means. If he had a trade he could follow this, and many janissaries were part-time artisans. But a more attractive pursuit for many was to sign on as a volunteer in a private corsair ship for a share of the prizes. The balance of time, numbers, and resources spent between subduing hinterland tribes and pursuing the *corso* was one aspect of that duality inherent in Barbary society. Some rulers saw the glory, the purpose, and the profit of their post in collecting tribute from the tribes; others in building up a powerful corsair fleet. Resources directed to each activity thus varied considerably, but it was prudent for any ruler to put at least some resources into the *corso*. The janissaries were inclined to think that it was not only more glorious to attack Christians, but also more profitable, since the only share of tribute that they received from the inland raids was in the form of their pay, which they expected to receive anyway. A ruler who made war too much against the Moors, and was not sufficiently inclined towards the *corso*, would soon become unpopular.[21]

Despite the military and naval orientation of the Barbary states it is important not to think that all activity in Barbary was directed to predatory ends. The military and naval elements in the society were small in relation to total numbers, and Barbary, like anywhere else, had an economy. Indeed one of the main elements in the success of the Barbary corsairs was the fact that the bases that they had chosen had fertile hinterlands. As the Dey of Tunis observed to Admiral Blake in 1655, 'we have our subsistence from the land without needing anything from the sea'.[22] Most visitors remarked on the cheapness of foodstuffs in Barbary during years of normal harvests, and attributed this fact quite rightly to the fertility of the land. 'This is indeed a land fair to look upon', wrote the daughter of an early nineteenth-century British consul in Algiers, 'and all that it wants is to be governed by hats instead of turbans.'[23] From the basis of a sound agriculture a flourishing trade had grown up, exchanging mainly foodstuffs and raw materials for the manufactured goods of Europe and the products of the Ottoman Empire. Tunis, in particular, was a prosperous commercial centre by the seventeenth century, exporting grain, vegetables, wool, hides, and wax in exchange for cloth, paper, hardware, spices, dyes, and wine.[24] Algiers was slower to develop, and its commerce in 1699 was described as 'peu de chose'.[25] In the eighteenth century all three of the Barbary regencies developed their trade, the profits and revenue from which tended to be substituted for those which had formerly come from the *corso*.[26] Little distinction was made between trade with friends and trade with the enemy. Passports, albeit of a limited number, were issued to the traders of all nations. 'The ports of this kingdom [Tunis] are free to all the world . . . The Maltese even, although the irreconcilable enemies of the Tunisians and of all the people of Barbary, come here laden . . . with their own flags displayed.'[27] One vital import for which Barbary relied on outsiders for the whole of its existence was shipbuilding and war *matériel*. Some of this was captured, some received in tribute, but most was brought in the normal way of trade, by Christian and Moslem alike. Tripoli took timber from Anatolia and Egypt, iron from Thessalonika, cordage from Smyrna and Alexandria,[28] but for munitions, pitch and many other such imports, all three regencies relied heavily on their imports from Holland, England, and the Baltic states, to the pious horror of Christian commentators.

Tripoli, the smallest and weakest of the three regencies, could nevertheless send out a very powerful corsair fleet on occasion.

The Barbary states were certainly military states, but they were military states built on a fairly sound economy. And the *corso*, originally the *raison-d'être* of the regencies, had settled down in the seventeenth century as just one, albeit one of the most important and profitable, occupations of Barbary. Time and custom had acted to control the more anarchic features of uncontrolled piracy, and had given the Barbary corsairs an organization that was fully institutionalized and accepted by all participants. The ships used by the corsairs for their depredations against Christendom were owned by private individuals or by the state. The prospect of a good return made investment in the *corso* a very attractive proposition for private citizens, and all classes of society were represented in the ownership of corsair ships. Shareholding in the ships was organized in exactly the same way as shareholding in commercial companies, and the two were regarded merely as alternative investments. The great period of private investment in the *corso* was the seventeenth century. The smaller fleets of the following century were mainly owned by the state, a trend which was sharply reversed during the chaotic and highly profitable period of the French Revolutionary and Napoleonic Wars. [29]

Although some of the galleys and ships used in the *corso* were built in Barbary itself, shipbuilding was a great problem for the Barbary corsairs. Neither the materials nor the skills required were plentiful in North Africa. Ironically both these shortages were made up by Christians. As we have seen, despite all types of prohibition, there was never much difficulty in buying timber, naval stores, and armaments from the maritime powers of northern Europe. Later in the history of the corsairs this supply was formalized in treaties with such countries as Holland and Sweden who guaranteed to pay a tribute in naval stores and armaments, in return for protection from attack. The shortage of skilled shipbuilding labour was made up by the use of Christian slaves and renegades. The very highest prices were paid in the slave market for a skilled ships' carpenter or cannon-founder. Another source of both ships and naval stores was through capture on the high seas. Such captured ships, converted for the *corso*, became particularly important from the seventeenth century onwards, when sailing-ships began to play a large part in the armament of the corsairs. As we shall see in the next chapter such conversion changed the ships completely and made them virtually unrecognizable. It is probable that the stream of prizes was sufficient to provide most of the large ships used in the *corso*. In 1625 Salvago reported that sailing-ships were never built from scratch at either Tunis or Algiers, there only being sufficient wood for galleots and other oared vessels.[30] This was probably the normal situation from his time onwards, though sailing-ships were built on occasion.[31]

The captains (*rais*) of corsair ships were chosen by the ships' owners, but before anyone could aspire to such a dignity, he had to be examined by a council of existing captains under the chairmanship of the Admiral. The origin of captains varied considerably, but one major source, particularly in the seventeenth century, was renegades from Christian Europe. In some years half or more of the captains were renegades or the sons of renegades, and these were often the most successful of the corsairs. Turks made up most of the rest of the number of captains, but there were also a few native North Africans (Moors). Corsair captains normally made a career of their job, though a particularly profitable cruise might lead a prudent corsair to retire prematurely.[32] The community of corsairs formed a powerful political *bloc* in all the Barbary states. They naturally favoured a policy of expansion of corsair activity at the expense of military expeditions against the inland tribes. Much of the party struggle within the state, particularly in Algiers, was between the *rais* and the janissaries. In Algiers the *rais* kept their houses in the west part of the city with their crews and suppliers grouped around them, as a precaution against attack from their political opponents.[33]

The crews of the corsair ships were a heterogeneous collection of renegades, Turks, and Moors, but one characteristic element of nearly all ships was the number of Christian slaves enrolled as crew. On the galleys, Christians, chained four or five to the bench, provided the motive power. But even on sailing-ships a large number of slave seamen were employed. While they had, of course, to be free to do their work, they were normally confined or chained up during battle.[34] In addition to the crew who actually sailed or rowed the ship, all corsairs carried a complement of janissaries. This was the real fighting element of a corsair ship, and the janissaries rarely had anything to do with the sailing of the ship. They sat quietly, smoking their pipes, until under the command of their Agha they were launched into the attack and boarding of an enemy ship. There was thus dual command on a corsair ship.[35] The *rais* controlled the crew, but the janissaries took orders only from their Agha. Since he could do little without the janissaries this placed the captain in an awkward situation, and it meant in fact that he had to do what the janissaries wanted, and go where they wished. However, despite the apparent dangers of this system of divided command, it seems to have caused few difficulties. The captain was in charge of navigation and the ship's artillery. The Agha was in charge of the janissaries. Together they set out to prey on their enemies.

* * *

But who were the corsairs' enemies? This is one of the trickiest questions in any study of the Barbary corsairs. For the Maltese corsairs it is simple: all Moslems were their enemies. But not all Christians were the enemies of the Barbary corsairs, despite the apparent religious motivation of their brand of warfare. To state the obvious, their enemies were the nationals of the countries with which they were at war. Initially this meant the Catholic countries which were at war with the Ottoman Empire. The line-up at the Battle of Lepanto gives a good idea of who they were – Venice, Spain, Naples, Genoa, Savoy, Malta, and Tuscany. With some of these countries the Barbary states never made peace or else did not do so until very late in their existence. In particular they were in a constant state of war with Spain, and that of course included Spain's European Empire,* until the late eighteenth century. But this comparatively simple statement of the corsairs' enemies is only part of the truth. What, for instance, was the definition of a 'national'? A modern concept, it was poorly defined in the seventeenth century, and was determined solely by domicile, proof of which was residence and marriage.[36] Such a definition could clearly give rise to much misunderstanding, but it was only part of the problem. There were two other major fields of confusion.

First, there was the problem of enemy goods in friends' ships.

---

* Spanish Flanders, the Balearic Islands, Sardinia, Milan, Naples, Sicily. Portugal was Spanish from 1580–1640.

'By the law and custom of the Mediterranean and Levant Sea, if the goods of enemies are taken in the ships of friends, the master of the ship shall receive his full hire, as if the ship unloaded at its destination.'[37] This is clear enough in theory, but in order to find out if there were enemies' goods in a friend's ship, it was necessary, of course, to search it. And this is where the trouble started. The right of the *visità* (the inspection of any ship, enemy or friend, to see whether there were enemy goods aboard) was a right naturally upheld by all corsairs, but disliked by all merchant captains. In the last resort a friend could, of course, resort to force to resist the *visità*, and once a battle was under way anything might happen. As far as the second half of the statement is concerned, what little evidence that exists suggests that the Barbary authorities were scrupulously correct in paying friendly captains for the freight they lost on enemy goods seized. But this in itself was a source of trouble. In 1661, for instance, the captains of six English ships allowed themselves to be boarded by the Algerians without any resistance. All the cargo was taken, except that belonging to Englishmen, and the captains were paid double freight on what was seized. What looked like correct practice to the Englishmen and Algerians, looked like bribery to the Venetians and Genoese whose goods had been seized. They protested at 'the unexampled impropriety of the act, all confidence being abused by the improper behaviour of the captains, to the prejudice of trade'.[38]

The second problem was the reverse of the first, the problem of friends' nationals and friends' goods on enemy ships. Nearly always such goods were considered a legitimate prize by the Barbary corsairs. The position of supposedly friendly nationals was a more tricky one. The criterion of capture and enslavement was supposed to be whether they fought against the corsairs or not. This was not easy to determine, and the usual decision was to enslave all the members of the crew, but not those passengers who belonged to friendly nations. The crew, theoretical friends or not, were a legitimate prize, because merely by being enrolled on an enemy ship, 'they fight against our people and wound them and kill them'.[39]

This is all to look at the problem of who was an enemy from the point of view of Barbary, but it takes two sides to make a war. Noticeable absentees from the list of enemies mentioned earlier were the three great seventeenth-century trading nations, England, Holland, and France. All three were in fact theoretically at peace with both Turkey and Barbary in the late sixteenth and early seventeenth centuries, but their concept of peace seems to have had a strange duality about it. On the one hand was the attitude of a trading nation who wanted to expand her commerce in the Mediterranean. Peace with Turkey and Barbary made good sense, and had the added advantage of encouraging hostility against Spain, often a common enemy. This was the attitude of most traders in the Levant, and it was the attitude of most statesmen who really thought the problem out. But alongside this attitude was another one, a hangover from the Crusades. The Turk was 'the common enemy', the scourge of Christendom. The Barbary corsairs were even worse; they were Turkish 'pirates' and should be swept from the seas. A good example of the clash of these two attitudes can be seen in 1671. English warships were then attacking Algerine shipping and a number of prizes had been taken. The English merchants who traded in the Mediterranean complained that the interests of the country were being prejudiced for the sake of glory. The Secretary of State, Lord Arlington, did not understand the merchants' attitude. He maintained 'that a war, so costly to the King, proved generally advantageous, as it facilitated navigation for all nations, and a peace restricting the advantage to the English alone would prevent the diffusion of trade, the corsairs being at liberty to harass other flags'.[40] The confusion implicit in the existence of these two attitudes towards the Turks was reflected in the English prize-courts. In the early seventeenth century Turkish and Algerine shipping was looked on as fair game, despite the fact that England was at peace with both states. Even after specific treaties had been signed in the 1620s, the question of whether Turkish and Algerine ships should be treated as pirates or public ships of a sovereign power was still undecided. Such attitudes lingered on until the early eighteenth century.[41] The same was true of the French, who if anything were even more unprincipled in their behaviour to their Turkish allies. The French regularly sent ships to fight alongside the other Christian powers of the Mediterranean against the

Turks and the Barbary corsairs, and they were also major financiers of the Maltese corsairs. Such ships may have flown Portuguese, Papal, or Maltese colours, but this was a pretty thin disguise.

Since the interpretation of peace and neutrality was so very much more liberal on the part of the Christians than of the Barbary corsairs, it is small wonder that a series of clashes often led to war. What is really remarkable is the patience of the Turks and Barbary corsairs. What the English, French, and Dutch called the intolerable impudence and impertinence of the 'pirates' was very often only legitimate and tardy reaction against the infringement of their sovereignty and neutrality by the Christian maritime powers. Two examples will suffice, one English and one French. In 1651 Stephen Mitchell, the English master of the *Goodwill*, contracted to carry thirty-two Turks from Tunis to Smyrna. On his way he met some Maltese galleys, and though, according to Boothouse, the English consul in Tunis, these had neither the legal right nor the physical power to enforce a search, he gave up his Turkish passengers for a large sum of money. The Dey of Tunis protested and Boothouse attempted to negotiate for their return. But to no avail. The Dey then authorized the capture of an English ship in reprisal, the proceeds of whose sale would pay for the ransom of the Turks. He seized the *Princess* laden with currants on her way from Zante to England. Cromwell instructed his Admiral Blake to present a demand for restitution which finally led to war between England and Tunis. Who was the 'impudent' party? Mitchell, who had committed no offence under English law? Or the Dey of Tunis? It is significant that in the eventual treaty there was a specific clause commanding English captains to defend their Tunisian passengers in the future, 'as far as is in their power'.[42]

The French example concerns eight Algerian Turks who had fled the Spanish galleys and sought refuge in a French port, France and Algiers being at peace at the time (1674). They were seized by the French and eventually sent to row in the Marseilles galleys. The Dey of Algiers protested through the French consul, who wrote to the Court. Colbert ordered the release of the Turks, but his instructions were not followed. The Dey then claimed the right to sell some French passengers who had been taken on a ship of Leghorn, in order to ransom the Turks. Negotiations went on and eventually in 1676 the French sent some Turks to Algiers. But only some of these belonged to the original party seized, the balance being made up by sick men who were not wanted on the French galleys. The French consul reported the Dey's disgust and said that he now planned to sell the Frenchmen whom he had captured, and with the money he received buy up sick Frenchmen to send to France. As in the English example the chain of events eventually led to a breakdown of negotiations, and finally war between France and Algiers.[43]

The confusion implicit in the dual attitudes clearly present in the minds of both Englishmen and Frenchmen regarding their behaviour towards the Barbary corsairs, and the frequent interpretation of the perfectly correct inspection of their ships by the corsairs as a hostile act, frequently led to such breakdowns in the course of the seventeenth century. The 'wars' that followed took on a stereotyped pattern. Barbary corsairs would seize as much shipping belonging to their new 'enemy' as they could while the going was good. And the naval powers would send an expedition to Barbary to 'teach the pirates a lesson'. There was an element of farce in these expeditions and indeed 'an expedition against the Barbary corsairs became the stock diplomatic formula for covering some ulterior and sinister design'.[44] Despite the quite considerable naval forces sent to the Mediterranean, few of these expeditions had much effect on Barbary. A few ships were sunk, Barbary cities were shelled from a safe distance, and eventually peace was signed and a new treaty was drawn up restoring the *status quo ante*. Great cries of triumph were heard in London, Paris, or Amsterdam and much attention was paid to the large number of captives released from slavery. But the fact that the captives were normally only released after payment of ransom by the 'victorious' powers was not usually given much prominence. Nor was the fact that the Barbary corsairs, despite their crushing 'defeat', seemed to be as active after the war as before it. Nevertheless, the growing strength of the western naval powers and the increased number of expeditions in the second half of the seventeenth century had their effects. Barbary abdicated the right of search on both English and French ships by the end of the century. And England and France learned to adopt a slightly more logical interpretation of such terms as 'neutral' and 'peace'. In the eighteenth century there were far fewer incidents, and a system of Mediterranean passes was adopted, display of which was sufficient to prevent the corsairs from insisting on the right of search.

These passes were normally engraved on parchment and were ornamented with the picture of a ship or otherwise decorated with marine deities. Through the engraving scolloped indentures were made and the scolloped tops were sent to the Barbary corsairs, or alternatively the latter were sent blank examples of the passes.[45] One problem arose from the fact that the ports on the Atlantic and Mediterranean coasts of France at one time used different formats for their passes. Since the corsairs only had blank examples of the Mediterranean format, they naturally assumed that Atlantic ships had forged passes![46] The other major problem, which bears witness to the general effectiveness of the passes, was the considerable trade in and fraudulent use of both English and French passes.[47] This became particularly serious after the English occupation of Gibraltar and Minorca. Foreigners settled temporarily in these places to gain the benefit of an English pass, and an observer in 1765 said that one-third of the trade carried in the Mediterranean under British colours was in fact done by Italians in no way connected with Britain.[48]

While attention has been drawn to the duality of English and French attitudes towards the corsairs, it should not be thought that the latter were all saints. The rulers of Barbary may have had a more honourable and correct view of the difference between war and peace than many Christian nations, but for all that it was sometimes extremely difficult to put such a 'correct' view into practice. One fundamental problem, common to Moslem and Christian alike, was the control of the corsairs themselves. The line between the profession of corsair and that of pirate was so narrow that it is hardly surprising that the corsair should often overstep it. Both Moslem and Christian resorted on many occasions to the torture of the officers of a 'friendly' ship to extract a confession that it was in fact an 'enemy' ship with forged papers.[49] When such prizes were taken home, however, Moslem practice often seems to have been more correct than that of Christians. The captains of corsair ships were examined, often in the presence of the consuls of friendly nations, on their return, and many a guilty captain was bastinadoed and ordered to return the goods wrongfully seized.[50] Although the courts of Malta often declared against the corsairs, this could often take so long that the plaintiff had gone bankrupt while waiting for a decision, and it was rare indeed for a captain to receive corporal punishment for his crimes. But Barbary was not always so honest. When the corsairs and owners of the corsair ships were a powerful political group in their own right, it was often politically impossible for a Pasha or Dey to support the side of justice. This was what Salvago found in 1624 when he tried to recover goods and slaves illegally seized by the Algerians and Tunisians in a raid on Venetian Dalmatia and the Venetian Islands. Despite a specific order from the Sultan to the regencies to return the booty, Salvago made no headway. Corsairs and shipowners who had benefited from the raid held high positions in the government. Their resources for bribing the Pasha were far greater than his. Futhermore the corsairs were able to present a fairly convincing case that Venice was in fact an enemy, even if no war had been declared. Venice had taken Barbary ships and galleots, and had decapitated the crews as pirates. Also, according to the evidence given by a group of Turks, former slaves on the galleys of Malta, Venice often gave assistance to the Maltese.[51]

Not only did Barbary corsairs themselves quite often break the rules, but also it was quite easy for a friendly Christian ship to think that they had been attacked by the corsairs when in fact they had not. Many Christians seem to have been extremely ill-informed on the political structure of North Africa, and tended to assume that all turbaned sailors were Barbary corsairs. This meant that many Christians did not realize that there were in fact three Turkish Barbary states, all of whom followed an independent diplomatic career. But this was only the beginning of the confusion. Moroccan rovers looked sufficiently like Algerians for reprisals to be taken against the latter for the actions of the former. And anyone could fly the Algerian flag if they happened to have one – Christian corsair, Moslem corsair, or independent pirate. As we shall see, the flying of false flags to lure their prey within easy reach was one of the commonest ruses used by both Barbary and Maltese corsairs, and naturally such a ruse could rebound on them. A final source of difficulty was that the authority of the rulers of Barbary did not always extend over the whole of their coastline. Regarding the seizure of a French vessel in 1700, the French consul in Algiers pointed out that it had been taken by the Moors living between Bougie and Djidjelli, a stretch of coastline which did not recognize the rule of the Dey. These Moors were in the habit of taking their captives up into the mountains and recognized no treaties that had been signed by Algiers.[52]

In conclusion it seems probable that the Barbary corsairs were better keepers of treaties than the Christians, though the latter often enough had ground for complaint. On the other hand the Barbary corsairs had a very cynical attitude to war. Since the *corso* was an important industry in Barbary, and since, as we have seen, the *corso* needed war to justify its existence, then there had to be war. Barbary could never be at peace with everyone. In the seventeenth century little difficulty arose on this front. Barbary had sufficient traditional enemies to keep her corsairs busy, and activity was frequently increased by the numerous short wars against England, France, and Holland. In the eighteenth century things were different. Both France and England had now denied the right of search to the Barbary corsairs, and both were strong enough to avenge any infringements of the new situation. Both were also increasing the proportion of third parties' goods that they carried in their ships.

In this situation Barbary frequently found that she needed new enemies. But on this subject there was often a clash of opinion between the actual rulers in Barbary and the corsairs themselves. For rulers had discovered that a peace treaty with a Christian nation, which included clauses by which the Christians had to pay tribute in return for peace, and therefore protection for their shipping, had many advantages. The revenue that would have been received from the *corso* was still received, but with little or no trouble. As the Dey of Algiers wrote to the King of the Two Sicilies when the latter wanted peace. 'How much will you pay to make up for the loss that this treaty will cause to the Regency?'[53] This was all very well for the Dey, but no one paid the corsairs a retainer during peacetime, and furthermore the janissaries soon got restless if too many peaces prevented the possibility of earning some pocket-money on board a corsair ship. Although the number of corsairs was much less in the eighteenth century, they still represented a powerful interest in the Barbary states, and the janissaries were of course potential makers of a palace revolution. So the Deys and Beys were quite often 'obliged to lessen the number of their alliances'.[54] The countries who suffered from what was very often a completely arbitrary declaration of war were the smaller trading nations. Holland was a frequent sufferer – peace with all three major trading nations being seen to be too much of a good thing. Later in the century new enemies became prominent as they expanded their trade in the Mediterranean – Sweden, Denmark, Hamburg, Prussia, and by the end of the century, the United States. It would be tedious to go into details of all the various wars and treaties, made not only with these states, but also with the Catholic countries of Mediterranean Europe, who had been the traditional enemies of the corsairs for two or three centuries.[55] The point is that the corsairs always had sufficient enemies to keep them employed, and those countries which were not their enemies (with the major exceptions of England and France) bought their peace by paying tribute. And this tribute, to round the system off nicely, was very often paid in those goods which the corsairs lacked but needed most – timber, pitch, guns, cannon-balls, etc.! As has been pointed out in the last chapter, this system suited France and England admirably, since it removed much of the potential Christian competition in the Mediterranean. In 1770, for instance, when the Danes attacked Algiers, the British Consul was the only Christian in the city who sent his janissary to help in its defence![56]

It can be seen that the question of who were the corsairs' enemies is not an easy one to answer, a point noted by Sir Henry Penrice in a legal opinion of 1716. 'For some nations are at peace with the Moors, others are at war; and with some of the Moors we are in amity, with whom our allies are at war, as the Dutch with the Algerines; in which case I presume, we are not to assist a friend against a friend.'[57] And even this was not the end of it for, as we have seen above, the nationals of the corsairs' enemies (even the Maltese) were often granted passes and safe-conducts which protected them from attack. These passes, like the English Mediterranean passes, were bought and sold or forged, thus complicating the situation still further. It was indeed a very awkward sea to sail in.

*   *   *

How big were the corsair fleets of the regencies? It is virtually impossible to give a completely realistic estimate of the size of fleets at any time because of the enormous problem of giving relative weights to different kinds of ships. Relative strength varied from 6o-gun ships-of-war with a fighting complement of 500 men to 3- or 4-gun felluccas with a strength of 20 to 30 men. Sheer numbers then will not present a very accurate picture. Many ships were also capable of being used for both commerce and the *corso*, and the decision to employ a ship for either use, or a combination of both, would depend on such factors as relative success in the past, the prices of trade goods, and the declaration of a new war or the signing of a new peace. Bearing these difficulties in mind a few general comments can be made.

Algiers always had by far the largest fleet and Tripoli nearly always the smallest of the three regencies. The fleets of all three showed a fairly continuous long-term trend of decline from the 1620s up to the beginning of the French Revolutionary Wars. A few estimates of the size of fleets will give some idea of their strength at various times. In 1624–5 Salvago, nearly always a fairly accurate observer, said that Algiers had 6 galleys and 100 fighting sailing-ships. Of the latter 60 were large with 24 to 30 guns each, and the rest were much smaller. At the same time Tunis also had 6 galleys, 10 to 12 brigantines (much smaller versions of the galley) and 14 large sailing-ships. Tripoli at this time had only 2 or 3 sailing-ships.[58] In the second half of the seventeenth century estimates for Algiers vary between 20 and 40 ships, of which a considerable number were still big with 30 to 50 guns. The Tunisian and Tripolitan fleets had about 10 to 15 corsair ships, made up of galleys, powerful sailing-ships, and weaker units. In the eighteenth century the fleets of all three regencies were smaller and the individual ships tended to be weaker. For example in 1737, Algiers had 8 sailing-ships with 6 to 18 guns apiece and 9 galleots. The

Tunisian and Tripolitan fleets were very small during this period, but all three could quickly increase the size of their fleets if there was good reason to do so. Algiers, for instance, had surges of activity in the late 1740s and the 1760s – periods incidentally when the Maltese corsairs were rather inactive. Finally both Algiers and Tunis built up extremely powerful fleets, both in numbers and in the strength of individual ships, during the French Revolutionary and Napoleonic Wars.[59]

Because of the small size of these fleets, and because of the immunity enjoyed by their countrymen, it is customary for English and French historians to play down the significance of the Barbary corsairs in the eighteenth century. This is not an attitude one would expect from the historians of other Mediterranean countries, or from the historians of the Baltic states. It is true that in the seventeenth century the Barbary states were in the same league as naval powers as England and France, and that in the eighteenth century they were not. But, for all that, the part that they played in their own league was of considerable significance – a fact which both British and French statesmen realized, and which explains the cynical policies which they adopted towards them. In the history of Italy, Portugal, or Spain the Barbary corsairs are of considerable importance right up to their eclipse in 1830. They did not need many ships, nor did they need very strong ships, to attack the shipping and the coastlines of such weak adversaries, a fact which should become clear from the discussion of their methods of operation in the next chapter.

CHAPTER 3

The Barbary Corsairs in Action

In the sixteenth century the Barbary corsairs were the allies of the Turks in a general maritime war between Islam and Christendom. Operations in this period were often pursued in very large fleets and attacks were sometimes made on the Christian coastline by armies of literally thousands of men landed from the ships of the corsairs and of the Ottoman navy. During this period whole towns were often sacked and enormous hauls of captives made to be carried back to slavery in Barbary. By about 1580, however, this period of general warfare was over.[1] Barbary was now distinct from the Ottoman Empire in its activities. Only when the Turks were actually engaged in maritime warfare against a Christian power, such as during the Cretan War of 1644–69, did the Barbary States send ships to fight alongside their Turkish allies.[2] Otherwise the Barbary corsairs of this later period operated in small fleets or as individual ships. Their activities remained the same – to attack and capture Christian shipping or to raid Christian coastlines – but the scale of operations was much smaller. Raiding parties now numbered hundreds rather than thousands; slaves were taken in batches of twenty rather than a hundred; single ships rather than fleets were captured. For all that, it is quite likely that their total depredations added up to much the same, at least until the middle of the seventeenth century when opposition from the great naval powers of northern and western Europe became more intense.

47

It is with this later period of small fleets and individuals rather than with large-scale maritime warfare that this book is mainly concerned, since it is this small-scale warfare which is the exact parallel of the Maltese corsairs who will be considered in the next part. This is the period of the corsair proper, a man who, in the definition of the Italian naval historian, Guglielmotti, 'although a private individual, none the less (authorized with letters patent from his government) commands an armed ship, and runs the seas against the enemies of his country, in time of war, at his own risk and profit'.[3] As we have seen the logic of the Holy War was able to construe 'the enemies of his country' as the enemies of his Faith, and 'in time of war' as always!

The armament of the sixteenth-century Barbary corsair was the galley rowed by galley-slaves.[4] Such was the traditional naval weapon of the Mediterranean, and an effective weapon it was. Long, slender, fast and easily manoeuvrable, its main function was to deliver its complement of over one hundred fighting men alongside the enemy as quickly as possible. All its heavy artillery, as well as a great iron peak, were kept in the bows to clear the enemy's decks in order to facilitate boarding. Lighter swivel-guns were mounted in the waist of the galley to break up any concentrations of the enemy that had gathered to reject boarders. But really these guns were only meant to provide an introduction to the real battle – the hand-to-hand struggle on the decks of the enemy ship. To galleys should be added the smaller galleots, brigantines, and frigates – all oared vessels* fitted with sails.[5] In these smaller vessels many of the oarsmen would be free Moslems. Fighting strength per ton and speed were much greater than in a galley, and they were ideal for the quick capture of fairly weak adversaries.

All these ships carried sails and indeed sailing was their normal means of propulsion.[6] But against the wind, in a calm, or in action, they could call on their human motors. It has been estimated that a galley with fifty oars and five slaves to each

---

* The classification of these vessels was quite complicated but the normal method was to classify by the number of benches of oarsmen and the number of rowers to a bench (two oars). Thus a galley had normally 24–28 benches and 4–5 men to an oar; a galleot 17–23 benches and 2–3 men to an oar; a brigantine had 6–16 benches; a frigate 6–12 benches and fellucca 3–5 benches. The last three vessels normally had one man to an oar.

oar could do about five miles in the first hour of hard rowing, a speed which fell rapidly in successive hours as the crew became exhausted.[7] Naturally to achieve such a speed it was necessary to have a good crew of oarsmen and this was one of the main problems in the operation of a galley. Not many men are capable of pulling an oar for three or four, sometimes for fifteen or twenty hours, at a stretch, however much their lagging efforts may be encouraged by a boatswain's lash. But in the human material that they used for their oarsmen the Barbary corsairs had a considerable advantage over most of their Christian rivals. For a very high proportion of the captives whom they chained to their benches were the Christian seamen of the Mediterranean, a breed who were used to pulling an oar from their earliest childhood. In the late eighteenth century, for instance, gentleman travellers from Sicily to Malta were amazed at the hardiness of the Maltese boatmen who rowed them across, sometimes rowing for twenty hours at a stretch with no boatswain's lash to force them.[8] Italians and Spaniards, too, were considered excellent oarsmen, unlike the English, French, and Dutch, 'people exempt from the oar because they are too feeble'.[9] But the splendid Christian oarsmen of the Mediterranean did not row on Christian galleys. Few free men would choose to put up with the filth, discomfort and harsh discipline of a galley. On a corsair galleot or brigantine, however, it was a different matter. Here, with less discipline, less weight to pull and a greater prospect of booty, many a free oarsman could be found. As we shall see, the galleots and brigantines used in the Maltese *corso* were normally rowed by free men, and so often were those of the Barbary corsairs. The Turkish North African was considered by the superintendents of the French galleys to be the best oarsmen of all, 'tall, extremely vigorous, and very resistant to fatigue'.[10] They regularly held key positions on the benches of French galleys. How much harder they would row as free men facing the prospect of booty!

However, from the early seventeenth century there was considerable innovation in the fleets of the Barbary corsairs. While the navies of Mediterranean powers still clung to the galley as a fighting weapon, the rising powers of western Europe had long been experimenting with the new concept of a fighting ship-of-war, square or lateen-rigged sailing ships with a heavy complement of guns. Nothing could be more different from the galley. The galley relied on its speed and manoeuvrability to ram and board its victim. The ship-of-war relied on its guns to batter its victims into submission. In the stormy waters of the Atlantic the ship-of-war had long proved its superiority to the galley. But in the Mediterranean the advantages were less obvious. The high incidence of calms and light winds during the summer fighting season; lack of sea-room; the defects of early naval artillery and the poor practice of naval gunners – such factors had meant that the Mediterranean powers had stuck to the galley. As late as 1571 the major naval battle of Lepanto was fought almost entirely by two enormous galley fleets. And right up to the late seventeenth century most Mediterranean powers used galleys as the main complement in their fleets.

Not the Barbary corsairs however. From the early seventeenth century they began to incorporate the fighting ship-of-war into their armament. The introduction of such ships into the fleets of Tunis and Algiers is normally credited to English and Dutch pirates and privateers thrown out of work by the ending of the Spanish Wars.[11] Between 1604 and 1615 it is estimated that there were several hundred Englishmen operating on corsair ships from Tunis. Most of them were renegades but some, notably Captains Ward and Sanson, were corsairs for a long time before they changed their religion. They seem to have provided a hooligan element in their adopted homes. The Sieur de Brèves wrote in 1606: 'the great profit that the English bring to the country, their profuse liberality and the excessive debauches in which they spend their money before leaving the town and returning to war (thus they call their brigandage on the sea) has made them cherished by the janissaries above all other nations. They carry their swords at their side, they run drunk through the town ... they sleep with the wives of the Moors ... in brief every kind of debauchery and unchecked licence is permitted to them.'[12] But gradually the Turks began to control the English and by the 1620s the art of navigating and fighting with a ship-of-war had been learned sufficiently thoroughly for the local corsairs to be able to dispense with these turbulent northerners.[13]

Barbary galley. Note the lack of a forecastle and the single mast.

Sailing-ships made an enormous difference to the potential scope of the corsairs. No longer were they confined to the Mediterranean. It is from this date that their depredations in the Atlantic and the English Channel began. From Iceland to the West Indies no Christian ship could feel completely safe. Furthermore the introduction of the sailing-ship freed the corsairs from the normal time-table of Mediterranean naval warfare. Even in the days of the galley the Barbary corsairs had less fear of the winter than their Christian rivals. Haedo describes the corsairs 'laughing at our galleys whose crews at this season [winter] are amusing themselves feasting in the ports of Christendom'.[14] With sailing-ships winter cruises could be considerably enlarged in scope.

Nevertheless the introduction of the sailing-ship did not mean the eclipse of the galleys, galleots, and brigantines from the fleets of the corsairs. A sailing-ship was fine for the capture of other ships on the high seas and it was fine for carrying a great complement of soldiers for a raiding party. But it was of little use for much of the work of the *corso*. It was of little use in a calm, for instance, or against the wind, or in shallow water. Even when the wind was blowing, it had to be blowing quite strongly for a sailing-ship to out-distance a galley which, as we have seen, could do five miles in the first hour. In the open sea the galley would soon tire, but in the Mediterranean, with less sea-room, it was that first hour that could be vital. And so the galley, or more accurately its diminutives, the galleot and the brigantine, were retained alongside the sailing-ship by the corsairs. From 1737 onwards the passports of Algerian corsairs, protecting them from attack by French warships, have survived. Although Algiers was by this date a poor shadow of its former glory as a corsair centre these passports give an idea of the continued importance of the galleot. In 1737, for instance, passports were issued to 8 sailing-ships and 9 galleots, in 1740 to 12 sailing-ships and 6 galleots.[15]

Although both the galley and the fighting sailing-ship had been developed by Christian navies they underwent a subtle change in the hands of the Barbary corsairs. Whether built from scratch in Barbary or converted from a prize nearly all ships operated by the Barbary corsairs were lighter, faster and lower in the water than their Christian equivalents. Their galleys, for instance, had one mast instead of two, more oarsmen in proportion to their length, no forecastle, no non-functional decoration and only one big bow-chaser cannon instead of the Christian three.[16] On the sailing-ships, too, everything was sacrificed for extra speed. All but the largest ships had holes cut for oars to give the corsair extra speed in pursuit or flight. Sails were out of proportion to the masts, castles were much lower than in Christian ships, decorations and ornaments were confined to the flags alone, provisions were minimal, even the number of guns was less than on an equivalent sized Christian ship. For, as the Venetian Giovanbattista Salvago reported to his masters in the middle of the seventeenth century: 'the whole military art of the Barbary corsairs consists in boarding, since they can do more with musketry than with artillery',[17] or at the end of the eighteenth century the Frenchman Venture de Paradis wrote: 'the corsairs do not amuse themselves by firing cannon; they seek to board the enemy ship'.[18] Such a policy made good sense, since the capture of live men and an undamaged ship was clearly to the advantage of the corsairs. On the other hand it made it difficult for the corsair to stand up to the fire of a well-armed ship. But speed can be used in defence as well as attack, and it was not easy to catch a corsair.

Since, as we have seen, the emphasis was on boarding, the real power of the corsair lay in its complement of soldiers. The complements were very large, 140 to a galley and 100–200 to a sailing-ship in the seventeenth century.[19] Armed with musket or bow* and scimitar the soldiers took no part in the sailing of the ship, but waited for their moment of glory when led by their Agha they stormed across the bulwarks of their potential victim.

With their speed and manpower the Barbary corsairs had enormous advantages over their main prey – commercial trading vessels. Although Dutch and English, and some Venetian ships were extremely strongly armed, the majority of

---

* The bow and arrow was used by the corsairs well into the eighteenth century, just as it was by the Tartar horsemen on the northern borders of the Ottoman Empire. In the late sixteenth century the Turks claimed that the bow could send thirty arrows in the time required to load and discharge a firearm.[20] Though the speed differential no doubt became less with time it is interesting to note that it was only the invention of the revolver that was able to counter the fire-power of the Plains Indians.

Mediterranean merchant shipping was very weak indeed. This can be seen by an analysis of Maltese merchant shipping. Of all nations the one most exposed to the danger of attack by the corsairs, one would have thought that the Maltese would have done what they could to protect themselves. And yet a register of Maltese shipping in the late seventeenth century shows that there was only one powerful ship in the entire fleet of 100 ships trading between Malta, Sicily, Italy, and the western Mediterranean.[21] Of a group of medium-sized ships – tartans, frigates, and brigantines – only the tartans were even moderately well armed. Most of these had at least one cannon, some of them had three or four, and they normally carried at least half a dozen swivel guns to repel boarders. Frigates were much lighter armed. They had no cannon and usually only one or two swivel-guns. Only a few of the brigantines had even that. And the smallest ships of all – mere rowing boats – carried only hand-arms. Economic considerations must have determined the quantity of arms that a merchantman could carry. Not only were arms expensive, but cannon, for instance, took up much space that could have been filled with cargo, and also if they should be fired would be more than likely to 'shiver the timbers' unless further expense had been given to reinforcing the ship. Men, too, were expensive and very few merchantmen had a crew of over twenty. Thus most merchant ships carried sufficient arms to push off small-time pirates and casual marauders, but relied for their defence against anything stronger on flight and a strong faith in the Almighty – while their employers protected themselves by taking out marine insurance, naturally at extremely high rates. Insurance covered them against loss from 'the sea, fire, the winds, Turks, friends, and enemies and every other misfortune whether caused by God or man'.[22] The rate for the 60 miles to the south coast of Sicily was 2 or 3 per cent, to Leghorn 5 per cent and for Pantelleria, 150 miles straight towards the headquarters of the Barbary corsairs – 6 per cent.

As we have seen, the corsairs made prizes in two main ways, by capturing other ships and by raids ashore. From the material available it is not possible to describe their normal routine of operation in as much detail as can be used for the Maltese corsairs. Most of what we know comes from the descriptions of captured voyagers or from the frightened eye-witnesses of their raids ashore. One would not expect a high degree of objectivity from such witnesses describing perhaps the most exciting events of their life, and writing for an audience that liked its tales to be dramatic. Most of the evidence seems to indicate that the voyages of Barbary corsairs were quite short, rarely exceeding two months.[23] Venture de Paradis, for instance says that the Algerians made two cruises of 40–50 days each, leaving Algiers at the end of March and October.[24] It is unlikely that they were quite as regular in their time-table, but it is probable that the length of cruise is fairly accurate. One of the most important needs of a fast wooden ship which wants to remain fast is regular careening and scraping and waxing of the bottom. To quote Salvago again: 'If a corsair ship has sighted a merchant ship, one could say that it has caught it and taken it, since the corsair ships are always freshly careened, have very high masts with triplicate sails and are very light, being without cargo, and without barrels of wine and salt meat, provisions abhorred by them.'[25] The Venetian was perhaps a little pessimistic but there is clearly much truth in his observation. As far as careening is concerned the logbooks of Maltese corsairs show that they careened their ships at least once every two months.[26] Since Barbary corsairs searched for prizes mainly in Christian waters where there was little opportunity to careen in safety, it seems probable that their normal practice was to leave port, snap up a prize as quickly as possible and return home before their efficiency and speed was impaired. Back at home they could careen and re-arm and be ready for sea again in eight to ten days.

Even when away from home the corsairs did not remain at sea for the whole of their cruise. There is plenty of evidence that, like their Maltese rivals, they had safe places in the territory of their enemies where they could shelter and take on water. Haedo mentions Formentera in the Balearics, Saint-Pierre near Sardinia, Stromboli, and the Lipari Islands as places where the Barbary corsairs could find shelter.[27] To these might be added the island of Lampedusa between Malta and Tripoli, and no doubt scores of other isolated islands and creeks in the western Mediterranean and the Atlantic. But none of these places were as safe for the Moslems as the Greek islands were for the Christian corsairs.[28]

Having left their base in Barbary, either alone or in small fleets, the corsairs set course for a likely catching area. There was a certain amount of division of spheres of interest between the ships of the three main corsair cities.[29] Algerine ships tended to head for Majorca and Gibraltar and then cruise on the Atlantic side of the Straits, or alternatively go from Majorca to the coasts of Sardinia, Corsica, Italy, and Sicily. Tunisian ships normally followed this second route or else headed for the seas between Crete and North Africa or between Crete and the Morea to catch ships on their way to the ports of the Levant. The Tripolitan ships kept to the east coast of Sicily, or else went to the same catching grounds in the Levant as the Tunisians. Various factors tended to limit the number of cruises made by the corsairs into the Levant. First, as we have seen, Algiers had by far the biggest fleet and the Levant was not a normal cruising area for the Algerines. Secondly, once treaties had been made with the English and French, the main kind of Christian shipping in the Levant was Greek shipping carrying Turkish or Greek goods. Since the Greeks, although Christians, were Turkish subjects their seizure posed serious political problems, and so few Greek ships were seized. Levantine cruises thus became less important from the second half of the seventeenth century onwards, and even when they were undertaken would normally involve a combination of a privateering and a commercial voyage. A cargo of pilgrims would be taken to Cairo and rice, beans, and Indian textiles brought back. If a prize was taken as well, so much the better.[30]

In both the eastern and the western Mediterranean the movement of most shipping was governed by the rhythm of the seasons which made the task of the corsairs in finding a suitable prize very much easier. In December, for instance, the corsairs might set a course for the coast of Andalusia, knowing very well that the wine and fruit were exported by the Dutch and English ships at that time.[31] Since both sides knew the seasons it was quite common for such fleets to be protected by convoy, but the problems of convoying a fleet of merchant ships are notorious and the corsairs normally had little difficulty in cutting out a prize.[32] If the captured ship was sizeable the

Galleots towing their prizes home to Tunis.

corsairs would arm her with a prize-crew and send her back
to Barbary; otherwise once the cargo, passengers, and crew
had been transferred to the corsair ship the captured merchant
ship would normally be sunk. And so the process would go on
until the corsair was dangerously overloaded, or needed to
careen.

Knowledge of the trade-routes of the Mediterranean meant
that there were certain places where the corsairs were far more
likely to make prizes than anywhere else. Such were the island
of Sapienza, known as 'the corsairs' look-out', where the corsairs could lie in ambush for the Christian ships coming home
laden from the Levant,[33] Saint-Pierre and Cape de Gatt in the
western Mediterranean – all places of particular danger for
Christian merchant shipping, but places that it was difficult to
avoid.

In the first half of the seventeenth century, especially, the
corsairs made many cruises outside the Mediterranean. Their
normal cruising grounds were just outside the Straits and
along the Portuguese, Spanish, and French coastline up to
about the latitude of Bayonne. But sometimes cruises were far
more enterprising than this. In 1617 the corsairs pillaged the
island of Madeira and ten years later a Dutch renegade led an
attack on Iceland. Nor was England or Ireland safe. In 1634
the same Dutchman raided Baltimore and is reputed to have
taken 237 slaves. In the 1640s and 1650s there were several
raids in the English and Bristol Channels, including the famous
descent on the Cornish coast in 1654.[34] Later treaty relations
with the northern and western European naval powers
restricted the scope of the corsairs' activities in the Atlantic and
the English Channel, but captures were made beyond the
Straits right up to the nineteenth century. In 1809, for instance,
a fleet of Algerian corsairs made a rich haul of mainly Portuguese prizes before returning home through the Straits.[35]

Because of their superior strength, their speed, their avoid-
ance of powerful enemies, and their habit of boarding rather
than out-gunning an enemy the Barbary corsairs very often
captured their victims without a shot being fired. From sight
of a potential prize to boarding and successful capture could be
a matter of minutes as the corsair darted out from the conceal-
ment of a headland. If the victim should run, as most did, the

chase could be longer, but, as has been indicated above, the advantages of speed were all on the side of the Moslems and so unless the fugitive could make port, run aground or escape in the darkness eventual capture was more than likely.

Many Europeans have left accounts of their capture by Barbary corsairs. One of the most vivid is that of Le Sieur du Chastelet des Boys which appears in the description of his many travels published as *L'Odyssée* in 1665.[36] Des Boys was sailing near Bayonne when a sailor sighted from the masthead a caravel being driven by both sail and oar. At first the ship was taken for a Biscay frigate, but as it got closer they could see that the flags were pointed and not square, 'covered with crescents, suns, and stars which made us realize it was a Barbary corsair'. Des Boys' ship was made ready. The guns were run out, muskets were distributed to the passengers, daggers and pistols to the crew. The sails were spread out and sprinkled with water so that they might hold the wind better.

Opinion was divided on what to do next. 'Some felt it best to sail for the coast; others, young and impatient, to defend themselves, even to wait for the enemy, whose vessel was as small as ours, and could not have had more than six cannon altogether. Others were angry that we had not changed course already, and even the least able did not lack for ideas in the search for safety and the common interest.' Finally it was decided to change course at night and this was done, the ship running to the east until daybreak. But at sunrise the caravel was still in sight. Now there was no thought of anything but flight. But, just as all hope seemed lost, the situation changed completely. Through the sails six big ships flying the Dutch flag were sighted. The fugitives headed for their protection and the caravel turned tail.

Des Boys continues: 'But, alas, as soon as we were within musket shot, the Dutch flags disappeared and the masts and the poop were simultaneously shaded by flags of taffeta of all colours, enriched and embroidered with stars, crescents, suns, crossed swords and other devices and writings unknown . . . Now was the time to surrender or defend ourselves. Some climbed into the rigging, others stayed in the 'tween-decks by the guns, and the carpenter went down into the hold to mend such holes as the enemy's artillery might make during the fight.

'The flagship of these six ships, so recently thought to be Dutch, was armed with 38 cannon and 6 big perrier-guns, and had already fired four volleys at us . . . when redoubling their terrible yells of "*Mena pero*" [surrender, dogs] they gave us the whole broadside, and smashed our bowsprit with angel-shot. The cry of "*Brébré, mena pero*" rose higher and higher as they drew so near that with their muskets they wounded one of our sailors, and killed one of the foreign passengers. The rest of the crew, terrified, lowered the sails and waved their handkerchiefs as a sign of surrender. The soldiers, still less resolute, laid down their arms. The deck and the waist of the ship were deserted and the hold filled up with fugitives.

'The boats of the enemy ship and of the caravel, which had just caught up with them again, were lowered into the sea, and they boarded us. The barbarous and motley adventurers, with whom the boats were filled, threw themselves into boarding our desolate petacchio, and into climbing up our wooden walls, without any resistance; a few sailors handed them the boarding ropes, in order to curry favour, and to save their lives after they had lost their liberty . . . The most tight-fisted debased themselves and offered up their small change; silver was no longer precious to them. Gold, less cumbersome, and easier to be carried or hidden, was concealed in various ways. Some made bracelets of it, in order to encircle their arms, and to obscure its glitter in the shadow of a shirt-sleeve, and thus to frustrate the clairvoyance of the corsairs . . . Some swallowed pistoles, crowns, and other pieces of money . . . But most of the silver, the bejewelled coats, gilded swords, embroidered belts, boots, letters and other marks of wealth or quality, were thrown into the sea, either in spite and dislike of seeing their goods possessed by an enemy, or in order to avoid, by disguising themselves, their enemies' demands for a high ransom.'

Simultaneously the corsairs were searching the ship and the passengers. Not much escaped them except those possessions thrown into the sea. Boxes were broken open with axes, passengers were stripped and some of the swallowed money was recovered by turning their prisoners upside down and shaking them. Later the crew and passengers were cross-questioned to discover any further hiding-places, and also to discover the rank and wealth of the passengers. The process of cross-questioning and torture was scientific and wasted the minimum of time. First the captain was beaten on the feet to 'reveal the smallest details of the cargo of the ship'. The captain gave little away but the first mate was less hardy. He told where some money was hidden and gave information about the passengers. A few more selected beatings as individuals incriminated their comrades soon gave the corsairs as much information as they needed. Finally the slaves and booty were shared out between the corsairs' ships and they set sail along the Spanish coast, flying the Spanish flag, on their way back to Algiers.

The use of false flags, so effective in the capture of Des Boys' ship, was the commonest stratagem of all in these uneasy centuries. By sending the janissaries below deck and pretending to be a peaceful commercial ship or Christian privateer the corsairs often completely fooled their victims, so that a prize would run right alongside the corsair before realizing that it had been tricked. This happened, for instance to the American brig, *Polly*, in 1793. She was hailed in English by a man 'dressed in the Christian habit ... the only person we could yet see on her deck'.[37] False flags were also used by the corsairs' victims but often such stratagems backfired. In 1692, the French Consul at Algiers reported the arrival of a corsair with a Portuguese prize laden with corn. The corsair had met the Portuguese at night and had hailed in Dutch. The Portuguese had two flags and two passports, one French and one Portuguese. Thinking that the corsair was a Dutchman and knowing that Holland was at war with France they threw the French flag and passport into the sea. This was, of course, a big mistake, since French ships were safe from capture by the Algerians but Portuguese were good prizes.[38] The fact that a corsair could hail in Dutch or English was no accident either. The Algerine ship which captured Emanuel d'Aranda in 1640 had an English renegade captain and members of the crew could speak Turkish, Arabic, Spanish, French, Flemish, Dutch, and English as well as Franco, the lingua franca of Barbary – a mixture of Italian, Spanish, French and Portuguese.[39]

Des Boys' ship at least made a show of resistance, but it would clearly have been foolhardy to do more when opposed by seven corsairs. The reaction of most merchant ships on seeing a corsair was to turn and run for the coast, or even, so terrible was

the corsairs' reputation, to haul down their colours immediately
and wait for the inevitable. The corsairs who captured the
Italian poet, Filippo Pananti told him that they had no thought
of capturing the brig on which he was sailing to Sicily, but
'seeing our total inactivity, and a seeming disposition to
approach, rather than get away, they thought us enchanted'.[40]
Pananti's ship was near the coast, and such a reaction would be
more common when a small merchant ship was caught in the
open sea with little chance of escaping the speedy corsairs.
Passive acceptance of one's fate is not necessarily a Moslem
trait. Travellers at sea must have expected to face the possibility
of capture and the remark of the English renegade who captured d'Aranda is a fair summary of the situation. 'Patience,
brother, it is the fortune of war: today for you, and tomorrow
for me.'[41] Certainly the corsairs were not unopposed and some
ships put up a fantastic resistance. The Dutch had a particularly
good reputation in this respect, and were renowned for their
habit of blowing up the powder magazine when capture
seemed inevitable.[42] And often of course it was the corsair
himself who was the potential victim. But normally their speed
was as effective in avoiding capture as in taking a prize.
Cervantes makes his corsair say in *El Trato de Argel*, 'Yes, but
pursuit by the Spaniards is not a serious matter. Their ships
are hampered by their own weight . . . We are armed lightly
and are as free as flame. They chase us? We can go well even
against the wind; we haul down our sails and all the rigging,
and we leave them behind easily.'[43]

Virtually all accounts of capture by the corsairs mention the
terrifying noise that the janissaries made as they closed in on the
potential prize. Hurling abuse, banging the sides of their boats,
clapping their hands – the noise itself was sufficient to make
most men drop their arms. And all descriptions mention the
actual boarding as the strange-looking, fanatical men of 'all
the races sent forth from the African continent' swarmed over
the sides of the ship. This was the supreme moment for the
turbaned warriors in their flowing robes. Wearing no armour,
bare-armed, with their great curving scimitars grasped in their
hands they normally made short work of any resistance, as they
swept through the ship.

The process of searching the ship, described by Des Boys,

was naturally a regular procedure in the corsair business. Accounts of voyages make numerous references to the attempts of passengers and crew to conceal their identity and to hide their most valuable possessions. An amusing story is told of the French numismatist, Vaillant. His ship was approached by a Sallee Rover and in order to sweeten his captivity he swallowed twenty gold coins. But the wind got up and they managed to evade capture. Back in Lyons he visited his friend M. Dufour, also a collector. Cross-questioning revealed that the coins were the heaviest possible. Dufour's first reaction was to make a bid for them, despite his apprehensions at the effects on his friend's stomach. 'Is it possible that you have cared to load your stomach with a weight of as much as five or six ounces, and of a matter so solid?' he asked. Vaillant replied, 'You speak like a man who is at ease in his study, and who can see only from 100 leagues the horrors of slavery. If you had been in my place, you would probably have swallowed, not only the coins, but the ship itself, if it had been possible, to sweeten the bitterness of captivity.'[44]

By the seventeenth century, when eventual ransom was the normal lot of the corsairs' victims, the main interest of captured prisoners was to conceal their rank and wealth so that their ransom might be calculated at the lowest possible figure. Des Boys describes the jettisoning of marks of quality, but attempts to fool the corsairs often went to far greater lengths. Nobles changed clothes with their valets, disguises were worn and so on.[45] Many writers left advice to those who might be so unfortunate as to be captured. D'Arvieux advised new slaves to 'say that they do not expect to be ransomed, that their relations are too poor for that, that having been accustomed to live by their work, it is all the same to them in which country God sends them, since they must always work to live ... ''[46] But the corsairs were well aware of most of the tricks. D'Aranda told how the corsairs looked at his hands to see if they were fit for hard work and his teeth to see if he could chew galley biscuit.[47] Hands and teeth, indeed, were normally sufficient to indicate a man's station in life, if not his bank balance. Examination of the hands could tell more than this, though, since skilful reading of the palm could show how long a slave would live and whether he would escape![48]

Apart from searching the passengers and crew, the captain

and the purser (*khodja*) were always quick to get hold of the ship's books and to seal the cargo in order to prevent their men from sacking that as well. But on the score of pillaging captured ships the Barbary corsairs had a better reputation than most privateers of the period. It was the universal custom of corsairs that certain goods such as the possessions of captured sailors and passengers should be the personal reward of those who captured them.[49] Other goods such as any cargo below deck and the contents of the captain's cabin were reserved either for the general share-out or for particular persons who had customary rights to them. The normal practice of the Barbary corsairs was to pile goods that were destined for the general share-out around the mast. Many writers were surprised at the high standard of honesty shown in doing this. D'Arvieux went as far as to say that the Barbary corsairs did not pillage at all.[50] This seems rather unlikely though the punishments for the individual found defrauding his mates were characteristically savage. None the less the general behaviour of the corsairs when capturing a ship was very much better than that of their Maltese rivals, and incomparably better than that of a contemporary English privateer.[51] The strong discipline of the janissaries and the scrupulously fair division of booty in the Barbary ports were the main reasons for this. D'Arvieux writes: 'It is surprising that people as brutal and barbarous as the Algerians can keep so much order and justice as they do in their brigandage. One never sees the least difficulty amongst them over the division of the booty.'[52]

The corsairs also treated their captives much better than one might think. Many of these were taken straight on as sailors, divided into watches under the eyes of the soldiers.[53] Although when off-duty they were normally confined, they seem to have been chained up only when the ship was actually going into action.[54] Passengers were generally treated with respect; indeed, kind and flattering words were a good way of getting a captive to drop his guard and reveal his station in life. Women were almost invariably well treated. Anyone who touched a woman in a sensual manner ran a very great risk of being bastinadoed,[55] and Pananti goes so far as to advise future captives to give any gold or other valuables they might have to the female passengers 'as the Turks hold their persons

Pollacca. This sort of prize could easily be converted into a corsair.
Stromboli was a favourite hide-out of the Barbary corsairs.

sacred'.[56] Most of the discomfort for a captive on a corsair ship
arose from his own misery at the reality of his capture and the
thought of long years of slavery ahead of him, and the poor
conditions of the ship itself. The ship, already full of fighting
men, had little room for captives, and so if the latter were
confined it was normally in such foul and evil-smelling places
as the cable locker. As we have seen the corsairs took few provisions on board, and so there was little for their captives, and
what there was would probably not be to their taste. Pananti,
for instance, complained bitterly of the eternal couscous, and a
bite from a fresh onion could seem like a luxury after a few
days.[57] All passengers, too, were struck by the general lack of
comfort on board the corsair ship. Even the Rais himself might
be seen 'sitting upon a matt on the cabin floor'.[58] Such discomfort
and overcrowding naturally became worse the more captives
were taken, and became a real hazard to the seaworthiness of

the ship on some occasions, as the weight took the freeboard to dangerously low levels and heavy seas washed over the decks. This was particularly likely to be the case after a successful shore raid. The Spanish agent in Tunis reported the return of the corsairs after a raid on the island of Saint-Pierre in 1798. Four Tunisian ships and a galley, with a total of 1,000 men, raided the island and took 950 slaves, of whom 702 were women and children. The Spanish agent asks his correspondent to imagine what they endured, 'penned like sheep', on the return voyage to Tunis. Smallpox was rife amongst them, all were nearly naked, exhausted, dying of thirst, and suffocating from the excessive heat.[59] And if this was not bad enough think of the journey of the 800 slaves whom Morat Reis brought back from Iceland!

But such raids were exceptional in the seventeenth and eighteenth centuries. Most raids were now on a smaller scale which makes it difficult to estimate their total impact. Italy, particularly the southern provinces, and Sicily were almost certainly the areas which felt the greatest weight of the raids by the corsairs but there are records of raids throughout the western Mediterranean during this period as well as on the Atlantic seaboard and in the Atlantic Islands.[60] But most raids in the Atlantic were conducted by corsairs and pirates based on the ports of Morocco, in particular the famous Sallee Rovers, with whom we are not here concerned.[61]

The tactics of Barbary raiding parties varied considerably with the size of the fleet involved. When the numbers were large it was quite common to seize a strong-point and hold it for several days, while sending raiding-parties out into the surrounding countryside, before eventually re-embarking. Although naturally the main object of such parties was to collect booty and slaves, nearly all accounts record much religiously motivated destruction. Churches were broken into and ransacked, crucifixes trodden into the ground, images destroyed, and a common feature was for the raiding parties to bear off the church bells in triumph. Small parties from single ships or small fleets did not normally indulge in such noisy diversions. Landing at night they normally made a quick march inland to surprise a sleeping village, hoping to be back on their ships before a general alarm had been sounded throughout the countryside. A common feature of many raids, and one which was often essential to their success, was the use of local guides. Since, as we have seen, Barbary had such an enormous population of renegades there were in most North African cities potential guides for much of the Christian Mediterranean coastline. Indeed there are several documented cases of Christians, with a grudge against their neighbours or their masters, sailing for Barbary with the specific intention of apostasizing and returning with the corsairs to guide a raiding party. In Sicily, Calabria, and Corsica such actions had become a recognized extension of many a local vendetta.[62]

Although many thousands of men, women, and children were literally pulled from their beds during the three centuries of the Barbary corsairs' existence, not all raids were successful. The element of surprise was normally sufficient to ensure success, but the dangers of making night raids, particularly the danger of losing one's way, are fairly obvious. Nor were the inhabitants of the Christian coastline completely supine in the face of repeated raids by the corsairs. The easiest form of defence was to evacuate the coastline, and indeed much of the southern European littoral did become deserted during this period. More constructive was the building of watch-towers and the concentration at key-points of defensive forces who could quickly be brought to an attacked area. Such defences worked occasionally, and many spectacular successes against the corsairs are recorded in local chronicles.[63]

An example of one such defence-system in operation can be seen from the chronicle of the city of Catanzaro in Calabria.[64] In 1644 a squadron of galleys led by a local renegade, who wished to revenge himself on a former neighbour who had offended his honour, disembarked at night. But the local population had received adequate warning of their arrival and had fled, so that not a single slave was taken. The corsairs had to be satisfied with sacking and burning the houses, and ransacking the church. The next year the corsairs arrived again with an even larger raiding party. Once again the locals had been warned and had made their escape. Once again the corsairs sacked and burned, this time extending their activities to neighbouring villages. But on this occasion help was on its way. The governor of the province with 400 cavalry, 'the flower of

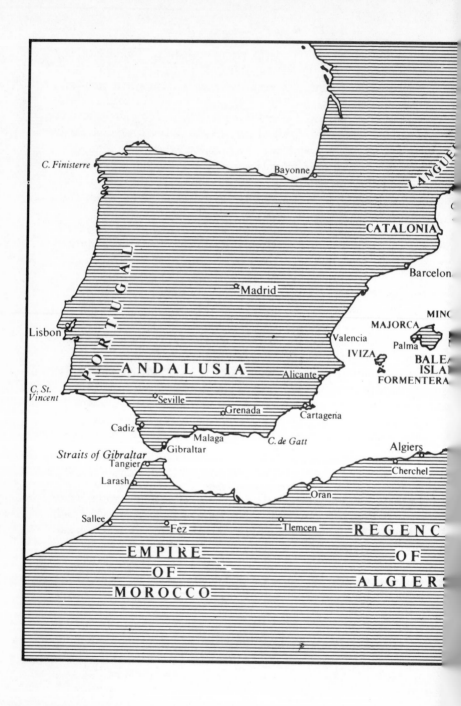

the nobility and of the most respected citizens', rode down towards the corsairs. Even so, all nearly ended in disaster, for the corsairs, with remarkable discipline for night raiders, fell back onto a reverse slope and lay in ambush for the cavalry. Only the good sense of one of the knights, 'a soldier of experience who had grown old in the wars and knew the country very well', saved the horsemen from running straight into the trap by advising his commander to send scouts out ahead. Their ambush discovered, the corsairs retired in good order while the guns of the galleys gave them covering fire. Only one squadron who were driving a herd of cattle back to the ships ran into serious trouble. Attacked by the locals, they left their booty and fled, leaving five prisoners behind. Reading this account one is struck by the remarkable discipline of the raiding party, esti-mated by the chronicler to be 3,000 strong [almost certainly an exaggeration], which, at night and in a strange land, was able to fall back to its ships with the loss of so few men. This discipline and the element of surprise were normally sufficient to ensure that the raids of the corsairs were only too successful. The dismal notice of 40 slaves taken here, 30 there, 200 there is what the chroniclers normally had to record.[65]

The Christians had developed defences against the corsairs at sea as well as on land. We have already mentioned the convoying of merchant fleets and the strong armament of large merchant ships. But the main line of defence at sea were the navies of the corsairs' enemies. For some of these navies the seeking and capturing of the ships of the Barbary corsairs was virtually their only function. Such were the galleys of the Papal Navy operating from the ports of the Papal States and the galleys of the Knights of St Stephen from Leghorn.[66] Both these navies had several successes against the corsairs, but over the whole period the most consistently successful opponents of the Barbary corsairs were the galleys and ships of the Order of St John in Malta.[67] Year after year they made cruises whose main objective was the capture of Moslem shipping, and in particular of corsair ships. And every now and then they made a significant capture.

But such successes, though much trumpeted in Christian Europe, were comparatively rare and the normal end to the cruise of the Barbary corsair was the more or less triumphant return to his home port. With flags flying and guns blasting off – the general noise being related to the size of the prize – the corsairs brought their booty home. And their unwilling passengers were normally impressed by what they saw, especially by Algiers, 'that proud city . . . that retreat of the men who have made God bankrupt'.[68]

CHAPTER 4

Disposal of the Booty

'The Turks, but above all the corsairs of Algiers, Tunis, Tripoli, and other places in Barbary, make war for gain rather than glory.'
LE SIEUR DU CHASTELET DES BOYS.[1]

'But they say that this money from the *corso* does not profit them much, for the bars and whores eat it up very quickly.'
VENTURE DE PARADIS.[2]

As we have seen, the activities of the Barbary corsairs in the sixteenth century formed part of a general maritime war between Islam and Christendom. At that time, glory as well as gain entered into the motivation of the corsair. But, by the 1580s, the *grande guerre*, to use Braudel's phrase, was over, and for most of the rest of their existence the Barbary corsairs, like their Maltese rivals, were mainly motivated by gain. By 1650, as the French historian, de Grammont, rather regretfully remarked, the Algerian corsairs 'were only scourers of the sea, half merchants, half pirates, considering their profession as an industry which should be exercised as prudently as possible, and avoiding, by all imaginable means, the necessity of fighting'.[3]

Organized plunder needs rules. Even the individual pirate needs some arrangement for sharing his booty with his crew. When legalized piracy had attained the scale and permanence of the operations of the Barbary corsairs, the rules had to be fully institutionalized and understood by all participants. From God to the lowest cabin-boy, everyone with an interest in a Barbary corsair ship knew what they could expect when the booty was shared out. According to the Koran one-fifth of the booty should go to God.[4] In practice this proportion was normally one-seventh or one-eighth, and went to God's secular representative in Barbary, the State. Further fixed proportions of the booty went for the upkeep of the port, to the port officials, brokers and to marabouts (the Islamic equivalent of Christian saints).[5] Then, when these payments had been made and the ship had been cleared of any outstanding debt, the net value of the booty was divided into two equal portions – one for the owners of the corsair ship, and one for the crew.[6] The owner might of course be the State itself, in which case the owner's share would be added to the State's share as the representative of God. But, especially in the seventeenth century, a high proportion of Barbary corsair ships was owned by private individuals. Sometimes the owner was the captain himself, but more often ownership rested in syndicates who made an investment in the *corso*, just as they might have done in any other type of business. Such investors included 'rich merchants, powerful servants of the State, high officials in the armed forces . . . but together with them were shopkeepers, artisans, and small savers who had faithfully pledged their own capital in part-ownership of a corsair ship'.[7]

While the owners' share was divided *pro rata* of each individual investment, the rules for the division of the crew's share were more complicated. First of all there was much that did not enter into the general account at all. 'When a ship is taken by boarding, all the gear of the sailors [and in fact the passengers] can be pillaged, and everything in the cabin belongs to the captain; but neither the captain nor the crew must ever touch the cargo or the ship's equipment.'[8] Apart from what they could grab on boarding, individuals were also occasionally granted bonuses for special services, such as being first on board a defended prize, or being the watchman who first sighted a ship later captured.[9] The rest of the crew's share was divided into several hundred parts and individuals had rights to a certain proportion of these. By the late eighteenth century, for instance, the captain had a right to 40 parts, sailors to 3, janissaries to 1½, and cabin-boys to 1. An indication of the importance of captured Christian seamen on board Barbary corsair ships is that they, too, were entitled to 3 parts, the same as a free Moslem seaman.[10] This fact intrigued the Italian Pananti. 'It is remarkable,' he wrote, 'that all Christian slaves, who may have been on board an Algerine when any capture is made, are entitled to their share of the prize; it being presumed their good fortune contributed to the event!'[11] Another feature of the division of prizes in Barbary which surprised Christian observers was the marked absence of dispute, once the division had been made.[12] When there was trouble it was normally because of a greedy Dey or Pasha who wished to bring the State's share somewhat nearer to the Koranic one-fifth. Writers commented, too, on the speed of justice. Everyone pleaded their own case and there was no appeal. D'Arvieux wrote: 'Our lawyers, attorneys and other people who gnaw on mankind . . . would die of hunger in this country'.[13] A familiar comment for a seventeenth-century Frenchman! Certainly Barbary must have made a strong contrast to contemporary Malta where the law courts were full of disputes between corsairs, and where many a litigant died of old age before receiving a decision on his case.

What happened to the booty itself? The biggest single item was often the captured ship, its armament and its equipment. In Barbary the State tried hard to keep this part of the prize for itself, to counteract the chronic shortage of shipbuilding and war *matériel*. Ships and munitions could then either be sold or armed as corsair ships on the State's own account. The corsairs themselves, however, disliked this practice. It was contrary to the normal custom of corsairs in the Mediterranean, and it naturally reduced the amount of prize-money to be shared between crew and owners by a very considerabe amount. By the late seventeenth century the corsairs had developed a method of forcing the rules to be changed. Since the prize ship brought them no gain, and at the same time meant that they had to deplenish their crew to man it, they developed the habit of destroying prizes, once cargo and crew had been transferred to their own ships. This benefited no one, and so the rules were sometimes relaxed, especially when private individuals owned a high proportion of the Regency's corsair fleet.[14] However, whether the prize went to the state or the owner, it was either itself fitted out as a corsair ship or was sold. Many smaller ships which were not suitable for the *corso* went straight back into Christian hands. In 1651, for instance, the Dey of Tunis sold a captured pollacca to three Maltese merchants who loaded it with grain and took it back to Malta.[15] In 1696 the Tripolitan corsair, Mamet Mezzaluna, sold a prize barque that had been built in Malta to two Italians. The corsair promised not to seize it again before it reached Christendom![16]

The cargo of captured ships was sold, normally by auction, in the ports of Barbary. Some cargoes found a ready outlet in Barbary and were bought in the normal way of business by the local population. Prices would normally depend on the state of the market, but were occasionally inflated by a belief, encouraged by the corsairs, that the mere possession of goods seized from Christians was of spiritual value to the purchaser.[17] Many cargoes, however, had no market in Barbary, and would have sold for extremely low prices if Christians had not been prepared to make a profit out of their unfortunate co-religionaries' loss. Sometimes Christians bought prize-goods direct at the auction, but this was frowned on, and occasionally the purchaser was later punished, so it was more normal to buy from intermediaries.[18] These were often Jews who had formed considerable colonies in all the North African ports. Haedo estimated that there were 150 Jewish households in Algiers in the late sixteenth century.[19] In 1717, a lean time for the Algerians, the French consul reported to his masters that 'the Jews, who number about 10,000, appropriate all the little business that is done in this place; they are even owners of corsair ships'.[20] The Jews who specialized in prize-goods and ransom were normally 'French Jews' or 'Christian Jews' from France or Leghorn, and often of Marrano origin. They were better treated than the rest of the North African Jews and were often under the protection of the French consul.[21] They distributed the Christian prize-goods throughout the Mediterranean, either by selling them direct to Christian merchants in North Africa, or by forwarding them to their Jewish correspondents in the busy entrepôt of Leghorn. In Barbary there were facilities for changing marks and altering bales so that

'the goods stolen by those pirates are bought by the agents of
Leghorn merchants at easy prices and sent forthwith to Leghorn'.[22] The prize-goods dealt in reflected the normal trade of
the areas patrolled by the corsairs. In the Mediterranean
these were normally of little value – wine, grain, fish, hides, and
other foodstuffs and raw materials, though a cargo of silks,
cloth, or cash could soon make a corsair's fortune. On their
rarer visits to the Atlantic and the English Channel the corsairs
occasionally made much richer prizes, such as the *Empress
Elizabeth* of Ostend captured in 1728 on its way back from the
East Indies with a cargo of coffee, muslins, tea, and porcelain.[23]

Despite these occasional lucky coups there is little doubt that
over time the main income of the corsairs arose from the sale
of the crews and passengers of captured Christian ships, or
of the slaves taken during their raids ashore. The trade in men
is one of the oldest trades in the Mediterranean, and rarely
can it have been so flourishing as in the second half of the
seventeenth century, when Moslem and Christian corsairs
alike found a ready outlet for their merchandise. Throughout
the history of the *corso* this trade had two main aspects. Captured slaves were sold, mainly to co-religionaries, for the work or
services they could perform; or, alternatively, they could be
freed on payment of ransom. Ransom and sale were closely
inter-related activities, as we shall see.

The slaves captured by the Barbary corsairs rarely had to
wait long before their first acquaintance with the slave market,
a focal point in most Moslem cities. Their captors had little
interest in maintaining them for any longer than was necessary,
unless they were someone of apparently great importance, who
if sold too quickly might not fetch his proper price. And so, after
the State had chosen its share of each new batch, most of the
rest were soon brought to the market. Here, the morning was
normally given over to inspection while the auction itself was
held in the afternoon.[24] Many writers have described the
indignity of the inspection and sale of slaves in Moslem cities.
Often nearly naked, the slaves were prodded and pushed, made
to run and jump to see what sort of a physical specimen they
were. Once again, hands and mouth were examined to see
whether they were fit for work. Further cross-questioning could
be expected, to determine whether the investment might yield

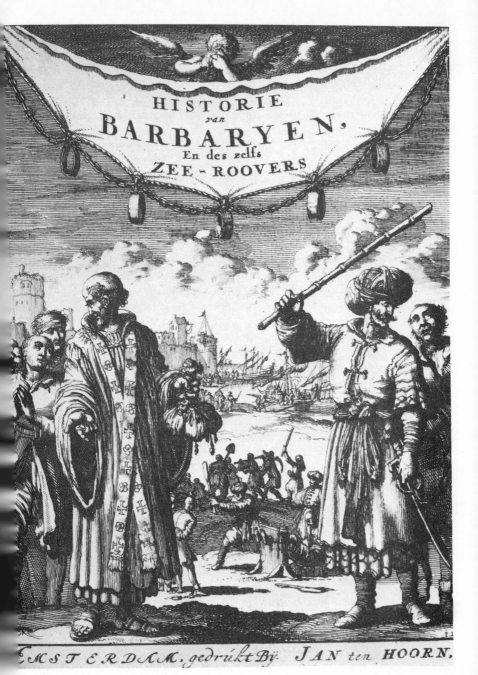

Arrival of the Redemptionist Fathers at Algiers. This is the frontis-
piece to the Dutch edition of Father Dan's famous *History of Barbary*.

a high return as a result of a good ransom. But this was all for men. Women, contrary to popular belief, were treated with much more decorum. In Constantinople, for instance, while the men were sold nearly naked, 'the women are completely covered' but could be viewed more intimately in a house set back from the market.[25] And in Algiers they were placed in a 'concealed latticed shop'.[26]

The inspection of slaves finished, it was now time for the auction. The auctioneers, paid by commission, were skilled at their job and knew how to inflate prices by singing the praises of individuals. Slaves who might be expected to fetch high prices – gentlemen, beautiful women, priests, skilled craftsmen, etc. – were sold individually. Others were sold in batches. The range of prices was considerable. The median slave was probably a fairly young man, with no education or skill, apparently fit to labour or pull an oar for many years. The old and the sick and the very young might well fetch no more than a quarter of his price, whilst skilled craftsmen, especially those skilled in the operation of building ships, might fetch four or five times as much.[27] And then occasionally the corsairs would capture someone who would sell for an enormous price – a nobleman, a Knight of Malta or a beautiful woman – though normally such treasured slaves would have already been picked out by the Dey as part of his eighth. D'Aranda has described well the actual process of his own sale. 'An old and very decrepit auctioneer, with a staff in his hand, took me by the arm, and led me to different parts of the market.' As he was being exhibited, D'Aranda was asked questions about his station in life, and was once again put through a physical examination. 'Then they made us all sit down, and this old auctioneer took the first in the line by the arm, walking three or four times round the market with him, crying "*Arrache, arrache*", which means who will offer more.' When it came to D'Aranda's turn, 'I heard several people offer money, without however understanding what they said . . . but in the end the bargain was made for 200 patagons.' But the Pasha had the right to buy any slave at the final price bid, and so all the slaves were taken in front of him, with the price of their sale marked on their heads. The Pasha picked out d'Aranda and placed him with 250 other slaves, the crew of his galley.[28] This second display of the slaves to the Pasha could be a trying time for the successful bidders, especially speculators who, by playing down their value, had got a potentially valuable slave at a low price.

By the seventeenth century the State or the private individuals who acquired slaves in the market nearly always fixed a price for their eventual ransom. Often this would only be the purchase price itself, or else the price *plus* a small mark-up. But if the sellers believed that they had acquired somebody with great assets or rich relations in Europe, then naturally the ransom was raised accordingly. Unfortunately for the slaves, the information service in Barbary, though good, was by no means perfect, and ransoms were often set at ridiculously high prices. And it was often virtually impossible for the slave himself to persuade his new owner of the poverty of his background in Europe. For set alongside these truly poor men with a high ransom on their heads were the truly rich telling exactly the same stories to prove that they were really poor. The whole business of ransom was thus extremely arbitrary.

A letter of 1758 from a Lazarist Father to the Venetian magistrate in charge of the funds raised by public charity to ransom his fellow-citizens throws some interesting light on the economics of the ransom market. He pointed out that the price fixed for a ransom depended on the status of the owner of the slave. The higher was the rank of the slave-owner, the higher would be the ransom asked. The highest of all might be asked by the Dey, though other high-ranking people liked to emulate him. 'The Dey considers as a glory and a manifestation of grandeur the fact of having a great number of slaves; he will never lower his price and he has no love of authorizing ransoms. That is his fantasy, and as the government is despotic, no one will make him change his mind.' In these conditions a glut in the slave market would not have the effect of lowering the price of ransom asked by high-ranking persons – rather the opposite since there would now be less need for income from ransoms. Amongst lower-ranking persons, however, the laws of supply and demand would be felt. The Father saw only one way of lowering the high prices which were being asked when he wrote his letter. It was as ingenious as it was impractical. This was to put a complete stop to the ransom of all Christians for several years, while at the same time ensuring that all Moslems enslaved in Christendom were ransomed only at the prices then current for Christians in Barbary. 'But', he pointed out, 'it would have to be absolutely general: perhaps the Regency would then open its eyes.' Even if the loss of income had no effect on the Dey, it might well stir the soldiers to revolution – an event which would probably in itself lower the price of slaves.[29] Although he could not match the splendid imagination of the Lazarist, a Trinitarian had some good ideas to offer the same Venetian magistrate a few years later. He suggested that slaves should bribe the Dey's doctor to speak to the Dey and obtain an advantageous ransom by letting him suppose that his slave was in danger of death. This was what happened to Don Alessandro Visconti, a gentleman of Milan. His ransom had been fixed at 3,000 Venetian sequins. Unable to procure this sum the poor gentleman spent eight years in slavery. After going to hospital he was ransomed at the end for 530 sequins, including all the money spent during his captivity and his passage to Milan![30]

Before discussing the conditions of slaves in Barbary it is necessary to look at the matter with a sense of perspective. First, we are talking about the seventeenth and eighteenth centuries – a period when man's humanity to man, slave or free, was not a particularly pronounced feature of his behaviour. Secondly, much of what we know about Barbary was written by men who had a very definite interest in painting as black a picture as they could. This was particularly true of the Redemptionist Fathers who told lies about the condition of the slaves 'in order to excite the charity of the Faithful'.[31] Thirdly, slavery is a traditional institution of Islam, but one which took many different forms. There were three different sorts of slave in Barbary, and there were three different sorts of slavery. The Christians captured by corsairs were considered as prisoners-of-war. They could be ransomed. They could be repatriated if peace was signed between their own country and the Regency where they were enslaved.[32] And, if they apostasized, they could if they were lucky, look forward to a high social and political position in the State. An intermediate position was held by the white slaves imported from the Levant. Mainly Georgians and Circassians, they were regarded as objects of commerce, and not prisoners-of-war, and so could not be ransomed or repatriated. But like the Christians they could rise to power in the State. Finally there were the Negro slaves. Marched up from Kano or Bornu, changing master at every major trading centre, the Negroes eventually reached the North African coast after a journey on foot of some 2,000 miles. For some even this was not their final destination. Changing master once more they were shipped to the Levant. But most remained in Barbary. Fairly well treated, they had no hope of ransom or repatriation, no hope of social or political preferment, and even if freed on their master's death they remained for ever in an inferior position.[33]

The Christians, then, were the only slaves who had a hope of ransom. But while they waited, sometimes for ever, for their ransom they were set to work by their new masters. The conditions of their existence were determined very largely by the sort of work that they were made to do. Nearly all accounts agree that the very worst work and the cruellest conditions were suffered by those slaves who were fated to row on the galleys, or work in chain-gangs ashore on heavy construction work. Though the life of a galley-slave may have been somewhat exaggerated by writers in the past, there can be little doubt that such a life could be a veritable hell on earth. When slaves provided the motive power to win a fortune or to escape from death or slavery, it seems certain that their masters must soon forget their humanity, even if they probably fed and clothed them better than is suggested in most accounts. Slaves cost money, and it seems unlikely that they would be allowed to starve or die of exposure unnecessarily. None the less the very nature of the occupation meant a very harsh life in cramped, noisome, and extremely exposed quarters. When the galley-captain was a psychopath who took a coarse pleasure in inflicting pain, such as Bekir Pasha, then life was worse than harsh.[34] But to most captains the slave was probably treated in a similar way to his horse or donkey ashore. If he starved it, or flogged it to death, then he would have to buy another one. On the other hand if he flogged it, it seemed to work harder. The same attitude is apparent in the treatment of slaves engaged in heavy labour. Work that might have been done by mechanical or animal power in northern Europe was done by slaves in Barbary. Slaves were used as stevedores, as quarrymen, as the motive power for pulling carts or ploughs, and for much other

heavy work. One task which was never-ending was the rein-
forcement of the mole which protects the harbour of Algiers
from the north wind. Built by Kheireddin Barbarrosa from the
ruins of the Spanish fort, Le Peñon d'Alger, it was continually
being washed away by the action of the sea. Several generations
of slaves worked in quarries two miles inland to break the
necessary stone, carted the stone on sleds to the Marina and
loaded it into lighters to be placed behind the mole.[35] Chained
together, and kept at their tasks by an overseer with a whip,
such slaves were perhaps the most to be pitied of all.

But not all slaves, nor even a majority, were engaged in such
tasks. Barbary economy and society rested on slavery, and slaves
could be found in practically every occupation. Individuals
who bought slaves as an investment used them as household
servants, clerks, or shop assistants. Slaves were engaged in high
positions in the government. And in all these occupations,
where the whip was not likely to bring forth any better per-
formance from the slave, the conditions of life were probably
fairly bearable. Islam teaches kindness and pity towards slaves,
and there are many instances of slaves being treated much
better in Barbary than they had ever been as free men in
Christian Europe. D'Arvieux said of the slaves of Mehmed Beg,
the son of the Pasha of Tunis, that they were so well treated
that they had forgotten their own country, 'where they knew
they would never be so much at their ease, as they were with
him'.[36] Often, indeed, it might be hard to tell who was slave
and who was master, so important did the slave become in the
domestic economy of Islam. It is wise, therefore, to treat with
caution the horrific descriptions of the life of slaves in Barbary.
Horrors there certainly were, but life could be pleasant as well.

Although the number of slaves declined fairly rapidly in the
second half of the seventeenth century and in the eighteenth
century, as a result of a quicker turnover through better organization of ransoms, and of the decline of the corsairs themselves,
slaves must sometimes have formed between 10 and 20 per cent
of the total population of the great cities of Barbary.[37] This fact
naturally posed considerable problems of discipline and control.
A rigid code of regulations governed the life of the slave, and a
strict check was kept on his movements. Very violent punishments were meted out for any transgression of such rules.

Christian slaves being examined and shown off in the slave market at Algiers.

European ships which visited the Barbary ports had their sails
and oars removed to prevent slaves trying to escape. And, at
night, slaves were confined indoors. The slaves of the State and
of the most powerful citizens were held in special slave-prisons,
known as *bagnos*, where individual slave-owners could also lodge
their slaves for a fee.

Conditions naturally varied from *bagno* to *bagno* but on the
whole they appear to have been quite reasonable. Some *bagnos*,
such as the Grand Bagno of Algiers were enormous complexes
of buildings able to hold up to 2,000 Christian slaves.[38]
D'Arvieux has left two excellent descriptions of *bagnos* in Tunis
and Algiers, and a modern writer comments that he makes
them sound like 'a more rascally version of a debtor's prison
in the time of Dickens'.[39] Of a *bagno* in Tunis d'Arvieux writes:

> One finds on entering a great square or oblong courtyard
> surrounded by stalls; these serve for the slaves to keep their
> taverns. The back of these shops is divided into several small
> rooms, which are occupied for the most part by the priests
> of the various nations who take care of the slaves . . . One is
> very safe in these places, and free to come and go as one
> pleases. The main gate is opened at daybreak and is shut
> very late.
>
> The courtyard is furnished with many tables, always full
> of soldiers, sailors and other idle or dissolute people who
> go there to drink wine, sing, smoke, or talk business . . . The
> slaves who run these bars pay a fairly considerable sum to
> the Concierge of the *bagno*, who, in return for this tribute,
> protects them and makes those who refuse to pay for their
> drinks pay on the spot . . .
>
> At the end of the courtyard opposite the main gate is the
> prison, a big building divided into three parts, the middle one
> serving as a Church and the two others as lodgings for the
> slaves.

In their lodgings the slaves had their beds suspended one
above the other with rope ladders connecting them. The slave's
bed had to serve not only as a place of rest but also to keep
all his possessions.[40] D'Arvieux did not find the *bagno* in Algiers
quite as attractive. Although the organization of the *bagno* was

similar, the lodgings were 'places of horror, where smoke from the cooking-fires which are prepared on all sides, noise, cries, blows and tumult reign everywhere'. Here again the beds were heaped up one on top of the other.[41] Many years later things seem to have got even worse, for the American, Foss, reported that to sleep inside at all the slaves had to pay rent to the concierge, or else 'sleep in the open *bagno* where they have nothing but the firmament to cover them'.[42] The concierge (*guardian-basci*) of the *bagno* was the functionary who maintained discipline, kept the place clean and saw that the various gangs of slaves got off to the right work in the morning. Such a position could make a man a monster and terrible punishments were occasionally meted out to recalcitrant slaves. But normally his influence was little felt, and his agreement to a bending of the rules could be purchased for a small sum. By the seventeenth century, a general relaxation of attitudes towards Christian slaves had ensured that most of the bigger *bagnos* were able to provide considerable comforts that must have made the life of a slave much easier to bear. Chapels – Catholic, Protestant, and Orthodox – served mainly by captured priests or visiting Redemptionist Fathers existed in most *bagnos*; bars and shops of the type described by D'Arvieux were normally allowed; medical facilities were provided, and later slave hospitals were built. Above all there was the possibility of relaxation.[43] No one has given such a vivid description of life in the *bagno* as Emanuel d'Aranda. He enjoyed himself so much that even when he was living outside he used to go to the *bagno* for the entertainment – to listen to the slaves of Dunkirk, who recounted their adventures at sea, to the Dutch who knew the East Indies, Japan and China, to the Danes and Hamburgers who spun yarns about their experiences whale-fishing off Greenland. And if this was not to his liking, he listened to the Spaniards telling of Mexico or Peru, or the French of Canada and Virginia. 'For almost all the slaves are men of the sea.' [44] What he says rings true, and it seems clear that slavery could be an education, as well as an intolerable hardship.

Whether his life was harsh or comfortable nearly every slave must have been preoccupied with the thought of liberty and return to his homeland. The chances of escape were few, though some spectacular stories have been recorded,[45] and the only other way home was through the payment of his ransom, or through exchange for Moslems held in a Christian land. Collection of his ransom money, often set at inflated levels, was therefore the main interest of most Christian slaves.

The institution of ransom required a very considerable organization, and a network of individuals who specialized in this business had grown up throughout Islam and Christendom. Men were needed to communicate between the captured slave and his family or business associates. Specialist moneylenders provided ransom money against the slave's future expectations from inheritance or business. Facilities for the remittance of cash to Barbary were established. Shipowners carried freed slaves back to their homelands on credit. Alongside these individuals to whom ransom was just a part of their business which paid well and made use of their existing commercial contacts between Islam and Christendom, there also existed organizations whose only function was to arrange ransoms.[46]

Most famous amongst these were the Redemptionist Fathers, orders established in the Middle Ages to arrange ransoms, alleviate the hardships of the slave's life and to save him from the temptation of apostasy. The orders were financed by bequests and collections from all over Catholic Europe, and the Fathers made regular visits to the cities of Barbary. Rarely, however, did they have sufficient money actually to pay the ransoms of slaves. Their finances were normally exhausted by the expenses of travelling round Europe collecting funds, of the voyage to Barbary and the long period of bargaining that their arrival in Barbary usually entailed. They, therefore, normally travelled round particular areas collecting funds and advertising their forthcoming visit to such and such a city of Barbary. Relatives and friends could then arrange to pay for the ransoms of slaves through the intermission of the Fathers. On such occasions as the Fathers had collected sufficient money to pay for ransoms themselves, they had the terrible task of choosing which of the many slaves who presented themselves as most deserving should be freed. Redemptionist Fathers also stayed in Barbary to ease the problems of ransom. They made lists of the slaves who were brought in and sent extracts to the Redemptionists in the slaves' provinces of origin. On receipt

of the ransom money they made arrangements to see the Dey
to close the deal. They made sure that there was no trickery
when the ransom itself was realized. Two witnesses stood by
while the former slave received his receipt and certificates of
his liberty ratified by the French Consul. Once ransomed the
slaves were sent on a Christian ship to the Redemptionist
Father at Leghorn who saw them through quarantine, con-
fessed them and sent them home. As an interested party
remarked: 'It is much better to trust the ransoms to the priests
that God has chosen for that end, than to address oneself to
heretic merchants and Jews who do it only for their own interest
and who, besides making you pay higher ransoms, take a
commission of 14 per cent which could more usefully be employed for other ransoms.' [47]

Many other religious and lay institutions also provided means
of organizing ransoms. Cities and provinces had ransom
organizations, financed like the Redemptionist orders by
charitable gift or bequest. These were organized in much the
same way, sending off negotiators to Barbary at regular intervals. A tax on shipping at Hamburg financed the *Sklavenkasse*
which arranged the ransom of seamen captured on the city's
ships. Similar arrangements were made in Lubeck and other
northern seaports. Swedish sailors paid a portion of their
earnings into a kitty, instituted by their Mediterranean consuls.[48] Private bequests were also made for the same purpose,
such as that of an English ironmonger in the early eighteenth
century, from the investment of whose fortune £21,000 was
paid out in ransoms between 1734 and 1785.[49]

But charity and taxation were not enough, and the ransom
of most slaves had to be found out of their own resources, or
from those of friends or relatives, or else was borrowed from
professional money-lenders. It was consuls in Barbary who
made most of the arrangements described above by the Redemptionist Father, or else it was those 'heretic [and Catholic]
merchants and Jews' whom he warned his readers against.

One way of financing one's own ransom was to work for it in
Barbary itself. It was a very common practice for the slaves
owned by individuals to be allowed to set up their own business
in Barbary, paying a percentage to their masters and retaining
the rest themselves. The bars in the *bagnos* were organized in this

way, and so were businesses of all kinds outside, such as shops and small workshops. Even those unfortunate slaves who propelled the corsairs' galleys made some gain, since, although their share of the booty as slaves normally reverted to their masters, it was customary for the latter to give some back. Another way in which slaves could acquire money and goods in Barbary itself was by stealing. According to some accounts this amounted to a very considerable business, in which the concierge of the *bagno* often acted as fence. The main victims were the Jews, and slaves were often encouraged in this pursuit by their Turkish masters.[50] Not all acquisitions went towards ransom. Slaves needed money for other things, often indeed for their own food. Above all, with money it was possible to avoid being sent on the galleys, by paying for a substitute.[51] Money could be acquired from abroad for maintenance as well as for ransom, and much of the business of merchants in Barbary consisted in buying the bills of exchange drawn by slaves on their friends or business associates in Europe.

It could take a long time to accumulate a ransom in Barbary itself, and so most people depended on raising the money at home. The records of deeds registered before the French consuls at Tunis, which have been calendered by Pierre Grandchamp, are full of references to such business.[52] Often it was necessary to sell property or anticipate a future legacy, and thousands of powers of attorney connected with such transactions were taken out. However it was raised, the money had to be transferred to Barbary somehow or other. This could be done by a bill of exchange drawn in the slave's home town in favour of the slave himself, or of a merchant in Barbary who had already advanced the money. Or the money could be entrusted to a merchant or sea-captain whose business took him to Barbary. In 1662, for instance, two Armenian merchants who were about to make a voyage from Malta to Tunis received 1,625 pieces of eight from Jean Daniele, a Frenchman. Daniele was making the payment for the ransom of slaves in Tunis, whose deeds authorizing the payment were first registered before the French consul in Tunis and later ratified in Marseilles.[53] Such merchants and sea-captains were often prepared to lend the ransom money to the slave. And so we find in 1651 that a Maltese sea-captain, a former slave of the Dey of Tunis, received from another Maltese captain 378 pieces of eight to pay his ransom and other expenses. He promised to repay the money *plus* 25 per cent interest within fifteen days of his arrival in Malta.[54]

Perhaps the most comprehensive ransom network of all had been built up by the Jews. In the records of the French consul at Tunis there are over 400 deeds recording the payment of ransoms by Jews acting on orders from all over Christendom. The Jewish ransom dealers collected their money *plus* interest, *plus* commission, through their correspondents in Christian cities, especially Leghorn and Marseilles. The letter from a Lazarist father to a Venetian magistrate, which has already been quoted, discusses the problems of this sort of business, and in particular the problem of who should bear the risks at different stages of the transaction. If the Venetians insisted on paying no money out until the slave had arrived back in Venice, then they would be forced to operate through a particular Jewish merchant who had a near monopoly of trade between Algiers and Venice. His monopoly position made him expensive and he was also suspected of having come to an arrangement with the Turks to inflate ransoms, to the advantage of both parties, since his commission was a percentage (normally 14 to 15 per cent) of the ransom. If the Venetians made arrangements to pay the money to the Jews in Leghorn, then the greater competition for the business would lower the cost. 'However,' said the business-like father, 'there is the maritime risk. For if the slave should die at sea [between Leghorn and Venice], he would die at the expense of the Venetian confraternity who had forwarded his ransom money.' [55] This Jewish ransom network rested on a great web of credit, and, although well organized, was occasionally prone to disaster. The crash of the Jewish banker, Giuda Crespino, the main agent of North African Jews in Leghorn, caused widespread ruin and spoiled the organization of the ransom market for years.[56]

It could be difficult to fix up a loan from Barbary, and appeals to friends and relations often fell on deaf ears. In such cases it was possible for slaves to return to Europe themselves to arrange their own ransoms. Slaves were often allowed to return with no security beyond their signature to a contract drawn up before the French consul in Barbary. Others arranged for their wife or children to be sent to Barbary, to act as hostages in their absence. Others acted as the representative of a group of co-citizens, the remainder being left in Barbary as security for their colleagues' good faith. There was even a kind of bonded warehouse at Leghorn for slaves waiting for their ransom. Maintained and guarded by the Grand Duke, the slaves could be returned to Barbary if they had not paid their ransoms in a stipulated time.[57] Once in Christendom in person it was often much easier for the slave to raise money, normally as a business transaction. Such money was often remitted to Barbary in goods, enabling the slave to swell his initial loan by means of commercial profit. Although some people naturally took advantage of the trust implicit in safe-conducts for slaves to raise their own ransom, there are not as many recorded cases as one might think. There were normally hostages remaining in Barbary on whom vengeance could be taken. Even if there were no specific hostages, there were always co-citizens of the welsher. The harsh treatment meted out to a poor Florentine in 1624, who was kept in chains in a waterlogged underground prison for ten months, after a fellow-citizen had failed to send his ransom money from Florence, must have been some cheek on such behaviour.[58] Moslems who allowed their Christian slaves to go abroad were obviously acting in a sensible enough manner. For most slave-buyers capital gain was more important than yield when they invested in a slave, and the quicker they received such gain, the better the business.

Since, as we shall see, the Barbary corsairs were only one side of an institution which had its exact parallel in Christendom, there was also considerable opportunity for the exchange of slaves. Slaves would not necessarily be exchanged on a one-for-one basis. Indeed the exchange rate in the seventeenth and eighteenth centuries was nearly always in favour of the Moslems.[59] One Christian for three or four Moslems was quite a common arrangement, a fact to be explained partly by the greater wealth of Christendom and partly by the fact that slaves had a status value as well as an economic value in Islam. Exchanges could be arranged in a number of ways. A Christian slave in Algiers, for instance, might be able to find a Moslem who had a relation or friend enslaved in his own home town, or at least in his country. Such was quite common for the Maltese and other specialists in the Christian corsair business or for the citizens of countries who maintained galley fleets. Complicated negotiations would then follow as the ownership of the two (or more) slaves involved was transferred, so that eventually a straight exchange could be made. Sometimes such negotiations could be brought to nothing in unusual circumstances. In 1604 the Maltese Leonardo Mansico, whose daughter Paolina was a slave in Tunis of the Turk Mustafa Agha, arranged with Mamet Mustafa, whose daughter Fatima was a slave in Malta, that each should ransom the other's daughter, and then the two girls could be exchanged. Mamet ransomed Paolina and sent her to Malta on a Venetian ship, whose captain promised to return with Fatima. Fatima, however, had married a Maltese boy and refused to return to Tunis![60]

It was not necessary for exchange to be so complicated, however. Slaves who were granted safe-conducts to arrange their own ransoms often did this by finding a Moslem slave in their homeland, and fixing up an exchange. The same was done the other way round. In 1627, the Grand Master of Malta issued a safe-conduct to Ibrahim bin Mansur of Rosetta to go to the Levant, 'to seek and bring back the ransoms of some Turks and Moors, who are slaves of the Order of St John and private persons; and whilst he is there to negotiate the ransoms of various Christians . . . who are slaves of the Infidels in those parts.'[61] Specialists in this business existed – often Armenians and Greeks who belonged to both worlds – such as Captain Paolo Paterno of the island of Chios who received a safe-conduct 'to sail from here [Malta] to Constantinople and other places in the Levant and back, and to deal both in Islam and Christendom in the ransom of slaves, Christians as well as Moslems.'[62] Naturally the Captain would expect a handsome commission for his work, but it was he and his colleagues who were the most likely people to shorten the time of enslavement of those so unfortunate as to be captured.

Not all slaves wanted to go home. Some did so well in Barbary that they had no desire to leave. A slave who made a success of business in Barbary might well pay off his ransom, and continue as a free Christian merchant. Much commoner than this was the path of apostasy. As we have seen, renegades, 'professional Turks' as they were called,[63] played a very important part in the government and economy of all the North African regencies. Haedo lists the motives 'which to the so great loss of their souls, push them to abandon the true path of God'. For some it was cowardice at the thought of slavery, for others the taste for a free life, for all the vices of the flesh so much practised amongst the Turks.[64] Allowing for the prejudices of the Spanish Benedictine, this is a fair summary, though amongst the vices of the flesh should be listed the desire for economic betterment. Certainly few Moslems had an interest in the conversion of slaves – rather the reverse since apostasy might lose them part of their ransom, or at least delay its payment. Only in particular cases, such as when a Moslem wanted to add a Christian woman to his wives, was there much evidence of forced conversion. Even in such cases resort was more often to exhortation and promises than to force. Indeed, far from there being much evidence of forced conversion, there is considerable evidence of the reverse – of pretended apostates being forced to deny their apostasy through torture.[65] So far had business sense rather than the desire to add to the numbers of the Faithful triumphed in the motivation of the inhabitants of Barbary!

Nevertheless, many a slave did apostasize successfully. This did not mean instant freedom, but it normally facilitated the negotiation of a ransom, and usually lowered its level. Often, indeed, a master gave his freedom to a converted slave. Once a free Moslem, the former Christian slave was able to enjoy the benefits of the Barbary economy – to set up as a merchant, to become a Barbary corsair himself. And in these pursuits he often had very great advantages over native Moslems. Often well-trained in Europe, and retaining their contacts with their former Christian associates, many renegades did well in business. Great merchant-houses were established with branches in Christian cities run by the Christian relations of the renegade. In the *corso*, too, the superior seamanship of Europeans and their knowledge of Christian waters and the Christian coastline were important elements in the success of the Barbary corsairs.

Barbary in its hey-day must have been extremely attractive to the more unruly elements in European society. Nowhere in Europe was there a place with such a degree of social mobility; nowhere were so few questions asked about one's past. And few places held out such hopes for a prosperous and adventurous life. No wonder that slaves apostasized! No wonder that many free men came voluntarily to Barbary with the firm intention of going over to Islam! Later, of course, remorse might take the renegade, but return was difficult. The punishment for an unsuccessful attempt at flight was invariably death. Nevertheless many renegades did return to the land of their birth.

One such successful return to Christendom was made by the Maltese renegade, Osta Mameto Guivara. Employed as a barber by the Pasha of Tunis, he maintained contacts with his homeland through his two brothers, Vincenzo and Serafino Piccanino. Despite a successful business career, in which the three brothers traded in prize-goods and arranged ransoms, Osta fled Tunis with some other renegades in 1661, 'pushed by remorse'.[66] No doubt he brought some of his gains with him, but it is doubtful whether his bribe to the Christian authorities was as large as that promised by an English renegade, who, in 1663, was issued a safe-conduct by the Order of St John to travel from Alexandria to Malta. In return, the forty-year-old Englishman, who had repented of his errors, promised to bring to Malta ships, goods, and slaves belonging to his unsuspecting Moslem business associates.[67] Hardly surprisingly the Inquisition did not take very kindly to the renegade who had lived a life of luxury in Islam by preying on his former co-religionaries, and such a bribe could ease his acceptance back into the Faith. But the difficulty of return and the possibility of remorse were hardly likely to deter a young man, so little indeed that the French Commissaire de la Marine wrote to Colbert from Algiers advising him 'to recommend to captains not to let anyone ashore here; for the Provençals will put on a turban as easily as a nightcap'.[68]

No figures exist which would enable an estimate of the length of time spent in slavery by the captives of the Barbary corsairs to be made. Many, of course, died in captivity. For others slavery could be very long. A seventy-five-year-old Ragusan was ransomed in 1662 after forty-three years of captivity.[69] But by the seventeenth century, this was exceptional. Ten years could normally be considered as a very long period of slavery. Many slaves were ransomed after only a few months. As we have seen, the institutions of capture and ransom were well organized, and the Barbary corsairs had an interest in maintaining a fairly rapid turnover. For, to repeat the quotation at the beginning of this chapter, 'the corsairs of Algiers, Tunis, and other places in Barbary, make war for gain rather than glory'. The same could be said of their rivals, the corsairs of Malta, who will be considered in the next part.

PART THREE

The Maltese Corsairs

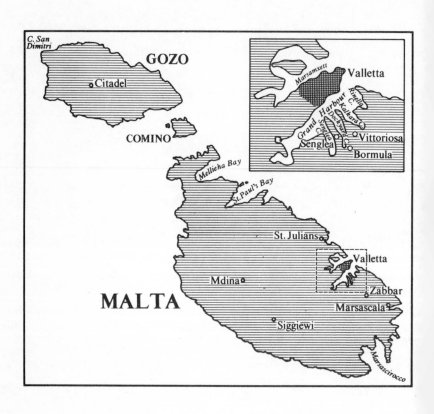

CHAPTER 5

The Capital of Christian Piracy

For an island whose balance of payments depended on plundering shipping, Malta was admirably sited. Almost exactly in the centre of the Mediterranean, the island commands the narrow part of the sea that lies between Sicily and Tripoli. So long as the Maltese remained vigilant it was difficult for shipping to sail from the east to the west Mediterranean without them being aware of the fact. For this reason, if for no other, Malta has always been of considerable strategic importance.

But Malta has other advantages as a privateering base besides its site. Chief amongst these are the island's fantastic deep-water harbours. On each side of the narrow tongue of rock on which the capital, Valletta, has been built, the sea pierces for over two miles into the heart of the island. To the east lies the famous Grand Harbour. Joining Grand Harbour at right angles are the four creeks of Rinella, Kalkara, Senglea, and Dockyard – all with further deep-water anchorages. To the west lies Marsamxett Harbour with further creeks running off the main waterway. This whole complex of anchorages could be protected from attack from the open sea by the fact that the gap between the tip of the rock on which Valletta stands and the land on each side across the mouth of the two great harbours is in each case less than a quarter of a mile in width, so that eventually a string of three forts was built which could command with ease both entrances. Not that the defences

of Valletta stopped here. For during the sixteenth and seventeenth centuries Valletta and the cities on the other side of the
Grand Harbour were built up into the most impregnable fortress in Europe. Year after year more and more of the island's
beautiful golden limestone was quarried to erect the great
man-made cliffs that supplement the city's natural defences and
remain a marvel to the modern visitor. Bastions, cavaliers,
curtains, and ravelins rose up from the water on every side.[1]
To storm the city with seventeenth- or eighteenth-century
siege weapons would have been impossible, as long as the walls
remained manned. As the Reverend Henry Teonge, chaplain
of H.M. Frigate *Assistance*, who visited the island in 1675
wrote: 'Here needs no sentry for there is no getting over the
outermost wall if lease were given . . . and were an army of
men in the midst of the city, yet their works were but in the
beginning, for each house is a castle.'[2] The harbours of
Valletta were not only protected from the attacks of man, but
also from the worst vagaries of the weather. For, although both
the great harbours were open to the north-east wind, the
notorious storm-bearing *gregale*, shipping had only to take
shelter in the creeks to be completely protected from the
weather. And if the weather made entrance to the harbour
impossible, there were always other harbours on the island.
On the easternmost part of the island the two-mile inlet of
Marsa Scala provided protection from the weather, if not from
man till the late seventeenth century. In the south-east lay the
great bay of Marsa Scirocco, protected from the Turk by its
own forts, while in the north-west were Mellieha and St Paul's
Bays – all adequate anchorages for sea-going shipping.

Thus the first requirement of the privateer or pirate, a
powerful base, was fulfilled. Once in the island's harbours he
need fear neither wind nor Turk. In peace he could go about
the business of unloading his booty and preparing his ship for
yet another foray against the Infidel. Not that all the island
could be defended as the great nerve-centre of Valletta could.
As a result of the danger of incursion from the sea the whole of
the west of the island was virtually uninhabited, and as late as
1614 a powerful Turkish raiding party of some 4,000 men
could land at Marsa Scala and ravage the country as far
inland as Zabbar before being driven off.[3] The sister island of

Gozo was also liable to attack. For these reasons the vast majority of the population of the islands clustered close to the great fortresses, the Citadel of Gozo and the great complex of, fortifications that surrounded Valletta.[4]

Being a small and rocky island, Malta's main problem was not protection, but food and water. This problem grew in intensity as the island's population more than quadrupled to over 100,000 in the course of the seventeenth and eighteenth centuries.[5] Much had been done to improve the position since the first arrival of the Knights of St John in 1531. The island that was described as a barren rock at that date had changed considerably by the time of the arrival of the Englishman, Sir William Young, on his summer's excursion in the year 1772. He wrote:[6]

Malta is about sixty miles in circuit; a mere rock, in many parts absolutely bare, in others covered with a foot and an half of very rich mould; a great deal of which hath been brought from Sicily, and of which the proprietors are extremely tenacious; walling their several possessions into small squares, to prevent the earth being washed away by a heavy rain into their neighbour's territory; so that the country from an eminence has the appearance of a large chess-board. The whole island is a fine example of what industry can draw from an ungrateful soil; every spot is occupied; the whole is a rich picture of villages, pleasure-houses, and gardens.

And indeed the incredible industry and patience of the Maltese peasants had its rewards. Virtually all visitors remarked on the excellence and abundance of the Maltese fruit and vegetables, just as they do today. Despite the small size of the island game was also quite abundant, for Malta lies on the migratory routes of many species of birds, and the islanders had acquired great skill with net and gun. Fish too were fairly easily caught in the surrounding waters. The problem of the water supply to Valletta had been fairly satisfactorily solved by the construction of a very elegant aqueduct in the early seventeenth century. But still there remained the problem of bread. In the mid-seventeenth century Cardinal Federico Borromeo estimated that the island grew barley and wheat sufficient for six months of the year's consumption.[7] By the late eighteenth century, with the rise of population, this proportion had fallen to only four months.[8] For the rest the island was dependent on imports. Not that the islanders would necessarily starve during a siege. Enormous bell-shaped underground granaries had been built in Valletta and elsewhere to hold reserve supplies. But the lack of self-sufficiency, not only in corn but in other essentials such as naval stores, meant that Malta could not exist in splendid diplomatic isolation. The main supplier of corn was Sicily, and export was a privilege, not a right, so that the rulers of the larger island, first the King of Spain and later the Bourbon King of the Two Sicilies, could exert considerable diplomatic pressure on Malta through the threat of withdrawing their licences to export. In the eighteenth century Malta was supplementing her imports from Sicily by imports from her erstwhile deadly Moslem enemies in North Africa, but the threat and danger remained.

During the period which we are considering, although privateering remained the second most important occupation of the people after agriculture, Malta was also developing as a commercial centre of considerable importance. Her position on the commercial routes to the Levant and her marvellous harbours made her an ideal staging-point and entrepôt for commercial shipping. In particular, it was French merchants who took advantage of Malta for this purpose. As French commerce in the Levant developed to a dominant position in the late seventeenth and eighteenth centuries, so Maltese commerce developed in its turn. Over five hundred miles nearer to the ports of the Near East than Marseilles, and, unlike the former, safe from Turkish reprisals against French merchants, Malta became for Marseilles what Leghorn was for the English and Zante for the Venetians. A thriving business in both eastern and western goods grew up and a large French merchant community settled in Valletta and in the Three Cities of Vittoriosa, Senglea, and Burmula (Cospicua). This French orientation of the island was so great that by the late eighteenth century a historian can write: 'Malta, by 1789, was, in reality, a dependency, a colony in fact, of France. Her possession was then considered as indispensable to the primacy of French commerce in the Levant.'[9] As we shall see this commercial development was very fortunate for Malta, for the invisible earnings from commerce were able to make up for the declining earnings from privateering as the eighteenth century wore on, and thus helped to provide the quantities of foreign exchange needed in order to purchase grain to feed the people and luxuries to satisfy the tastes of the merchants themselves and their aristocratic rulers.[10]

In a world of nation states and increasingly large territorial units, Malta was an anachronism in the seventeenth and eighteenth centuries. Her rulers were the Knights of the Order of St John of Jerusalem, also known as the Knights Hospitaller, a military and nursing order created during the Crusades with charters from the Pope to engage in constant warfare against the Infidel. In 1522 the Knights of St John had been forced to surrender their stronghold of Rhodes to the Turks, and after nine years of wandering round the capitals of Europe searching for a new home had been presented with the island of Malta by the Emperor Charles V. The Knights were the younger sons and younger brothers of the great families of Europe, and it was virtually impossible for anyone to aspire to join the Order unless he had at least four quarterings of nobility. These Knights took vows of chastity, poverty, and obedience, and were expected to aid the Order in its objectives of nursing the sick and fighting the Infidel. One of the Order's most recent historians has written:[11]

> To enter the ranks of the Hospitallers, no religious vocation was needed, no aptitude for hospital work, for fighting, for administration, for holiness. The intrinsic nobility of the candidate, revealed by an unsullied pedigree, was, in the glorious legend of Europe's aristocracy, sufficient to ensure his capacity for all these things.

Despite a gradual decline in standards as the centuries passed and the knightly ideals of the Middle Ages became more and more only a memory, the same historian can, very fairly, sum up the Knights of the eighteenth century as follows:[12]

> Such, then, were the Knights, a mixed company of expert sailors, good administrators, philanderers and loafers. Many were bored, most were rich, on the whole they were brave.

In earlier days they had shown a quixotic valour that was deeply tinged with buccaneering: the savage mien of soldiers fighting in a war in which quarter was neither expected nor asked for was softened by their duties in the Hospital, where the proudest and bravest were required to wait upon the sick, however humble or dirty. They were in Malta to promote and assist the legend of Europe's aristocracy, and they carried into the late modern age the principles for which Europe's aristocracy had been created.

The Order was a republic of aristocrats who elected their own Grand Master,* who then became ruler of both the Order and of the Maltese islands. In both these roles he was subject to a considerable curbing of his power, in theory and in practice. As ruler of the Order he was subject to the ultimate authority of the Pope who had his representative on the island in the person of the Maltese Inquisitor. From the first arrival of Inquisitors in Malta they had been at daggers drawn with successive Grand Masters, and we shall see when we come to consider the diplomatic history of the corsairs that Papal curbing of the Grand Master's power could be made effective. As lay ruler of the islands the Grand Master owed feudal vassalage to whoever should be the ruler of Sicily, the King of Spain and later the Bourbon Kings. Any desire to ignore this vassalage and to go against the wishes of his feudal superior could very speedily be checked, for, as we have seen above, Malta was dependent on Sicily for her corn supply. Increasingly during the seventeenth and eighteenth centuries a third sovereign who could curb the power of the Grand Masters was added to the Pope and the King of Sicily. This was the King of France. This source of pressure did not arise as a result of any legal status, but of hard political fact. For as the period wore on Malta became more and more a French dependency. More than half the Knights were French, a large number of the merchants on the island were French, much of

---

* Note the close resemblance between the political structure of Malta and the Barbary states. Both were military republics who recruited their soldiers from outside. Both elected their rulers. Both kept the local aristocracy firmly under control. One major difference was in their source of recruitment. No Moslem writer would have described the Knights of St John as the 'excrement of Christendom'!

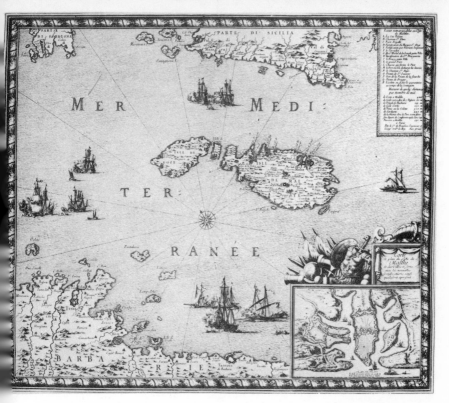

Malta, Barbary, and southern Sicily. This map illustrates very well the strategic importance of the island.

the island's trade was done with France. Malta just could not afford to offend the king of France.

There were three main ways in which outsiders could put pressure on the Knights in their stronghold. Firstly, by his spiritual position, the Pope could exert moral pressure on the Knights. And if they should defy him he could bring to bear the disciplinary weapons of the Church, such as the threat of excommunication. Secondly, as we have seen, the rulers of Sicily could exert pressure by threatening to withdraw the licence to export grain. A third weapon, and perhaps the most effective of all, lay in the financial organization of the Knights. From the time of its inception the Order had been mainly dependent for funds on the pious bequests of generations of European Christians. Most of these bequests were in the form of land, and by the seventeenth century the Order owned lands all over Europe. These lands were grouped into what were known as commanderies which were placed under the administration of a Knight Commander. Commanders lived on the proceeds of the land, but also acted as factors for the Order and were expected to keep the lands in good order so that they might be handed over to their successors. From the revenues a portion, known as Responsions, was sent to Malta for the upkeep of the Order. The continuance of such Responsions was absolutely vital for the existence of the Order, but since the lands from which these revenues arose were scattered all over Europe, the Order depended on the goodwill of European sovereigns, not only for their share of the revenue, but also for their continued ownership of the lands themselves. One of the first actions of Henry VIII, after leaving the Roman Catholic Church, was to seize the lands of the Order in England, and the threat that other sovereigns might follow this example was a powerful diplomatic weapon, exploited particularly adroitly by the Republic of Venice. Indeed in the end the collapse of the Order as an effective political power came as a result of the seizure of their lands in France, when the Loi Spoliateur was passed by the Revolutionary government in 1793. The Grand Masters of Malta had to be careful to behave in a proper way towards the other sovereigns of Europe, if they wished to remain solvent.

The outward and visible sign of the Order's obligation to engage in constant warfare against the Infidel was the Order's navy. This remarkable institution, out of all proportion to the size of its island base, reached the peak of its strength relative to other powers in the second half of the seventeenth century. In 1685, for instance, the Order's navy consisted of eight of the strongest and best equipped galleys in the whole Mediterranean, together with a number of small sailing-ships and auxiliaries.[13] The main duties of the navy were to go out on two or three cruises every year, searching for Turkish and Barbary shipping, and in particular for the ships of the Barbary corsairs. In addition the navy was expected to form part of any Christian maritime force against the Turks. In the seventeenth and early eighteenth centuries this normally meant an exceedingly strained alliance with Venice, in the numerous wars that she fought against Turkey between 1644 and 1718.[14]

Early in the eighteenth century the Order decided to add a

squadron of ships-of-the-line to her navy, at the same time reducing her commitment to the galley. This new type of fleet was probably at its strongest in the early 1740s when it comprised six ships-of-the-line (three of sixty guns each) and four galleys. From this date onwards, however, the Order's navy began to decline in strength for the remaining period of the Order's rule in Malta.

As the front line of Christian hostility against Moslem naval power, the Order's navy was quite effective in the seventeenth century. Although it had its fair share of disasters when galleys were captured or shipwrecked, the overall balance of victories was certainly in the Order's favour. But, in the following century, the navy as a fighting force began to decline in importance. The last land engagement of the Knights against the Infidel was in 1707, and its last expedition against the Turkish navy in 1716.[15] For the rest of the century the navy very rarely ventured into the Levant, the scene of much of its former glory. Cruises were mainly confined to the western Mediterranean, and, although the occasional Barbary corsair was captured, much of the navy's activity was confined to such mundane matters as escorting princes and convoying Malta's vital supplies of food.

Although the Order's Treasury received a stream of prizes and slaves as the result of the navy's depredations of Turkish shipping and attacks on Turkish coastal towns, this was never enough to finance the extremely expensive galleys, and the navy remained a constant drain on the revenue of the Order. Almost always the navy was far and away its biggest single item of expenditure. Some relief arose from the custom which had developed in the early seventeenth century of rich Grand Masters and others setting up foundations whose object was to finance the building of galleys. The capital of such foundations was so arranged as to provide sufficient income to build a new galley every eight years, which was as long as one could expect a galley to remain effective.[16]

The human element in the Order's navy came from a number of sources. First there were the Knights themselves, the front-line troops of Christ. These warriors had the responsibility of carrying into the modern age the ideals of knightly chivalry and bravery in action. Brave they certainly were, and their capacity for stubborn resistance in the face of overwhelming force had given them the reputation of the finest soldiers in Christendom. The supply of thirty Knights for each galley was guaranteed by the institution of the Caravan. A Caravan was a tour of at least six months' active service in the galleys, and no Knight could receive promotion in the Order until he had served four Caravans. In the eighteenth century standards of knightly valour seem to have declined, and it was found that most Knights preferred to do their service in the safer and more comfortable ships-of-the-line to the detriment of the galleys. To counteract this it was agreed that each Caravan in a sailing-ship had to last one year.[17]

Apart from its complement of Knights each ship or galley carried a contingent of paid soldiers, 180 for a seventeenth-century galley, and a crew of sailors to sail the ship. These men came from all over the Christian Mediterranean, but a major source, especially of the seamen and gunners, was Malta itself. Finally, the galleys, of course, were rowed by slaves. The main source of these was the Moslem prisoners taken by the Order's navy itself and by the Maltese corsairs. But each galley's crew was leavened by a certain number of Christian oarsmen. Many of these were convicts, some from Malta but also including contingents from such places as the Papal States, who often sent condemned men to serve their sentences in Malta. A third class of galley-slave was the *buonavoglie*. These were free, but normally desperate, men who volunteered as oarsmen on the galleys. Treated like the slaves, they were very often debtors, who were paid a lump sum on signing on, and whose minute salary was then withheld until its book value had accumulated sufficiently to repay the original lump sum. Only then were they free to leave the service. *Buonavoglie*, who were sprinkled amongst the Turks on the rowing benches, were regarded as a protection against mutiny, and were normally unchained and armed when the galleys were hard-pressed in action.[18]

Many rude words have been written about the Order's navy and there is no doubt that, particularly in the early seventeenth century, they behaved very like corsairs, if not pirates, in their rampages through the seas of the Levant. 'Corsairs parading crosses', one Venetian dubbed them.[19] In this book, however, I decided to give them the benefit of the doubt, and refer to them as a navy, and not as corsairs, though there is indeed very little difference between their activities and those, for instance, of the state-owned ships of the Barbary corsairs. The reasons for this distinction are rather technical than realistic. First, the navy was guilty of behaviour which could not be true of any self-respecting corsair. It did not make a profit! Secondly, they paid their crews and did not share their prizes out amongst them. To quote Elizabeth Schermahorn:[20]

> In those days, whether you were blessed as a martyr or cursed as an outlaw depended upon your motives and intentions, rather than on your methods. If you plundered strongholds, and seized the property and persons of your enemies, in order to fill your own coffers, you were a Corsair, and hopelessly damned; if to fill the Treasury of the Religion, in the interests of Christianity and to win means for carrying on the Holy War, you were a Knight without reproach and your soul flew straight to Heaven when it left the body.

Finally there is a distinction in organization between the Maltese navy and the Maltese corsairs which one does not find in Barbary between state-owned and private ships.

Malta was a centre for corsairs long before the arrival of the Knights. Corsairs had been licensed to attack Moslem shipping in the days of direct Sicilian rule and there was no change in this practice when the Knights took over in the sixteenth century.[21] By the end of the century corsairs of all nations were taking advantage of the island's position and resources to fit out at Malta. Indeed so many corsairs were fitting out at Malta that it was felt that a tighter control should be kept on the issuing of licences, since the provisions and war *matériel* that the corsairs took on board were causing the possibility of the island itself and the Order's navy facing shortages. At one time the idea of forbidding any corsair at all to arm at Malta was considered. But the Grand Master and his Council, seeing how the *corso* had been encouraged by his predecessors, and how ships armed by the Knights and his lay subjects provided exercise in maritime warfare and at the same time increased the commerce, prosperity, and numbers of his population, decided to maintain the *corso* and to set up a tribunal to iron out its abuses.[22]

This tribunal set up in 1605 consisted of five commissioners chosen by the Grand Master. Known as the *Tribunale degli Armamenti*, it was to remain the body responsible for the organization and jurisdiction of the corsairs down to the eclipse of the institution in 1798. In order to restrict the number of corsairs using Malta as a base, and also to give the Grand Master a greater measure of control, it was laid down that no one could fit out a corsair ship in Malta which was to fly the flag of any foreign prince or state. For corsairs who wished to fly the flag of the Order an elaborate set of rules was framed. These rules covered the method of licensing corsair captains, the rights of the various claimants in the disposal of the booty and the procedure for bringing suits before the tribunal in the event of litigation. A clear definition was made of those people whom it was legitimate for the corsairs to attack. Both ship-owners and captains had to swear not to attack 'ships, mer-chandise, goods and persons of Christians, nor of any other person, even an Infidel, who displays the safe conduct of the Grand Master or of any other Christian princes, under penalty of making up all the damage'.[23] These oaths, for whom a pledge stood surety while the ship was at sea, were of the greatest importance, and it was on the basis of breaking the oath rather than of contravening the statutes themselves that corsairs ignoring these regulations were prosecuted. Prosecutions against corsairs and the normal litigation involved in the corsair business were brought in the tribunal itself, but there was pro-vision for two stages of appeal. First there was appeal to the *Tribunale dell'Udienza*, a court composed of the Grand Master, Knights Grand Cross, and judges of the Grand Court of the Castellania, the Maltese lawcourts. In virtue of the Order's subservience to Rome a second appeal could be directed through the Maltese Inquisitor to the Papal Courts in Rome.[24]

For the first half of the seventeenth century the system laid down in 1605 appears to have worked quite well, though the Maltese authorities had to reiterate the clauses forbidding Maltese subjects to arm corsair vessels flying the flags of other princes. There was considerable litigation, of course, and some diplomatic problems arose, particularly as a result of the wrong-ful seizure of Venetian ships, but compared with what was to follow this was of little significance. But from the middle of the

seventeenth to the middle of the eighteenth centuries the
Maltese corsairs were constantly getting themselves into trouble,
and were forced to fight a continuous diplomatic rearguard action
against the King of France and the Pope. Eventually they were
shorn of much of their power by these two potentates, and by
1750 the Maltese corsairs appeared to be virtually extinct as an
institution. The troubles which they faced arose partly from the
undoubted abuses which the corsairs themselves had introduced
into their business, but also from changing circumstances in the
Mediterranean, as commerce between Christian and Moslem
increased and as religious intolerance became less marked outside Malta. Most of the diplomatic problems of the corsairs
came under three heads.

First there was a constant temptation for the corsairs to
attack not only Moslem shipping, but also to attack Christians.
Although this was in direct contradiction of their oath, the
corsairs justified their activity on various grounds. The Christians were not really Christians, they were only pretending to
be Christians. If they were Christians, the goods they were
carrying belonged to Turks, and thus it was legitimate to seize
them. Or even if they were Christians and the goods that they
carried belonged to them, they were Greek Orthodox and therefore schismatic, and therefore heretics, and therefore enemies
of the Faith, and thus liable to depredation. During the
seventeenth century these unfortunate Greeks and the representatives of the other minority Christian groups in the Levant,
such as the Maronites, were on their own and their only hope
of recompense was to come to Malta and sue the corsairs in the
island's courts. It is some measure of the justice of the courts in
Malta at this time that many Greeks who sued for wrongful
depredation actually won their case and recovered damages.
In the eighteenth century, however, while Maltese attitudes
hardened towards the Greeks, the latter found a powerful
protector in the Pope. The second type of problem which the
corsairs faced arose from the danger of reprisals. Whilst as
Maltese, secure in their fortress, they need fear no reprisals
except when actually at sea, the fact that they were Christians
and also often Frenchmen frequently led to the Turks taking
reprisals against Christians, and in particular Frenchmen, as a
result of the depredations of the Maltese ships. Finally the

corsairs ran into trouble as a result of their insistence on the right of the *visità*, the right to stop any ship, Christian or Moslem, and demand to see if there were any Infidel passengers or cargo on board. Such an infringement of their dignity particularly annoyed the powerful maritime nations.

At no time in the seventeenth century were Maltese corsairs allowed to operate wherever they liked. The letters patent licensing their activities stated that they were allowed to make war on the Infidel either in the Levant or Barbary or both. Both these terms had strict definitions, but in general we can say that the Levant meant the Mediterranean east of the Adriatic, and Barbary meant the north African coast. In other words no Maltese corsair was allowed to operate in the western Mediterranean north of a line from Gibraltar to Sicily, nor in the Adriatic. In 1647, as a result of depredations in the waters of the Holy Land, which had led to reprisals against pilgrims, the Council of State decreed that no corsair should sail or take prizes in waters within ten miles of the ports of Jaffa, Acre or Saida.[25] Fifty years later this restriction on the area of operations in the Levant was extended to cover the waters up to fifty miles from the coastline.[26] Such restrictions were particularly frustrating and frequently disobeyed, since the waters of the Holy Land were amongst the richest in potential prizes in the whole Mediterranean. In the course of this period further geographical restrictions were placed on the corsairs by a closer definition of the limits of 'Barbary' and of what were to be regarded as Venetian waters.

While the area of search was thus gradually reduced a more serious source of frustration came to a head in the 1660s. The trouble now arose as a result of the development of French commerce in the Levant. Both Louis XIV and his minister, Colbert, were determined to build up French commerce in this area, and as a result of their success more and more of the ordinary Moslem trade of the Levant was carried in French ships. The loss of so much potential booty was not at all congenial to the corsairs and they stepped up their inspection of French ships. Diplomatic reaction from Paris and Marseilles was rapid. The King himself demanded the release of three Jews captured without safe conducts on a French ship by the Chevalier de la Barre in 1663.[27] This and other cases led to a long battle of words between Malta and Paris.[28] Louis demanded the restitution of the ships and the cargo, the release of the passengers, and a prohibition of any further examination of French ships by the Maltese corsairs.

The Grand Master could not possibly accept this without greatly weakening the corsairs and he made his case as strong as possible. The special envoy sent to France in 1665 to discuss the first case was instructed to make the point that:[29]

Ships armed for war against the Infidel with the flag of Christian princes may visit any ship, even Christian ones, and seize the goods of Infidels found without safe-conducts. If this is permitted to all the others, so much more should it be permitted to the Religion [short title for the Knights of St John] whose job is to attack the Turks by all means possible ... If the French King does not allow this, then other Christian princes will follow suit and in this manner not only will the institution of the Religion be prejudiced, but also its subsistence, these prizes often providing a great part of its maintenance.

In answer to this statement of the rights of corsairs to visit Christian ships the Grand Master was asked by Colbert whether Dutch and English ships were also subject to the *visità*. The Grand Master replied that 'nothing was more certain than that we never fail to visit and seize English and Dutch ships when we find ourselves the strongest'.[30] A few weeks earlier he had, however, admitted that this was rare when he wrote to the Ambassador de Souvré in Paris, 'regarding the inspection of English ships, it is true that we do not visit them, but that is because they are stronger than us, otherwise there would not have been one ... which would not have been seized, if it was found loaded with Turks or their goods'.[31]

Indeed English merchant ships were more powerful than French ones, so perhaps the Grand Master was making a good point when he wrote:[32]

Since the corsair vessels of the Religion are almost all French, their gain enriches your subjects, and also provides the subjects of the Crown with experience at sea, and indeed

captains and sailors of fame and valour have always graduated from this school to the service of France.

But the King remained determined, and the Grand Master
had to agree to restore the prizes, but asked for an understanding that French ships would not carry Turkish goods
between Turkish ports. But in the end the desire to maintain
the Turkish alliance, to build up French commerce in the
Levant, and to prevent reprisals against French citizens led
Louis to demand the cessation of inspection of French ships by
the Maltese without giving any firm undertaking that these
ships would not carry Turkish goods. And the need for the
Grand Master to remain on good terms with the King of
France meant that finally in 1673 he had to agree to this. In
that year the Grand Master and his Council, 'to conform
to the will and disposition of His Most Christian Majesty . . .
unanimously voted that corsairs that have armed, or shall arm
with the flag of the Religion, meeting French ships cannot take
off them Infidels, nor the goods belonging to them, nor visit
them for that purpose, nor maltreat them . . . '[33]

Thus at one blow much potential booty was made safe from
the Maltese corsairs. Once the Turks appreciated that, for the
most part, the corsairs were prepared to obey the orders of their
Grand Master, they naturally resorted more and more to
employing French shipping for their coastwise trade. Since
English and Dutch shipping was protected from the corsairs
by their strength, the consequent decline in profits led the
corsairs to redouble their efforts against the other non-Moslem
carriers of Moslem goods. In practice this meant the Greeks,
the most important suppliers of carrying services in the whole
Levant. The Greeks had no King Louis to protect them from
the indignity of the *visità*, and so the corsairs stopped and inspected every Greek ship they could lay their hands on. And
certainly much of the cargoes of Greek ships did indeed belong
to Moslems, and thus could be defined as good prize to the
Maltese. But often the ownership of cargo, and indeed the
religion of passengers and crew were not too easily identifiable.
There is no doubt that Greeks carried Turkish cargo registered
under the names of Greek men of straw, that what appeared
to be Greek ships had false papers and in fact belonged to

Malta. Valletta and Grand Harbour from the land. The three peninsulas pointing to Valletta are Senglea, Vittoriosa with Fort St Angelo, and Rinella with Fort Ricasoli.

Moslems, and that the Greeks themselves were often Moslems. Such deception was indeed normal in the centuries that saw the long war of the corsairs.

And so, debarred from searching French ships, the corsairs increased their efforts against the Greeks. At first, the Maltese authorities took a strict view of what was often illegal activity. But in the last twenty years of the century official attitudes changed. Greeks who sued for wrongful depredation in the courts of Malta now found it much more difficult to win their cases. This changed attitude of the courts naturally encouraged the corsairs to attack the Greeks even more often, and to worry little, or not at all, whether their cargoes were in fact Christian or Moslem. The only recourse of the Greeks against such unfair treatment was to appeal to Rome. Such appeals were often successful since Rome normally gave the Greek appellants a fair hearing. Although the Maltese were often able to delay the implementation of a Roman decision for many years, they were forced, eventually, to obey the dictates of the courts of their religious superior. So once again the Maltese corsairs were forced to change their tactics.

During the seventeenth century practically all the corsair ships operating from Malta had flown the flag of the Order of St John and had been licensed by the *Tribunale degli Armamenti*. But there had always been provision for Maltese ships to operate under another flag. This was the flag of the Grand Master himself. In his capacity as a lay ruler he was entitled, like other lay rulers, to commission shipping to fly his own flag. In the 1580s and 1590s, for instance, a large and successful fleet of corsairs had been fitted out to fight the Moslems by the Grand Master, Verdala.[34] While such practices had fallen into abeyance after the reorganization of the corsair business in 1605, there was no clause in the Statutes of the *Tribunale degli Armamenti* that said that they were illegal. To sail under the flag of a foreign prince was illegal certainly, but not to sail under the flag of the Grand Master.

What happened in the late seventeenth and early eighteenth centuries was that this practice was revived. The reason is made clear by a letter of 1704 from Grand Master Perellos to the Prior Sacchetti, ambassador of the Order in Rome. He wrote:[35]

'Ships have always been armed under the flags of our predecessors, and the suits of Greeks arising out of these . . . have
always been heard in our Grand Court of the Castellania . . .
without passing to the *Tribunale degli Armamenti* which was
set up only to hear those cases concerning ships armed with
the flag of the Religion.'

Now there was no appeal from the Grand Court of the Castellania, the Grand Master's own court, other than to the Maltese
Supreme Court of Appeal.[36] In other words there was no appeal
to Rome, and thus no chance for Greeks to reverse the original
decisions of the Maltese Courts. By the end of the seventeenth
century an even more suitable court for trying cases relating to
ships flying the Grand Master's flag had been established.
This was the *Consolato di Mare*, set up in 1697 to try cases arising
out of normal maritime commerce.[37] By the beginning of the
eighteenth century the *Consolato di Mare* had become established
as a parallel institution to the *Tribunale degli Armamento*. While
the latter arranged for the processing of licences for corsair
captains who wished to fly the flag of the Religion and tried
the disputes arising out of their activities, the former was processing the licences for corsairs flying the flag of the Grand
Master. And as in the case of the Grand Court of the Castellania, the *Consolato di Mare* was a lay court and there was no
appeal to Rome.
    Reactions to this defiance of papal authority were rapid, and
the Grand Masters were to fight a long battle against Pope and
Inquisitor during the next thirty years on the subject of the
Greeks and of the legitimacy of the *Consolato di Mare* as a prize
court.[38] The Popes refused to admit the distinction between the
two flags and declared their right to hear appeals, even from
cases which had been introduced in the lay *Consolato di Mare*.
Furthermore, the Popes and the Inquisitors denied the justification of the Grand Master to license ships to fly his own flag.
Although the Grand Masters fought hard to defend their
position it is clear that they realized that they had a poor case,
both in theory, and because of the undoubted moral and legal
pressure that the Popes could exert. And so we find that
although the Grand Masters continued to license corsairs to
fly the Magisterial flag they normally did so only for operations

in the waters of Barbary.[39] Since few Greeks sailed in these waters, the Grand Masters were thus able to postpone a final decision on the legitimacy of their flag for some years. But by the 1720s they were once again licensing corsairs to operate in the Levant under their own flag and the dispute with the Pope came to a head once more.

Meanwhile the problem of wrongful attack on Greeks remained, but now it was mainly a problem concerning ships flying the flag of the Order, and thus liable to appeal to Rome. In order to curtail the process of litigation and appeal the Inquisitors began to by-pass the first stage of appeal within Malta, and to issue mandates to the Greeks to appeal direct to Rome. The first instance of this was in 1713,[40] but thereafter it became very common practice, and since the appeals of the Greeks in Rome were normally successful it threatened the whole future of the *corso*. Just as forty years earlier the Turks had increased their use of French shipping, so they now consigned more and more of their cargoes under Greek names and in Greek ships. The Grand Masters complained, but to no avail. Even the plea in 1720 that 'it was only by a continual harrowing of Turkish shipping that the Christians were able to boast the greatest maritime skill in the Mediterranean' fell on deaf ears.[41] However, although the Maltese were unable to ignore the sentences of the Roman courts, they were able to place many impediments in the course of justice. Often Greeks were convicted of giving false evidence by the Maltese courts, and were imprisoned before they were even able to start their suits. Sometimes, of course, such convictions were made quite correctly, as in the case of the Greek Captain Angelachi of Salonika. He had falsified the deeds of his ship so as to make it look as if it was Greek rather than Turkish. However, several Turks gave evidence against him, and he was convicted of fraud by the Maltese courts. To get out of this he pretended to be a cleric, and as such exempted from lay jurisdiction. His case was then transferred to the Bishop of Malta's own religious court. Here it was decided that he was not a cleric and he was returned to the lay authorities who imprisoned him for three years.[42] On other occasions, however, it seems fairly certain that the charges against Greeks were put-up jobs intended to prevent their suits against the corsairs being heard. When such cases were heard they could be dragged on for years. And even if the Greeks took their case to Rome, and their appeal was successful, the *Tribunale degli Armamenti* could decree five-year delays of payment by the defendants, or other such impediments. As a result of such delays many litigants died litigating, or went bankrupt before successfully concluding their case.[43]

Nor was procrastination the only recourse of the Maltese to the actions of Rome. Since neither the flag of the Religion nor of the Grand Master appeared to give full protection to the corsairs in their attacks on Greek shipping a new type of subterfuge was developed in the second decade of the eighteenth century. This was to license Maltese corsairs under foreign flags, particularly those of the Grand Duke of Tuscany and the King of Spain. Both of these potentates kept agents in Malta to handle normal problems of diplomacy, and these agents, always Knights, were quite prepared to license corsairs in the name of their sovereigns.[44] Now it will be remembered that one of the most strongly worded clauses of the original statutes of the *Tribunale degli Armamenti* was that no foreign corsairs should fit out in Malta. The Inquisitors were constantly reminding the Grand Masters of this clause and of its reiteration in 1608 and 1681. In 1724 the hypocritical Grand Master Vilhena repeated the clause, 'that no one was to arm, nor to contribute to the armament of any corsair ship with the flag or *patente* of any foreign prince or republic on the pain of serving ten years in the galleys and confiscation of his ship and prizes'.[45] Hypocritical, because Vilhena himself was a major financier of these foreign ships.[46] But indeed, as the spies of the Inquisitors found out, these ships were not really foreign at all – 'that is a mere appearance, there is no room to doubt . . . the ships are built in Malta, the crews are Maltese, the owners and bondholders are all Maltese'. The evidence that the spies produced regarding six 'foreign' ships operating from Malta in the late 1720s and early 1730s is conclusive on this point, even down to sworn affidavits from the shipbuilders, and similar evidence can be pieced together from notaries' contracts some ten years earlier.[47] Corsair ships flying the Tuscan flag had owners and crews identical with corsairs flying the Maltese flag. But once a ship was flying the Tuscan or Spanish flag it was extremely

difficult to bring a successful action against the crew's depredation. For if Greeks were attacked by a ship flying the flag
of the Grand Duke of Tuscany, the Maltese *Tribunale degli
Armamenti* would not listen to their plea, since the Tribunal had
no jurisdiction over the Tuscan flag. Nor was it worthwhile
pleading the case before the Tuscan agent in Malta because he
had no jurisdiction in the island, and even if he had, the only
appeal would be to the tribunals in Florence. But even if the
Greeks obtained victory in Florence, that would not help them,
because Florence had no jurisdiction over Maltese subjects
(i.e. the real financiers of the ships) in Malta.[48] A nice piece of
legal trickery for what was really nothing more than piracy.
The noose round the necks of the Greeks was in fact even
stronger, since Tuscan corsairs were only required in their oath
to desist from attacking Roman Catholics.[49] Orthodox Greeks
were not protected by the Tuscan courts as they theoretically
were in Malta. Indeed as Grand Master Zondadari wrote to the
Bailiff Spinola, the ambassador in Rome, if the ships and goods
of schismatic Greeks were made lawful prizes for the Maltese,
as they were for the Tuscans, then the whole problem would
be solved.[50] But the Popes, good Catholics though they might
be, were not prepared to license a Christian Order to hunt
down Christians. In view of the problems involved in suing
corsairs flying the Tuscan flag, it is hardly surprising that many
Greeks thought it hardly worth acting at all, and even if they
had a very strong case they might well agree with the action of
Giovanni Trimani who, 'in view of the expenses and the time
involved, and knowing besides that the result of this suit was
extremely doubtful', agreed to settle out of court.[51]

The use of the Tuscan and Spanish flags not only protected
the Maltese corsairs against successful litigation from the
Greeks, it also provided the Grand Masters with an excuse
to refrain from acting against corsairs who continued to
damage French interests in the Levant. Since the late seventeenth century French commerce had continued to grow in this
area, and although the Maltese very rarely attacked French
ships, they sometimes caused considerable damage to French
interests by their activities. In particular, since the Turks were
well aware of the fact that much of the mercantile money that
financed the *corso* was French, and that many of the corsairs

themselves were Frenchmen, they felt themselves perfectly entitled to seek reprisals from French merchants in the Levant for the activities of the corsairs. Complaints from Paris came to a head in the early 1730s when two corsairs, financed by Maltese money but flying the flags of Tuscany and Spain respectively, caused heavy charges to be levied on French merchants as a result of their attacks on Moslem shipping in Alexandria and the waters of the Holy Land. The Grand Master, Vilhena, said that he was sorry, but pointed out that he had no rights over the flags of other sovereigns, and that he could not order the Chevalier de Borras, one of the culprits, to disarm 'without putting ourselves in the wrong with the King of Spain'.[52]

But these subterfuges were at that moment being brought to a halt. From the mid twenties Greeks and Maronites who suffered from attacks by corsairs armed with foreign flags had ceased to attempt the farce of prosecuting them in the courts of Florence or Spain. Instead, they appealed direct to Rome and laid before the Papal Courts the details of the Maltese refusal of justice, together with evidence of the Maltese ownership of the corsairs. In 1727 the position was formalized when the Grand Master received instructions from the Papal Secretary of State that 'those attacking Christians in the Archipelago were to be tried by the *Tribunale degli Armamenti*'. Compulsory Letters and Mandates from Rome containing these instructions followed. Both the Spanish and Tuscan agents in Malta tried to resist the execution of such mandates. But Papal authority was too strong and they were soon forced to obey their instructions.[53] In 1732 the Grand Master himself gave up, and in August an edict was issued forbidding the use of Malta by corsairs flying foreign flags.[54] In the next year the Grand Master agreed to give up the use of the Magisterial flag as well.[55] Henceforth all corsairs in Malta were to fly the flag of the Religion and be subject to the *Tribunale degli Armamenti*.

A great improvement in the legal position of Orthodox Greeks came in 1733, when a famous legal decision in Florence (Federico di Giovanni *v.* Demetrio Licudi) declared that schismatic Greeks were not good prize, even for Tuscan corsairs.[56] But Greeks and other Christians in the Levant continued to be molested, despite legal decisions and despite the very specific safe-conducts issued by the Grand Masters. These occasionally have a very cynical ring to them, as if their issuers had little hope that they would be respected by their subjects. See, for instance, the introduction to the safe-conduct issued for a Maronite prince in 1740:[57]

> ... we cannot be led to believe that any of the said ship-owners [of corsair ships], by contravening our orders, and forgetting their duty and honour as Catholic Captains, should have the temerity to molest or damage the ships and goods of those that are of the bosom of our Holy Church: none the less ... [follows the safe-conduct].

And indeed from 1735 to 1745 the Maltese law courts are still full of suits brought by Greek Christians. In truth, as the surviving logbooks of the corsairs show, it would have been very difficult for the Maltese to make a living in the Levant without attacking Greek ships and Greek islands. For by the 1730s there were very few Moslem ships to be seen. With French ships protected by magisterial decree, English ships protected by their strength and Greeks fairly sure of a good hearing in the courts of Rome, if not in Malta, the great majority of Moslem merchants very sensibly shipped on Christian ships.

If French merchants were not to be subject to reprisals, and if Greek merchants were not to be molested, there was really only one answer – the abandonment of the *corso* in the Levant. Eventually continuing complaints from the French, the Pope, and other interested parties had their effect. In the early 1740s the Grand Master and Council decreed that no more corsairs should be licensed to cruise in the Levant. Theoretically, therefore, several centuries of Christian corsair activity in the eastern Mediterranean came to an end, though in fact as we shall see later there was a considerable amount of disobedience. Henceforth, although the *corso* was to last another fifty years, the only licences issued were for the Barbary Coast, or for a new type of patent which combined the right to trade and attack Infidel shipping. And indeed, this well illustrates the changes occurring in Malta in the course of the eighteenth century. Having attracted merchants as a result of its geographical position and its great prize markets, Malta now became more important as a trading than as a privateering centre.

We have seen how changed circumstances and particular diplomatic pressures acted together to make the Maltese *corso* slowly retreat from the extremely powerful position that it held in the maritime life of the Mediterranean in the first half of the seventeenth century. This gradual reduction of power was naturally reflected in the numbers of the corsairs, motivated as they were by desire for profits. It is extremely difficult to calculate the size of the Maltese corsair fleet accurately for any date. Records of the licensing of corsairs are fairly abundant, but when checked against other records they can often be seen to be incomplete.[58] Also, the records of licences issued in any one year will not cover all the corsairs active in that year, since licences were often issued for more than one year. Finally, as we have seen, many corsairs in the eighteenth century who should really be classified as Maltese corsairs were in fact flying foreign flags and thus do not appear in the normal records. As in Barbary, numbers alone will not in any case provide an accurate picture of the Maltese corsair fleet, since the ships varied very considerably in strength. For instance the thirteen corsairs who fought together in a fleet action in 1669 had an average of fifteen cannon a ship, but the largest ship had thirty-five and the smallest three.[59] Furthermore, from 1600 to 1750, although there was a tendency for the number of ships engaged in the *corso* to fall, there was also a tendency for the size of ships to increase. In view of these difficulties there seems little point in being too precise. The Maltese corsair fleet numbered about twenty to thirty ships of various sizes in the first three-quarters of the seventeenth century, ten to twenty from 1675 to 1740 with a tendency towards the lower limits as the end of the period approaches, and ten or under in the second half of the eighteenth century. A run of success, general warfare, or diplomatic problems could raise or lower the limits of these ranges in particular years.

Some idea of what such a fleet could mean when the Maltese *corso* was at its height can be had by an analysis of the fleet in the late 1660s when we have the most information. At this period there were probably thirty active corsairs operating from Malta. If we take the thirteen corsairs mentioned above as a random sample of this population we can gain some interesting information. For instance there were 1,774 men engaged in these thirteen ships. Grossing this up makes slightly more than

4,000 in the whole fleet. The population of Malta was about 60,000 at this date, and this figure includes men, women, and children. If we accept a ratio of 1 : 3 of adult men to the population, which is hardly generous for the seventeenth century, then one-fifth of the adult male population was engaged in the *corso*. This is, in fact, too high a proportion, since many of the crews of the corsair ships were not Maltese, but it gives an idea of the scale of the *corso* in relation to the Maltese economy. If we add an estimate of 3,150 for the crews, soldiers, and slaves in the Maltese navy the point is even clearer.[60] Finally, perhaps it is worth mentioning, that in 1697, for which year a register of merchant shipping has survived, there were ninety-nine sea-going Maltese merchant ships in operation with an average crew of thirteen men.[61] Bearing in mind the numbers of men who must have been directly engaged in servicing this enormous number of seafarers and their ships, there can be little surprise at the energy with which the Grand Masters attempted to protect the activities of the corsairs.

Malta as a centre of privateering compares very favourably with its much better-known rival, Algiers, from the second half of the seventeenth century onwards. Estimates for the sixteenth century put the Algerian fleet at about 50 or 60 units, and Father Dan estimated the fleet to consist of 80 ships in 1634, of which 70 were sailing-ships.[62] But by the period 1674–6 the Algerian fleet was only between 26 and 35 ships, including those owned by the State, i.e. virtually identical in size to the Maltese fleet plus the Maltese navy.[63] From this period onwards both the Maltese and Algerian fleets declined in size at a very similar rate. By the mid 1740s both had less than ten corsair ships at sea.

In view of the rough figures above it is with some justification that this chapter is entitled the 'Capital of Christian Piracy'. Marseilles, Toulon, Majorca, and other ports were great centres of privateering but they required a declaration of war by one Christian power on another to justify their activities. Only Malta, year after year, devoted the greatest part of her resources to the maintenance of the Eternal War against the enemies of the Faith. Both in employment and income the Maltese economy was very heavily committed to the pursuit of the *corso*, and in the remaining chapters of this part we shall see how this occupation was in fact organized and pursued.

CHAPTER 6

The Organization of the Maltese Corso

In Malta, as in Barbary, one of the most striking features of the *corso* was the extremely efficient way in which it was organized. Such organization can be seen very clearly in Malta, because of the survival to this day of much of the complicated documentation which lay behind every corsair cruise. So much paper work may seem strange for such an individualistic, even anarchic, type of business. But without efficient organization the *corso* could never have operated on the scale that it did. The Maltese and French businessmen, who invested large sums in the fitting-out of corsair ships, would never have done so unless they had been reasonably sure of getting a handsome return on their investment. And to achieve this, it was necessary not only for the ships to make rich prizes, but for those prizes to be returned to Malta for distribution amongst the various financial interests. However, big business alone was not responsible for financing the corsairs. An institution which combined, in such a satisfactory way, the greater glory of God and the possibility of gain was immensely attractive as an outlet for the small savings of hundreds of ordinary Maltese people. Indeed, embracing as it did the financial and crusading hopes of Grand Master, Knights, priests, nuns, businessmen, commoners, and crew, a Maltese corsair ship could be said to embody the collective desires of the whole island.

Naturally, it was not easy to organize an institution whose main function was licensed robbery on the high seas. There was much illegal activity, as the volume of cases brought before the Maltese courts show; but it was far less than might have been expected, considering the type of character who was inevitably drawn towards such a violent form of business. More striking was the matter-of-fact efficiency with which, year after year, ships were fitted out, sailed, made their prizes and returned to Malta to distribute them amongst the various financial interests. The main credit for this efficient organization must go to the Commissioners of the *Tribunale degli Armamenti*, the body set up in 1605 to run the corsair business.[1]

One of the main functions of the Commissioners was to report on the suitability of applicants for a *patente di corso* or licence to sail as a corsair.[2] The applications took a fairly stereotyped form: thus in 1707 Captain Leonardo Roy states that he had 'been nominated as captain of the corsair vessel called *La Rosa* to make a voyage against the enemies of our Holy Catholic Faith in the area of Levant and Barbary . . . for the space of five years'. He begs to 'be granted the flag . . . and the usual patents'.[3] Such applications were considered by the Commissioners on two main grounds, the condition of the ship and the fitness of the captain for the job. They inspected the ship to see if she was seaworthy, made sure that she was adequately provisioned and armed, and then checked the roll to ensure that she had a sufficient crew for the job. When comments were made about the captains in the report on their application, this was usually because they were new to the business (at least to the Maltese *corso*), such as Captains Borg and Grech whose report in 1704 said that they were 'persons experienced in the art of the sea and of the *corso*, one of them having previously commanded similar vessels in the Levant . . . and the other having sailed for several years with the Squadron of Galleys [of the Order] as a gunner'.[4] Nearly all applications for licences were successful. Presumably only serious people applied and because of this the Grand Masters and their advisers do not appear to have made any attempt to restrict the number of corsairs operating at any one time. It seems clear that it must have been the market, operating through normal supply and demand, that determined the number of corsairs.

Once the applications had been approved the letters patent could be granted to the corsair.[5] These were fairly specific, defining the time-limit of the patent, the geographical area in which activity could take place and those persons whom it was forbidden to attack. By the early eighteenth century the time limit was often five years, and even this could be extended if the expedition had not yet paid off its costs, such as in the case of Captain Rizzo, who applied for a two-year extension in 1720 'in the hope of having one day a happy encounter to make up for the past bad luck'.[6]

At the same time that the prospective corsair was filing his application for a *patente di corso*, he would also be engaged in the fitting-out of his vessel and the recruitment of his crew. Fitting-out brings us to the fundamental realities of the *corso*. Holy War or not, the whole institution was first and foremost a business venture. Corsair captains themselves might be saints or ruffians, but underpinning their operations was a sophisticated financial and commercial organization. For the capital involved in any one voyage could be extremely heavy. Normally the ship would be purchased by the financiers of the voyage, in itself a big item, but one which was only the beginning. Fitting-out and armament expenses were normally greater than the cost of the ship itself. Once the ship had sailed, plentiful working capital had to be found for the replacement of ammunition and stores, and for food for the crews whose number on a large ship might well be over two hundred It is clear that the original provision of capital often seriously underestimated the needs of working capital, on the optimistic assumption that this could be provided from the stream of prizes captured and sold. It is true that one of the commonest cargoes of captured vessels was foodstuffs, but it was certainly the lack of working capital on a disappointing voyage that led to much of the illegal capture of non-Moslem ships and cargoes. Indeed it was the custom of corsairs that if they found themselves short of food or equipment, they were entitled to stop any ship and demand what they required, even though this might leave a supposedly friendly ship short of vital equipment such as anchors or masts.

Six main groups of people had a financial interest in any corsair voyage. All these groups either provided services or capital for the fitting-out and operation of the particular voyage, or provided the services which enabled the corsair business to run at all, and all had clear rights in the division of the spoils at the end of the voyage. Since the number of people with a financial interest in the booty captured by any one ship might well run into hundreds, drawn from every locality and every class in the Maltese islands, and indeed from outside, the business of dividing the spoil was extremely complicated and often led to long drawn-out litigation. For the whole operation to go smoothly required a degree of honest practice and honest book-keeping that was at variance with the violent nature of the business involved, and mutual distrust and recriminations were a common feature of many voyages.

The first claimant on booty was the Grand Master of the Order himself. For the privilege of flying the flag of the Order or the Grand Master's personal flag every corsair had to pay 10 per cent of the value of his booty.[7] No doubt corsairs begrudged the 10 per cent that they had to pay to the Knights, but in fact the facilities that they were able to use in return for this payment were almost certainly better than those available anywhere else in the Mediterranean. Completely safe from the threat of enemy attack in the island's incredibly strongly fortified harbours, the corsairs could fit out in peace and draw on the special skills that Malta could offer. Dockyards, ships' chandlers, wholesale provision merchants – all the services required for fitting-out were provided by specialists. When the ship returned, what other port could provide such good facilities for the sale or redemption of slaves, as well as a wholesale commercial network for disposing of the prizes captured throughout the western Mediterranean?

The second claimant to booty was an institution known as the *Cinque Lancie*.[8] These five lances were five shares taken from the booty which were paid out to various people for spiritual and material services which they gave to the Maltese corsairs as a whole. The first of these shares went to the nuns of the Convent of St Ursula in Valletta 'who pray continuously for victory against the Infidel'.[9] More prosaically the second share went to the *algozino*, the official responsible for looking after the slaves in the *bagno* at Malta. The remaining three shares were distributed between various officials of the *Tribunale degli Armamenti*, the department responsible for running the corsair business.

The next claimants to a share of the booty were the captains and crews of the vessels. The share of the captain was known as the *gioia* and was fixed by statute at 11 per cent. Not all of this, however, accrued to the captain himself. Out of his *gioia* he had to pay some of his officers a premium on top of what they were entitled to receive as crew members. The most important such claimant was the pilot, a key person on board, and very often a Greek since so much of Maltese corsair activity was in Greek waters. His duties were to supervise the navigation of the ship, and especially to know the best places to water, to careen, and to find prizes. For the payment of the rest of the crew the commonest type of contract was known as *terzo buscaino*. By this it was agreed that of 'all the prizes that with the help of God are made in this voyage, deducting first the *dretti di ammiragliato* pertaining to His Excellency [the Grand Master] at 10 per cent, the *gioia* pertaining to the captain and the rights of pilotage at 11 per cent, and the extraordinary expenses, all the rest must be divided into three equal parts, two of which belong to the *armatori* [the holders of the equity in the voyage] and the other third to the crew of the said ship, the whole to be estimated by two experts . . . ' [10] The crew received an advance on their expectation of prize money and until they had repaid this they were unable to leave the service of the ship. Nor were they allowed to leave the service of the ship until the ship itself was free of debt, or had completed three cruises, whichever was shorter.

Apart from their expectations in the general share-out of prize money, some of the officers had rights conferred on them by the general custom of Mediterranean corsairs. These rights were extremely complicated and perhaps the best general impression of the sort of thing involved can be got by quoting the evidence given by Captain Balestrier of Majorca in a lawsuit of 1742:[11]

I have been engaged in the *corso* 33 years with ships flying the flag of Malta and other flags, and I know that it is always the practice amongst corsairs that money found on anyone in the hold and the goods taken, sleeping things, boxes and small quantities of money belonging to the passengers or sailors, that are loose and not sealed, providing that they are not part of the cargo, are all the perquisites of the Captain; and if

such goods are found in the cabin they belong to the lieutenant, those that are in the cable locker belong to the sergeant
and those in the galley to the steward.

It was also the privilege of various members of the crew to keep
goods pertaining to their trade. Thus the cook had a right to
the saucepans on a captured ship,[12] the surgeon to the medical
chest,[13] and the helmsman to an anchor, or if it was needed by
the corsair vessel to its equivalent in money.[14] None of such
articles entered into the general account but they were all
supposed to pay the rights of *ammiragliato*. In the confusion of
boarding it seems unlikely that such things as loose money,
wherever it was found, would find their way to the rightful
claimant, and that in fact the crew tried to lay their hands on
whatever they could get. Passengers and crews of captured
vessels were often stripped to the skin, even though they were
quite clearly Christians, since the value of a single gold ring
might easily exceed the total expectations of a soldier from five
years' privateering. This type of illegal activity was the hardest
of all for the authorities to check.

The two final claimants on booty were the bondholders and
the equity holders, the two financial interests who actually
financed the fitting-out and operation of the corsair vessels. The
division of interests between these two groups varied considerably from ship to ship. Sometimes a ship was financed almost
entirely by bonds with the only shareholder being the captain,
himself the owner of his own ship. On the other hand, an equally
common arrangement was for a syndicate of some half a dozen
merchants to own the ship and to finance the bulk of the fitting-
out from their own resources, selling bonds to other merchants
for the remainder of their needs. Whatever the arrangement
the bondholders held preferred stock and got paid off before
the shareholders. By far the commonest type of bond was the
bottomry bond, a kind of mortgage on the prospective booty.[15]
Such loans were made not only in cash, but also in the food and
equipment needed for the voyage. Thus a wholesale corn-mer-
chant would receive a bond in his favour for the ship's biscuit, a
spicer for medical stores, and ships' outfitters and ropemakers
for cordage, sails and spars. Even the ship itself might be acquired in this way with only a minimum outlay of cash. Some-

times it seems as though the whole island must have had financial interests as bondholders in the corsair voyages. Over seventy-five bondholders were interested in the voyage of a tartan in 1743.[16] Apart from merchants, shipowners, and underwriters from Valletta and the neighbouring towns, these included men and women from all over the island, as well as priests making investments on behalf of their parishioners.

The residual claimants to booty were the equity holders. Once all other claimants had been paid off and all expenses had been met, the remainder of the booty was shared between them *pro rata* of their investment. These investors in the *corso* '*a tutto risico*' form a fairly tight-knit group. They comprised mainly merchants, shipowners, and underwriters from Valletta and from the Three Cities of Senglea, Vittoriosa, and Bormula that lay the other side of the Grand Harbour, the community of corsair captains past and present, and some of the richer and more enterprising of the Knights of St John. Sometimes it is possible to delve deeper into the business lives of these men, and a logical pattern of operations can be seen.[17] The same merchant can be seen financing a corsair ship, bidding in the auction of the prizes of another ship, and buying or selling commercially the same types of goods for which he had bid in a prize auction. The distinction, for a businessman, between investment in the *corso* and investment in trade was wholly a matter of profit and loss, of calculation of the potential risks and the possible gains.

The system of financing corsair voyages outlined above was frequently complicated by the fact that corsairs often hunted in groups. A contract agreeing to form a *conserva*, as such groups were called, would be drawn up, and it would be agreed that all prizes captured by any of the ships involved would be shared.[18] When two or three ships were fitted out by the same syndicate, the accounting would be quite easy. The original investment would cover the fitting-out of all the ships, and the booty captured by any one of the ships would go into the general account. When the ships belonged to different financial groups, however, the accounting could be quite complicated. The best example is the division of the spoil captured by fifteen corsairs acting together in 1669.[19] In order to calculate the shares of each ship, account was taken of the number of guns, the size of the crew, and the size of the ship. Adding up the contribution from all these three categories, it was possible to calculate the share of each ship.

It can be imagined that for the Maltese authorities to keep control of the corsair business and to make sure that everyone got their right share was an extremely difficult task. They had not only to control the distribution of prizes in Malta, but also had to be able to keep a watch on what the ships were doing at sea. The only way to do this was to have someone on board each corsair vessel who everyone felt they could trust. This unthankful task fell to the purser or *scrivano*. He had to keep a set of books showing the shares of everyone with a financial interest in the ship, the expenditure that had been made in the course of the voyage, and a detailed record of all the prizes that had been taken. Before setting off on a voyage the purser, who was a public official, had to make an oath swearing to perform his office faithfully and truthfully. If later he was found to have been fraudulent the normal penalty was to have his right hand cut off.[20] The temptation to risk his hand must on occasion have been very strong, but although the writer has examined a large number of court cases concerning the *corso*, no example of a *scrivano* being sued for dishonesty has been found, so presumably they were either very crafty or very honest.

With the *scrivano*'s books in their possession, the officials in Malta were able to keep a considerable measure of control over the distribution of prizes. All prizes that were brought in had to go through a clearance procedure which often included quarantine, before being given the clearance certificate, known as the *pratica*. The cargoes, slaves, and ships were then sold, either privately, or more commonly, by public auction organized by the Magistracy. However the prizes were sold, a record was kept and the value of the prize and the name of the purchaser were registered in a special set of books. During this procedure the Grand Master's 10 per cent was deducted. The proceeds were then distributed, either directly to the interested parties, or else went into the bank or *cassa* of the *Magistrato degli Armamenti*.

The account books of this bank have not survived, but it is obvious that they must have included a daybook to record the incomings and outgoings of the bank, as well as a ledger in which running accounts of all interested parties could be kept.

The receipts of the bank were comprised almost entirely of the payments made by the purchasers of prize goods.[21] Thus in 1661 a French sea-captain deposited in the bank 856 *scudi*, the price of a Turkish ship sold to him in the public auction of prizes made in common by two corsairs,[22] or in the same year a Maltese merchant promised to pay within three months 3,287 *scudi* for coffee bought from another prize.[23] Disbursements included not only payments made to parties financially interested in the distribution of prizes, but also comprised a multitude of payments made to various people for expenses in connection with prizes. Thus it was a very common practice for corsairs to send their prizes back home in the care of merchantmen, and payments made to the captains of these ships for conducting 'a barque laden with barley and beans' or 'a frigate laden with grain' would all be recorded. Other sorts of payments would be to the warden of the slave prison, to the quarantine officials, or to the auctioneer.

At the same time those with a financial interest in the ship would be awaiting payment. As each prize came in, the money accumulating in the bank could be drawn on by the various claimants in the order of preference outlined above. Thus once the statutory deductions had been made the captain and crew could make a claim for their prize-money. And so we find a payment to Captain Treti in December 1676 'on account of and in diminution of his *gioia*' [24] or many years later in October 1742 to Maria, wife of Giovanni Rossi 'on account of the rights owing to her husband as first mate'.[25] Always pressing for payment and imagining that they were being cheated were the bondholders. The only participants in the booty with a fixed limit to their expectations, they were of course eager to get back their capital and interest as quickly as possible, since it was the time factor that was all-important. Thirty per cent on their investment was good business if they got it back in one year but over five years was a poor return considering the risk, since the normal rate of marine insurance in late seventeenth-century Malta was from 24 to 30 per cent per annum and the premium on commercial bottomry bonds from 40 to 50 per cent.[26] And so the shipowner and financier, Giorgio Camilleri of Valletta, must have been very pleased to receive on 20 August 1708 from the Bank 2,862 *scudi* from the effects of prizes made by Captain

Joseph Lia, in full payment of the capital and interest of two
bottomry loans he had made to him only three months previously, one for four months at 12 per cent and the other for one
year at 40 per cent.[27] Results were not always as happy as this
of course, and in 1661 we find Captain Agostino Vial negotiating with his creditors for an extension of two years to repay the
capital of some bondholders and of six months to pay the
interest.[28] After much negotiation the bondholders agreed
to give him one year for the capital and one month for the
interest, and Captain Vial was forced to borrow more money in
Valletta on the security of all his goods.[29]

Only when all the other interests had been paid off, and the
ship cleared of debt, could the shareholders start drawing from
the bank. This might be a very long time after they had made
their original investment. Once the ship had sailed they had no
control over the actions of their captain, and it is clear from
several lawsuits that the financiers were often suspicious that
their captains were not really trying as hard as they might.
Feelings of impotence, impatience, and suspicion must have
been common indeed amongst the financiers of corsair voyages
as they looked out of the windows of the counting-houses and
waited for a prize to be brought in. What was being done with
their money will be discussed in the next chapter.

CHAPTER 7

The Maltese Corsair in Action

With his letters patent in his pocket and his ship lying fully equipped in Grand Harbour, the Maltese corsair was now ready to set sail to fight the eternal war against the enemies of his Faith. Weeks of negotiation with the Tribunal and with his principals and creditors, of supervision of the fitting-out of his ship, of bargaining with corn-merchants and ships' chandlers were now over, and it must have been with relief that the captain went on board. For, although many captains were successful businessmen, their main function was to sail ships and make prizes, not to engage in mountains of paperwork.

The ships used by the Maltese corsairs were rather different from those of Barbary, and reflected a difference in tactics. The Maltese had a high reputation for gunnery, and relied fairly heavily on their artillery when they had to fight a battle against a well-armed opponent. This should be contrasted with the Barbary emphasis on rapid boarding in practically all encounters. For this reason the Maltese ships were generally heavier, higher-sided and with a greater complement of guns than those of their Barbary rivals, whose ships, as we have seen, were characterized by their extreme lightness and speed. For the same reason Maltese ships normally had smaller crews than a Barbary ship of the same size.[1]

Apart from this basic difference, the choice of ships by both groups of corsairs was very similar. Like the Barbary corsairs, the Maltese used a combination of oared- and sailing-ships for the whole of their existence. Over the period of two centuries considered in this book there was a slow change in the proportion of sailing-ships to oared ships, and there was a gradual improvement in arms, but overall the type of ship and the type of armament showed remarkably little change.

For most of the period a very clear distinction can be seen between the ships employed by captains licensed to raid in the waters of Barbary and those licensed for the Levant. Licences for Barbary were rarely for more than six months, and covered the summer fighting season which normally finished at some date in November. The normal practice of corsairs operating in these waters was to make a number of short cruises during the period of the licence, returning to Malta whenever they made a prize. Since distances were relatively short and the weather normally good, these cruises were perfect for the use of light oared-vessels – galleots, brigantines, and frigates. Fast and manœuvrable, they were ideal for cutting-out and boarding the lightly-armed merchantmen that were their main prey. Since they often worked in *conserva*, they would also have been a match for most of the more dangerous enemy ships that they might meet, and in the event of meeting a really strong enemy, their speed would have been sufficient to outdistance most of their pursuers, in view of the normally light winds of the summer months.

While oared-ships were the norm for a campaign in Barbary waters for most of the period, nearly all ships licensed for the Levant or for a joint campaign in both Barbary and Levant were sailing-ships. Although such ships were sometimes only licensed for the short summer season, the normal practice was for a licence to be for at least a year. By the end of the seventeenth century licences were for much longer, and during the eighteenth century the normal licence for a ship fitted out for the Levant was for five years. The conditions were clearly very different from those operating in Barbary. Very much further from home, and operating in waters that were theoretically under Turkish control, the corsair had to be prepared to face powerful enemies with little chance of running for home. Furthermore, his commission was to attack shipping in winter as well as summer, and although as we shall see, the corsairs were much less active in winter, they were still in Turkish waters and the Duke of Osuna's maxim that it was impossible

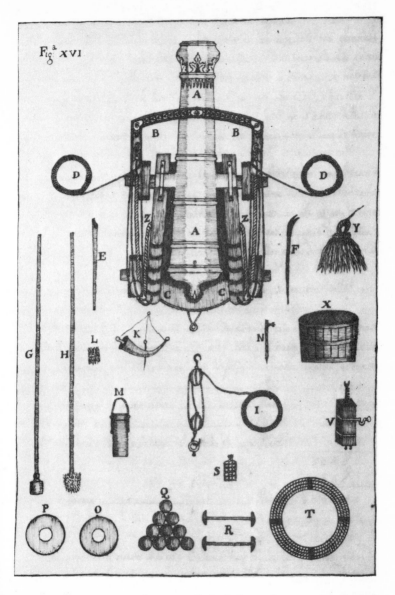

Cannon. Our sources give very little information on the size of cannon used on corsair ships, only the number of guns – up to forty or fifty on a large ship.

for galleys to stop sailing-ships in winter still applied.[2] While such factors as these, and also the need to carry a much greater number of men and far more provisions made it almost imperative to operate with sailing-ships, there were still advantages for oared-ships. These were often used for a short summer season at the beginning of the seventeenth century, and the same factors that made an oared-ship invaluable in Barbary waters in summer applied also in the Levant. For a sudden chase, for an operation in shallow waters, for towing sailing-ships during calms, etc. the oared-ship could do things which a sailing ship just could not do, and so a very common practice was for a sailing-ship to be licensed for the Levant in conjunction with an oared-ship. Sometimes these auxiliaries are mentioned in the letters patent, such as the brigantine of eight benches that was licensed together with a pollaque by a French Knight in 1623.[3] By the eighteenth century, however, these auxiliaries are not often mentioned in the letters patent, although it is clear from the logbooks of corsairs that most sailing-ships had one or two oared-ships under their command.[4] It was not, however, felt safe to allow some smaller ships to operate in this fashion, presumably because it was considered that they would not be strong enough to defend their weaker auxiliary. For instance, in 1708, the request of Paolo Cutaiar, captain of a tartan, to be allowed to use a fellucca or other small boat, which would not be permitted out of sight of the tartan, was turned down by the Grand Master.[5]

That the Maltese were not necessarily conservative in their choice of ship is shown by the fact that as early as 1601 Fra Giacomo da Liège fitted out a galleon from the 'west' (i.e. presumably from the Atlantic or the North Sea) – some years before the Barbary corsairs had made such a revolutionary move.[6] It is rare, however, that we get even such imprecise evidence as this of the origin of the ships used in the Maltese *corso*. It seems probable that most of the ships and galleys were built in Malta itself. Henry Teonge who visited Malta in 1676 recorded the launching of a new brigantine of twenty-three oars, which had been built on the shore at Malta, very near to the water. There were great celebrations and 'at last two friars and an attendant went in to her, and kneeling down prayed half an hour, and laid their hands on every mast and other places of the vessel, and sprinkled her all over with holy-water'. This brigantine was one of five destined to fight in Barbary waters.[7]

Most of the sailing-ships used in the *corso* bore the same generic names as those which predominated in French Mediterranean commerce.[8] The largest were normally styled *nave* or *vascello*, words which just mean a large sailing-ship. Then there was a whole range of medium-sized ships – tartans, pollaccas, petachios, and bertons, all ships of some 100 to 200 tons burden. These late seventeenth- and eighteenth-century pollaccas and tartans must be some of the most beautiful sailing-ships that have ever been built. With three or four raking masts and a combination of square and lateen sails, they were built for grace and speed. Some of these ships were certainly built in France, but probably the majority were either built or converted from prizes in Malta. The best evidence we have is a report made to the Maltese inquisitor on the origins of six corsair ships flying the Tuscan flag around 1730. Two of these ships were prizes which had been converted for use in the *corso*. The other four were all specially built for the *corso* in Dockyard and Senglea Creeks.[9]

As the period continues there is a slow tendency for the sailing ship to predominate in the *corso* relative to the oared-ship. By the second half of the seventeenth century it is extremely rare to find a predominantly oared-ship licensed for the Levant, unless as part of the equipment of a powerful sailing-ship. And in the eighteenth-century oared-ships on their own began to be rare in the operations in Barbary as well. Names which described oared-ships in the early seventeenth century such as frigate and brigantine are now clearly reserved mainly for commercial sailing craft, and the commonest oared-ship is the still powerful galleot or the new, small but extremely fast *speronara*. Some new types of sailing-ship appear in the eighteenth century – two of which, the *sambecchino* and the xebec, clearly betray their Moslem origins. But, even though sailing-ships predominated in the eighteenth century, many still had provision for oars as well. A four-masted tartan built for the *corso* in 1728, though provided with a heavy complement of sails, had also been pierced for twenty-two oars. No doubt the recent experience of the captain made him insist on this, for he had just returned from a voyage to the Levant on another tartan, and had only just managed to escape from two *soltane* of the Turkish

navy after a chase of twenty-four hours in which he had to jetti-
son much of his equipment. Twenty-two oars could make quite
a difference in such a predicament.[10]

Very rarely can we get much detailed information about the
armament of these ships. The best we have refers to the fifteen
ships that fought in a fleet action in 1669. All but three of these
ships had crews of over 100 men, and two had over 200. Their
main armament were cannons and swivel-guns. The largest ship
had 35 cannons, but most had between 10 and 20.[11] Further
information can be gleaned from some of the applications of
captains for a *patente di corso*. Thus in 1704 the *Santissimo Crocefisso*, Captain Vittorio Corbelli, was armed with 14 cannon, 20
breech-loading swivel-guns, over 100 hand fire-arms and a
wicked sounding collection of bludgeons, swords, and daggers.[12]
The three-masted *Santissimo Crocefisso e Sant'Anna* had a similar
armament of 14 cannon, 19 swivel-guns, and some 90 hand
guns.[13] Judging by the quantity of hand weapons, both these
ships probably had a complement of over 100 men. The complete crew-list of the *vassello*, *La Gerusalemme*, was attached to the
captain's application for a licence in 1708. This comprised 15
officers and 175 men.[14] The size of crew of a few other ships are
mentioned and these range from around 20 for lightly armed
brigantines and felluccas through two galleots with 46 and 60
men respectively to a *sambecchino*, the *San Paolo*, which was granted a five-year licence in 1726 with a crew of over 140.[15]

The two main enemies of the Maltese corsairs were the Barbary corsairs and the Turkish navy. We have already discussed
the Barbary ships with their emphasis on lightness and rapid
boarding. The Turkish navy, however, was quite different. In
the first half of the seventeenth century they relied mainly on a
very powerful galley fleet. Galleys could often be effective
against sailing-ships, but on several occasions Maltese corsairs
were able to defend themselves against incredible odds. In 1631,
for instance, a corsair on a lightly armed tartan with ninety
men and very few cannon was attacked at Cyprus by eight
galleys of the Bey of Rhodes. He defended himself for ten hours,
making great use of grenades from his height advantage, and
eventually forced the Turks to retire with great loss.[16] But the most
fantastic example is that of the Cavalier d'Hoquincourt. In 1665
Hoquincourt, captain of a powerful forty-cannon corsair ship,

Perriers or swivel-guns. Fairly light anti-personnel guns normally
carried in the waist of the ship to repel boarders, etc.

was surprised in Porto Delfino in Chios by the Turkish Armada of thirty-three galleys on their way to fight the Venetians in Crete. The Turks landed janissaries to fire from the shore and bombarded Hoquincourt with cannon from the sea. Yet, despite the fact that the ship's masts and sails were badly damaged, the poop covered in a hail of bullets and the hull punctured by more than 150 cannon-shots, Hoquincourt eventually was able to drive the Turks off with tremendous slaughter. As it happened he struck a rock a few months later in a gale and was drowned with about 170 of his crew. As the historian Dal Pozzo writes: 'A deplorable loss! Unworthy of a man with so much heart, and of a ship unconquered by the Turkish Armada'.[17] From the middle of the seventeenth century the Turks began to add sailing-ships to their galley fleet. Some of these ships were enormous and by the end of the century they were building three-deckers with 110 guns.[18] But the Ottomans had very great difficulty in manning these ships, and they suffered from a lack of skilled seamen. Navigation, for instance, was left to provincial Greek pilots 'who worked, however, in the most disadvantageous circumstances. For not only were they obliged to engage totally inexperienced assistants, picked up at the eleventh hour in the streets of the capital, so that they accounted themselves lucky to dispose of the service of Christian slaves and Maltese corsair prisoners; but they were threatened with death for the least misadventure.'[19] Turkish guns and gunnery were also defective, and although they had some successes, particularly under the command of the renegade Barbary corsair admiral Mezzomorte,[20] they were incapable of defending Ottoman shipping from the depredations of either pirates or Maltese corsairs.

The armament, crews, and vulnerability of the Moslem and Greek commercial shipping that was the main prey of the Maltese corsairs was almost certainly similar to that of Maltese merchantmen described earlier in the book.[21] Trade had to go on, towns had to be fed, but it was economically impossible to make all merchantmen strong. It is this fact that explains one of the paradoxes of the *corso*. The investors in a corsair voyage chose the vessel, arms, and crew in order presumably to provide the maximum fighting power for a given financial expenditure, and yet the Maltese corsair ships very rarely had to fight. Their superiority in firepower and men was so great over the vast majority of their victims, that if they could catch a merchant vessel, the latter nearly always surrendered without a shot being fired. This naturally suited the corsairs very well. They obviously preferred to capture ship, cargo, and crew intact, since it was the value of the prize that mattered rather than the glory of getting it.

When the corsair did have to fight, it was usually a bloody and cumbersome affair. The tactics of seventeenth- and eighteenth-century Mediterranean naval warfare were those of the bludgeon rather than the rapier. Before the invention of shells that exploded on impact, it was rare for a ship to sink another unless it was lucky enough to set fire to the magazine. The main objective was to board and capture the enemy rather than to sink her in any case. After a short period of firing sighting shots and manœuvring for the advantage of the wind, the ships would come close to each other and proceed to batter each other with poorly co-ordinated broadsides. As they pounded away they would concentrate first on the sails and rigging – chainshot being the most effective weapon for this. When the enemy was completely unsailable, with its masts broken and its sails and spars in an untidy jumble on the decks, sights would be lowered and the decks would be raked with grape-shot and musket fire. Finally the ship would close and board – and the last act of the battle would be a desperate hand-to-hand fight on the decks of the now helplessly drifting enemy. This was the time when the swords, bludgeons, and cutlasses listed in the armament would come into their own. This kind of bloody battle to the finish, though rare, was always a possible outcome of any corsair voyage, since some merchantmen were strongly armed, and even more there were cruising in the Mediterranean such determined enemies as the Barbary corsairs, the Turkish navy and the private men-of-war and galleys of Turkish provincial governors.

*　　*　　*

What were the tactics of Maltese corsairs and how did they acquire their prizes? Naturally, the first and most important part of tactics was to find a suitable prize. Here the Maltese corsair was at a great advantage. A very high proportion of all

Mediterranean shipping has always been engaged in the carriage of foodstuffs and raw materials to supply the large urban markets that are a feature of the area. Without this trade these cities would die, and thus the provisioning of the great Moslem cities of the Levant and North provided a constant source of gain to the Christian predators. No city in Europe could match in size the imperial capital at Constantinople, whose insistent demand for food drew ships from the whole eastern Mediterranean and from the Black Sea. Few European cities could compare with the other great cities of Islam – Cairo, Alexandria, Smyrna, Tunis, or Algiers. Added to these great urban markets were the islands of the eastern Mediterranean – often too small or too infertile to supply the needs of their inhabitants, and thus also dependent on maritime commerce for their food. Three main areas supplied these deficient markets. To the north the Black Sea had from the late fifteenth century existed as the major source of supply of foodstuffs for Constantinople. Here indeed the shipping was safe, for no-one but a madman would have dared to try to force his way past the 'two hundred mouths of fire' in the castles of the Dardanelles.[22] The other two areas were the Greek mainland of the Aegean and Egypt. It was the flow of ships from these two areas to the cities and islands of the Levant and North Africa that formed the major source of prey for the corsairs. And lest it should be thought that a cargo of rice or wheat was small recompense for the hazards of the *corso*, it should be remembered that rice is carried in ships, and that ships are sailed by men, and that it was from the sale of the ships and their crews, rather than the cargo, that the main income of the corsairs arose. Not that all cargo was food, however, for although the main function of Mediterranean trade might have been to prevent starvation, Moslem cities were centres of conspicuous consumption as well as the homes of hungry men. And so, in addition to more mundane cargoes, merchant shipping carried the foodstuffs and amusements of the rich. Chocolate, coffee, tobacco, and the spices of the East fetched better prices than rice or wheat, whilst the seizure of a cargo of jewels, silks, or concubines could mean instant wealth to the lucky corsair.

The nature of this trade and the geography of the east and south Mediterranean determined to a very considerable extent

Fire arrows. An effective weapon against sailing-ships.

the routes by which such cargoes were carried. Knowledge of such facts made the task of the corsair much easier. In the whole of the Mediterranean there were certain quite small areas where he was much more likely to find Moslem ships or Moslem cargoes than anywhere else. Whilst this fact made the corsair's job easier, it also of course made it more dangerous, since these facts were known just as well to the Moslem authorities as they were to him. And so whilst the first thing the corsair would do on leaving Malta was to head for such areas, he must always keep a constant look-out for the ships and galleys of the Ottoman Sultan and his provincial governors.

Of all the routes in the eastern Mediterranean the most vital and most heavily used was that connecting Constantinople with Egypt. Much of the trade on this route was carried in ships sailing together in convoy protected by the Turkish navy. The most daring, dangerous, and potentially profitable operation for a Maltese corsair was to attack this 'caravan', as it was called.

Normally this was left to the navy of the Order, but occasionally a particularly brave or powerful combination of corsairs
would attack the caravan, such as the fleet led by Gabriel de
Téméricourt who captured an enormous galleon and some
smaller ships in 1669.[23] Not all ships sailed in convoy on this
route, however, and the corsairs were nearly always able to take
prizes in their favourite catching grounds such as the sea area
between the Holy Land and Egypt, known as the waters of
Damiatta, and the area round Rhodes and south-western
Anatolia, known as the *crocieri* of Rhodes and the waters of the
Seven Capes. Further north the route became more dangerous
for corsairs, though a third area of operations lay in the waters
of Chios. Apart from this route the main areas of potential
prizes in the Levant were the waters round Crete and Cyprus.
In Barbary the favourite area was the waters between Tripoli
and Tunis, especially the stretch of water close to the island of
Gerba, known as the *Sechi di Palo*.

Whilst conditions of trade thus assisted the corsair, the political and religious situation in the eastern Mediterranean also
played into his hands. In a series of wars with the republics of
Venice and Genoa, the Turks had acquired sovereignty over
most of the myriad islands of the Aegean. But a statement of
sovereignty in a peace treaty is not of course equivalent to its
effective enjoyment. Many of the Greek islands had in fact
almost complete autonomy under their own priests or lords.
And thus despite the apparent dangers of operating in hostile
waters up to a thousand miles from home, the corsairs were in
fact able to use many of the Greek islands as forward bases.
The degree of security of these bases varied. At Larnaka in Cyprus
for instance, the corsair must wait to see if a white flag or a red
flag was flying before sailing in to take on water or dispose of
prizes.[24] But elsewhere islands were virtually Maltese colonies
set in the midst of Turkish waters. Such were Paros, Antiparos,
Delos, or Argentiera (Kimolos) in the Cyclades – havens where
the corsair could call for water or provisions, obtain information, careen, bury his dead in a Christian church or spend the
winter. Indeed relations were even closer than this since many
Maltese corsairs kept wives or mistresses in these islands, such
as Carlo Grech of Valletta who stated when being cross-questioned: 'I eat in taverns and in brothels . . . and the reason is

that, although I am Maltese, my house and family are in the Levant, so that I am here in Malta as a bird of passage.'[25]

What better way could be dreamed of for the subject Greeks to assert their nationality and their religion than thus to defy their Moslem masters? No wonder that the Greek shipping of the islands played such a dramatic part in the fight for Greek independence some twenty-five years after the eclipse of the Maltese *corso*. Indeed by the second half of the eighteenth century the Greeks had taken affairs into their own hands as Greek piracy became the scourge of the eastern Mediterranean, attacking not only Moslems but also English merchantmen and the Maltese corsairs themselves. It is perhaps worth remembering that Constantine Kanaris, a pirate from Psara, one of the so-called Naval Islands, was to become Prime Minister of Greece.

While some Greeks might assist the Maltese by providing them with a haven, others made their job much more difficult. These were the Greek merchantmen who carried so much of the trade of the whole eastern Mediterranean. In the sixteenth century a flourishing Turkish merchant marine had existed, actively engaged in carrying goods between Turkish ports, and indeed to Christendom. In the next two centuries this marine was to decline, partly as a result of the competition of Greek and western European shipping, but also as a result of the success of the Christian corsairs.[26] The chief beneficiaries of the decline of the Turkish merchant marine in the eastern Mediterranean were the Greek seamen. Whilst French, Dutch, and English shipping was predominant in trade carrying goods out of the area, the internal port-to-port trade was largely in Greek hands. Now since it was this port-to-port trade that was the main prey of the Maltese corsairs, this meant inevitably that there should be constant clashes between Maltese and Greek. The capture of a Turkish ship was a clear prize in the eternal war but the capture of a Greek ship posed very difficult questions. Who did the ship belong to? Who did the cargo belong to? Were there any Moslem passengers on board? Were in fact the persons posing as Greek Christians really Christians at all? Naturally such questions might not be posed in the politest way and naturally the answers might not be believed at all. As Captain Fra Gualterotti Bardi said in 1616:[27] 'The Greeks are always coming here to Malta to cry and pretend to be miserable, having been sent by Turks to recover their goods.' In this particular case the Greeks had every right to be miserable since Captain Bardi had stripped them and put them to sea in an open boat, but nevertheless it was a fairly obvious stratagem for Turkish merchants to consign their goods to ships belonging to Greek Christians and in the name of fictitious Greek merchants.

As the Turkish merchant marine declined still further in the eighteenth century, it was this problem of identification which did more than anything else to lead to the decline of the Maltese *corso*. The problem was intensified by the increase of French shipping in the Levant. The French, like the Greeks, carried Moslem passengers and cargo belonging to Moslem merchants. But the French (virtually the protectors of Malta) could not be treated in the cavalier fashion that the Greeks could. Furthermore the French with their strong political and commercial relations with the Turks were becoming less and less keen on encouraging the seizure of even Turkish goods in the Levant.

How did the Maltese corsairs operate under these conditions? As we have already seen, geographical and commercial factors limited the potential area of search for prizes. The corsair therefore sailed from Malta to these areas, normally via Zante and Cerigo if going to the Levant, or via Lampedusa if going to Barbary. Once in hopeful waters the normal procedure was either to anchor or to cruise about until a ship could be sighted. Now the chance of any particular ship being a good prize was very slim. Whilst they might seem empty by the standards of today, the waters of Barbary and Levant carried a considerable volume of shipping. These might be the large, well-armed and well-manned ships chartered by the English Levant Company to carry cloth to Smyrna, a Dutch flute, or from further north a big-bellied schooner carrying timber from Sweden or grain from Danzig. More likely there would be pollaccas, pinks or the ubiquitous tartans from Marseilles, Genoa or the ports of Provence. Occasionally a Venetian galleon or marciliana could be seen carrying on the city's declining trade with the Levant. But commonest of all would be the mass of Greek shipping – from the sizeable sambecchino and saique to the smaller saccoleva, caiassa, ciatturi, caique, and sambechinotto – engaged in

Grenades. Very effective when used by sailing-ships to drop dow
on to a galley.

fishing or the port-to-port or island-to-island trade that was the
lifeblood of the region. Occasionally a more powerful and potentially dangerous ship might be sighted – an English man-of-war,
a Venetian galley, or, more dangerous still, a Barbary corsair
or a soltana, caravel or galleot of the Turkish navy. The problems of identifying shipping at long range were enormous. What
looked like an English ship flying English colours might turn
out to be a French privateer or a Barbary corsair. A ship rigged
as a tartan might come from anywhere – harmless trading ship
from Marseilles, Neapolitan corsair, or potentially profitable
Moslem merchantman. All ships for their own protection carried a wide selection of flags and pennants so that they could
fly what appeared to be the most politic at any given time. Any
ship's captain worth his salt would carry papers and letters
patent, either real or false, granted by half a dozen potentates.
For it was a sea in which it was wise to be prepared for the
worst.

The first task of the corsair was therefore to filter the shipping to see if there were any potential prizes about. This might involve little more than running alongside another ship and hailing her to discover her port of origin, her destination, and her cargo. If possible this would also entail an exchange of information. A constant stream of news was vital to the corsair, even if some of it should conflict. Where were the good prizes? Had the passer-by seen the Turkish navy? Was the Turkish *soltana* loading janissaries for the Persian War still in Salonika or had she sailed? Where were the other corsairs? A casual meeting might elicit absolutely vital information, such as that England and Spain had declared war, or that even now there were three Turkish caravels out looking for his own ship.

While there was little that the corsair could do to the English and French ships, even if they were carrying Moslem passengers and cargo as they often did, the same was not true of the Greek ships. Here the filtering process was in earnest. The normal procedure was to send the felluccas or caiques, which as we have seen, were a normal part of a corsair's armament, to board and bring alongside any Greek ship which seemed suspicious or appeared likely to be carrying Moslem cargo. In one day the felluccas might leave the parent ship many times bringing back one or more Greek ships each time. Sometimes these would be released after a short period of questioning, sometimes the ship and cargo might be declared to be Moslem and would be seized, despite the protests of the Greek crew. Occasionally one of these ships would be forced to sail under the corsair's guns for days at a time – a manœuvre likely to unnerve the boldest spirit. The motive for this might be suspicion on the part of the corsair captain that the Greek was carrying infidel cargo, but much more often was a matter of simple blackmail. The Greek would lose so much time and would be so apprehensive of his future that he would pay a high sum to obtain his *pratica* or clearance certificate. Naturally this was made to appear a free gift, and it was much harder to establish this sort of injustice in the Maltese courts than a more straightforward case of wrongful depredation.

The testimony of Stefan Castello of Chios in 1661 provides a good example of such blackmail, as well as giving a good indication of the sort of trade common in the eastern Mediterranean.[28] Castello was suing Marcel Reverst, a Maltese merchant of French extraction, who was the *pleggio della bandiera** of Honorato Possen, captain of a petacchio fitted out as a corsair. In March 1659 Castello left Chios for Alexandria in a saique from Rhodes with 1,800 pieces of eight, some silver, and some cloth. He arrived in Damiatta where he did some business and increased his capital to 2,250 pieces of eight. He then, in company with two Greeks from the Black Sea and another Chiot, chartered a second Greek saique and loaded rice, flax, and other goods for Constantinople. On the 2 June they sailed and about seventy miles out to sea they met the petacchio of Possen. Possen seized the saique, even though the Greeks offered no resistance and protested that they were all Christians. The saique was forced to stay in company with the petacchio for fifty-five days until eventually Castello gave Possen 3,000 pieces of eight to release it.

Such incidents were commonplace in the time of the corsairs, but it was far commoner for the felluccas to effect a capture than for the parent ship itself. Although these auxiliary vessels were sometimes kept on board the parent ship or else sailed in company with their Captain their normal function was to be sent away for days at a time searching for prizes. When cruising independently they remained under fairly strict orders as the following extract from a log-book shows.[29]

'Once again we sent off the big fellucca armed with twenty-seven persons and commanded by the First Lieutenant, Demetri Nursella. He was given a passport signed by the Captain with the following orders: "He will go to the islands of Scarpanto and Scarpantone to plunder any ships belonging to the enemies of our Catholic Faith that he may meet, so long as they are weaker than him. Having made the tour of these two islands he will go to look for the frigate [i.e. the parent ship] at Kastelorizo in Caramania or at Fineka Bay. Not finding her there he is to proceed immediately to Provençal Island† and anchor to await the arrival of the frigate. This cruise shall not last more than three or four days." At

---

* The man who stood surety for a corsair captain's oath not to harm Christians.
† All these places are on a route from the east end of Crete to the north coast of Cyprus.

11 o'clock in the evening we sent the small fellucca armed with twenty-one persons and commanded by the Second Lieutenant Nicola Muri, to cruise towards the island of Scarpanto, and to return tomorrow morning, with or without a prize.'

If any ship should run at the appearance of the corsair ship or its felluccas, then this was clearly an admission of guilt and the chase would be on. It was rare for the parent ship to be involved in these chases, for the normal tactics of the victim would be to head for shallow water, but the light-draught felluccas powered by both oar and sail would chase. And if the victim should abandon ship and run on land, this was not necessarily the end of the matter – for most of the land was far from any danger for the corsairs. Indeed, all corsair ships specifically hired land pilots to guide them in their raids ashore, for slaves were not taken from ships alone.[30] Although raiding ashore was not such a specialization of the Maltese corsairs as it was of their Barbary colleagues practically every corsair voyage would include at least one such raid. The normal tactics would be to land the crew of a fellucca or the crews of several felluccas from ships in *conserva* and then march inland with a guide, provided either from their own crew or else a local guide hired for the specific job. A quick raid on a village, the seizure of slaves and then the march back to the ship would follow. Nearly all raids would be completed in a single night. Large-scale raids against fortified towns were normally left to the galleys of the Order. Corsair raids on land in the eastern Mediterranean were not without risk since the Turks kept cavalry stationed in the countryside and many expeditions ended in disaster with the slavers enslaved.

* * *

How did the Maltese corsair act in fulfilling the main function of his trade, the seizure of another ship? Here two factors should be remembered. First the normal prey of the corsairs were relatively small and lightly armed merchantmen. This meant that the seizure of a prize very rarely involved any battle at all. A hail, or at the most a warning shot across a vessel's bows, was

Brigantine. Small and very fast oared corsair ship. Together with the slightly larger galleot the commonest vessels used by Maltese corsairs in Barbary waters.

normally sufficient to make a prize come to and enable the soldiers from the fellucca or the parent ship to swarm on board the victim. Secondly, the most valuable item to be seized on most prizes were the passengers and crew, who could be ransomed locally or sold in the Maltese market for at least 100 *scudi* apiece. It was not, therefore, in the corsair's interest to kill, or even maim, such potentially valuable pieces of property. This attitude should be compared to that of a normal privateer whose prisoners could often be a positive embarrassment, as well as being a considerable expense. High-ranking persons might be ransomed, but the ordinary rank and file were a nuisance, since being Christians they could not be sold, and in any case had the right to be repatriated at the end of hostilities. The same sort of problem arose in the Caribbean, where the pirates and buccaneers who raided shipping of all nations, did not have an organized slave and ransom market in which to dispose of their prisoners. Not that the Maltese were particularly kind to their prisoners, even though these might ardently claim their Christian faith.

A very vivid description of capture by corsairs is given by the French gentleman, Jean Thévenot, travelling in the Levant in 1657. I will leave him to tell his story in his own words:[31]

'We sighted Mount Carmel and soon afterwards Acre, where we expected to be in a couple of hours, when we began to experience an example of the misfortunes to which all those who sail the seas are subject . . .

'Being then near Mount Carmel which juts a long way out to sea, we saw on the other side of the point a mast which we believed at first to be some bark at anchor near the land. But soon, seeing a caique full of men coming towards us, our Rais, who was Turkish, told us that they were Christians, and immediately got into the skiff and went off towards the land which was lined with Arabs, on foot and horseback, who were calling to us. And we were so close to shore that we could easily hear what they were crying to us in Arabic: "Come! It is a Maltese corsair." (Thus they describe all corsair vessels, since they often receive visits from those gentlemen.) And this time they were right. Those Arabs fired their muskets at them, which did not stop them coming towards us.

'As I knew that they were Christians, I persuaded a Greek, who had stayed on board and was holding the tiller, to lead us straight towards them, since I thought them my friends, and did not in the least want to go ashore where we would have been stripped by the Arabs, who stripped our Rais stark naked as soon as he stepped ashore. We had no arms at all; and if we had, we would have taken no care to defend ourselves against people whom we believed to be our friends . . .

'Very soon afterwards those gentlemen arrived. And although a Capuchin in our company cried to them from afar that we were French, and that on coming aboard they would see no one on the bark, that did not stop them from firing at our bark from close range a perrier loaded with musket-shot, and all their muskets.

'I will never name the Knight responsible for the sake of his honour. But this wretch deserved, for his evil conduct, to find thirty Turks in our bark, who would easily have overcome those people who had discharged all their weapons.

'After having performed this bold exploit, they climbed into the bark in great haste and we came out to make their acquaintance. But these young knaves, calling on God and devils alike to make themselves more frightening to unarmed men, did not want to recognize us at all, although they were all Frenchmen, and first of all occupied themselves with stripping us.

'As for myself, I was better served than a prince, for, although I said that I was French, I was surrounded by five *valets de chambre de malheur* who, for most of the time, kept a pistol at my throat and a sword on my stomach, and desired me at first to undress myself, but, one pulling from in front, one from behind, one on top and one below, stripped me stark naked in a flash. I thought I was finished with them, when they began to jab their swords at me. And seeing that it was for a cheap ring that I had on my finger, I took it off quickly and threw it to them, for I had already learnt something about how this sort of person behaved. Even after we were on their ship, one of them, noticing on my valet's finger a cheap gold ring, showed great displeasure that he had not taken it off. And when my valet told him that he could not get it off himself, he replied bluntly that he would soon cut the finger off to have the ring.

'Finally, after they had left me, having only my shirt on, I asked who was their commander. But no one answered me at all. However, after all this hubbub which was so strange to me, I began to feel the cold; and one of our monks, very kindly, covered me with his cloak, for they had not stripped the monks, although they had exhibited a strong desire to go through their pockets to see if they had any money. It would have been worth their while, too, for a Spaniard in our company had adroitly slipped his money into the sleeve of a monk, and thus saved himself from my fate. Afterwards, since they had even taken my bonnet off, I felt very cold on my head, as I had been shaving myself once a week in order to have my hair in the fashion of the country. I prayed them to give me a bonnet. Immediately they clapped on my head one of theirs, which had fallen into the sea, and which they had just pulled out.

'When all this disorder had quietened down, it was night. But so dark that our henchmen could no longer see their ship (which had sailed as soon as they knew that they were masters of the bark, for fear of having trouble from the land).

'However, the lieutenant, who was in charge of the gang that had taken us, had had orders to follow the ship with the bark as soon as they had captured us. So they lit several flares in the bows of the bark so that the ship might reply, and he would know where he was. At that moment I was much afraid that they would set fire to our bark which was fully laden with cotton, the bales being stowed one on top of the other. If that had happened they would all have saved themselves in their caique, and we would have been left to burn alive. But God looked after us. Their ship replied with a flare. And having come alongside, a quarter of an hour later, we climbed on board.

'At first the captain sent us to the poop, meaning to make us sleep in the open without supper, making the monks come down to his cabin. The latter having told him who I was, he came and called me by my name and told me to come down into his cabin. Giving me clothes straight away, he apologized profusely for the bad treatment I had received, assuring me that I would lose none of my things. And he said that he had seen me in Malta. Supper was not grand, as he had no provisions. However, he gave me his bed. And the following day, Monday 6 May, he went to great trouble to recover our gear. But it was in vain. He only returned to me my *capot*,* a pair of pants and a few similar bits and pieces. And still those rogues were mumbling, and said that if they had killed us, they would not have had to give anything back at all.

'Finally the captain told us that he would have to put us ashore, as he had not got enough food to feed us. Hearing this we begged him to let us go to our bark which was laden entirely on behalf of Frenchmen. But he told me that he was responsible for the bark to those who had fitted out his ship. So that he was resolved to put us ashore, though I pointed out to him that it would put us in danger of being burned alive if the Arabs should take it into their heads to take us for corsairs. He then had the caique prepared. But as it was not big enough for all of us, he decided to make two trips.

'As for myself, I was determined not to be in the first batch,

---

* Thévenot was very pleased with this article of clothing which he had bought in Samos some days earlier. 'A *capot* is a certain clothing of war, doubled in the same material, made like a camisole, going down to the knees; there are sleeves for your arms, and one puts one's head in a hood which is attached to it. All sailors have *capots*, and this article seems to me so necessary, not only for mariners, but for all those who go to sea, that I do not know how one could spend a long voyage without one: it serves as mattress and blanket; with a *capot* you can sit down and sleep where you are, and without it you would spoil all your clothes if it rained or blew. You can go in the open air with your *capot*, and inside a *capot* you fear neither water or cold.' [32]

Genoese fellucca. Felluccas packed with about twenty or thirty well-armed men made most of the captures of the Maltese corsairs.

fearing the worst. And indeed this trip turned out as I had imagined. For when they were fairly near to land in front of a fine village called Caipha,* which is at the foot of Mount Carmel they hoisted the white flag. But instead of replying to them with a white flag, someone fired several musket shots at them. And so they were obliged to return. The reason that they did not reply with the white flag was that there was in this village a French merchant who had come from Acre to buy goods. When he learnt from our Rais that he had had French passengers on the bark, he went to find the head of the village, and told him that if he flew the white flag, they would put us ashore, but take away the bark and its cargo. But if they did not, they would be obliged to let us go with the bark, not knowing what to do with us ...

'And so it was. For the captain finding himself very much disconcerted, after some hesitation, made us make for his acquittal a deed, in which we made assurance that the cargo of the bark belonged to Frenchmen. After we had signed it, he let us go with our bark, giving us three Greeks who he had taken before meeting us. We left him at mid-day and arrived at Acre at one in the afternoon, being very poorly equipped in all respects, and not even having a caique in which to go ashore.

* Presumably Haifa.

'M. de Bricard, French Consul, sent us one, and was kind enough to offer me money and clothing, for I had lost everything except for one bill of exchange on Acre which they left by good chance in an old suitcase . . .

'As soon as we arrived on land, the pasha made four French merchant ships which were in the port arm to go out after the corsair. For they had seen us captured from the port, and all the French merchants had recognized their bark which had a blue check sail. They put a hundred Turks on each of these ships. But the Consul who would have been much displeased to see so many Frenchmen enslaved, having asked the monks to pray to God for this business, gave orders to the Captains of the ships to do what they could not to capture it, and begged me to frighten the Turks who were going on board. This I did as well as I could: for, when the Turks, before going on board, asked me how many of them there were, I told them that there were three or four hundred, although there were not more than one hundred and twenty (but they had good arms and were well resolved to defend themselves).

'Finally the pasha himself boarded one of the ships, and went out towards the corsair who was anchored . . . the latter quickly cut his cable and, setting sail, got away as fast as he could. And the pasha, very happy to have chased them from his coast, returned to Acre.'

Such rough treatment was clearly commonplace, Christians or not, as the testimony of the Greek sea-captain, Caggi Pietro, in 1616 shows.[33] Pietro, a Christian from Lindos and master of a saique, said that he loaded his ship with rice in Damiatta to make a trip to Saide. About fifty miles out of Damiatta, he met the corsair ship of Captain Bardi, whose men came on board in the middle of the night and seized the saique. There were twenty-nine men on board, all Christians and not a single Infidel. These all proclaimed their religion and offered no resistance to the assault of Bardi's men. None the less, Bardi ordered that they should all be stripped naked, put in the saique's skiff and cast off to sea. And thus 'they were left on the high sea at the whim of fortune, to the misery and mercy of the sea and the winds, which by the Grace of God carried them to St Jean d'Acre where they had by alms and assistance been given some clothes.' They then made their way to the French consul to tell their story swearing to tell the truth on the Bible. Caggi Pietro's story was supported by affidavits, not only from the French consul in Acre, but by the French consul in Egypt, by the Greek Archbishop of Mount Sinai, and by Cyril, Patriarch of Alexandria. He was even able to produce copies in Greek and Italian of the purser's book from the saique. Clearly Bardi must have believed that they were Christians or he would never have put them in the skiff. It shows a certain gambling spirit that he did, since the chances of their surviving to sue him in the courts of Malta must have been about evens.

Apart from the violence associated with the seizure of a ship, a major source of further violence was the belief that somewhere on a captured ship there was a store of valuables not revealed in the initial search. No very sophisticated forms of torture seem to have been necessary to the corsairs; information nearly always being supplied at the threat of a beating. Thus when the Rais of a captured ship refused to show the whereabouts of some cash, the existence of which had been stated by one of his passengers, Captain Preziosi had him tied to a cannon, but before the boatswain had inflicted the first lash, the Rais thought better of his bold stand and the cash was soon found in the false bottom to one of the bunks.[34] As mentioned earlier, the corsairs, though tough and sometimes desperate men, had no interest in doing permanent damage to their prisoners. This meant that although capture was bound to be an unpleasant business, the captives could normally expect to arrive alive in Malta unless they had been badly injured during their capture. Whilst on board the corsair ship they would normally be shackled, and we can see in the inventory of the *Santissimo Crocefisso e Sant'Anna* made in 1706 provision for this in the form of chains, shackles, and handcuffs.[35] All the same it is clear that prisoners were not shackled all the time since on more than one occasion the logbooks revealed that slaves escaped, normally by jumping overboard. The slaves would have the services of the ship's doctor to attend to their injuries or illnesses. The latter had to attend to this business since the shareholders in a ship might well sue a ship's doctor for the price of a slave, if he died as a result of the doctor's

negligence, and thus deprived them of part of their expected
returns from a voyage. [36]

The corsair captain had four main choices open to him as
to the disposal of prizes. He could either keep cargo and slaves
on board his own ship until he could return to Malta to dispose
of them; he could send a captured ship home to Malta with a
prize crew; he could send cargo and slaves home to Malta in the
charge of a friendly merchantman or another corsair ship; or
finally he could ransom or sell ship, cargo, and slaves on the spot
in the eastern Mediterranean. The only real constraint on his
choice was that according to the rules governing the *corso* he had
to send really valuable prizes back to Malta. [37] It seems probable
that the majority of all prizes taken, at least in the Levant, were
sold or ransomed more or less on the spot. It was a quick method
of disposal and often the price received, especially in ransoms,
would far exceed what the corsair could expect on the open market in Malta. Relatives and friends would pay well for their
captured associates, and the captain was of course freed from
the necessity of maintaining slaves for the long period that
would elapse before their eventual sale in Malta.

The following extract from the ledger of prizes sold in the
Levant by Captain Geronimo Preziosi in the years 1739–41
gives a good idea of this process. [38] Captain Preziosi was the
captain of a sambecchino and was being sued by his creditors.
The prize ledger, which was called as evidence, is the only
example of such a document that has been found in the archives
at Malta.

		Piastres
27.12.1739	In waters of San Giorgio del Boro seized a caique of Napoli di Romania coming from Constantinople to Napoli with 20 quintals raw cotton, 90 ox-tails, etc.	
	+ silver money	80
	+ zecchini	198
3.1.1740	Argentiera. Sold cotton to Papa Francuci	77
9.1.1740	Delos. Sold ox-tails	87

		442

Piastres

20.1.1740	In the port of Palermo di Scopoli seized a saccoleva loaded with *giogionena* [a sort of cloth]	
24.1.1740	In port of Scargero ransomed saccoleva and cargo	1000
29.2.1740	In port of Psara ransomed Turk captured on above	245

1.2.1740	In port of Pellarizi seized a saccoleva and found 100 piastres	100
2.2.1740	In same place ransomed saccoleva	200

1.3.1740	In port of Psara seized saccoleva and found	640
Same day	Ransomed saccoleva to its own skipper	50

17.2.1740	In port of Lemnos seized saccoleva loaded with grain. We made biscuit with the grain between Paros, Antiparos and Argentiera. 300 kilos

8.4.1740	In waters of Hydra seized caique loaded with cotton and a Turk	
24.4.1740	In Zante. Sold cotton in port of Ceri	217.20

25.4.1740	Sent fellucca to land at Carenza. Captured one Turk

22.6.1740	In Giorgis. Sent the two felluccas for 2 carabos drawn up on land. Seized 8 Turks

25.7.1740	In Capo Charobi of Cyprus. Sent the two felluccas to land. Seized a Turkish woman	
17.8.1740	In Roads of Jaffa. Ransomed Turkish Cypriot woman to the Agha of that place	500

		Piastres
3.8.1740	In waters of Larnaka seized empty chiassa with 66 piastres on board. Half share to us*	33.25
31.10.1740	In waters of Kufonisi seized empty saicotta with 1,245 piastres on board. Half to us	622.20
3.11.1740	In port of Pattino ransomed saicotta. Half to us	150
10.11.1740	In waters of Psara seized empty saccoleva with 190 piastres on board. Half to us	95
16.11.1740	In waters of Volo, the fellucca seized caique with four Turks and capital of	784
3.12.1740	In waters of Samos the fellucca seized four saccoleve and took them to Arcio. Three of the four had capital on board belonging to Turkish merchants. These saccoleve came from Mytilene, Lemnos, and Chios and had three Turks on board	1585
7.12.1740	In Arcio ransomed the Mytilene and Lemnos boats	400
2.2.1741	In waters of Castrin ransomed one of the Turks from Salonika	400
6.2.1741	Ransomed other two saccoleve. Half to us*	300
13.2.1741	Received from Captain Cristofano* 54 *zecchini* and the proceeds of sponges sold at Argentiera	162
	+money coming from ransom of a caique	75
	+ our share of prizes in goods—soap, mastic, cloth	40

* Half share since they were at that time in *conserva* with another captain. See below 13.2.1741.

Christian corsairs running for harbour.

		Piastres
14.2.1741	Divided the Turks. Our share was twelve; four from Oran, two from Smyrna, two from Alexandria, one each from Cyprus, Gallipoli, Chios and Benghasi	
25.2.1741	Sent the fellucca to Missolonghi where it seized a caique loaded with oil, and ransomed it on the spot	75

This document, while it could hardly be called typical since it is the only example known to exist, gives a very good idea of the petty and ordinary nature of most activity engaged in by corsairs. How many other ships were stopped and searched to provide this meagre harvest of seventeen small ships we cannot tell, though the number must have been considerable.

If the prizes taken were more valuable, then it would be

worth while sending them to Malta. This would be true especially if the corsair managed to capture a fairly large ship. As we have seen, corsairs often carried large crews so the provision of a prize crew was not usually all that difficult, especially as it was often possible to use the Greek members of the crew of the captured ship. Often members of the crew of a corsair ship were specifically hired as prize captains (Captain Preziosi had two, a Frenchman and a citizen of Nice).[39] Or they might be appointed on the spot, such as Domenico Vigneri, constituted captain of a saique taken by Captain Maurizzi in 1658, and loaded with rice, flax, sugar, coffee, and other goods.[40] This must have been a large or very valuable ship and cargo since Vigneri sailed with a prize crew of forty-four. Taking a prize home was a dangerous task and a prize-captain had special rights in the division of the booty.

A study of the prize ledger of Captain Preziosi also points up another interesting feature of corsair activity. This was the fact that corsairs spent much of their time in harbour, not necessarily looking for prizes at all. This was something that obviously worried their employers, and the point is put rather well in the indictment of Captain Aloisio Gamarra in 1661 when his employers said that 'in the whole time that Captain Aloisio was in the Levant, he never lost a chance of attracting foreigners in conversation in the ports, of going on board other vessels continuously to play cards, eat and drink . . .'[41] Captain Gamarra's reply was that 'he tried as far as possible to remain in the *crocieri* and other good places to make prizes without having ever entered port unless to careen or to water, for bad weather and for other similar urgent reasons, as do all the corsairs . . .'.[42] Without going any further into the case against the captain which is considered in a later chapter,[43] he was certainly right in saying that this was what the other corsairs did. This can be seen clearly from log-books, especially of cruises in the Levant where corsairs often spent more than half the time at anchor in the ports of the Aegean, Crete, and Cyprus.

Corsair captains had many reasons for their frequent visits to the havens of the Greek Archipelago. It was here that they could sell their prizes, and get information from the 'Greeks of that place'. It was here that they could take on water and get fresh provisions. But perhaps most important of all, it was in

French soldier. Musketeers formed the main fighting element on corsair ships and were the equivalent to the janissaries on a Barbary corsair ship.

these havens that they could maintain their ships as efficient fighting weapons. To do this it was necessary, at least once every two months, to empty the ship, scrape and wax her bottom, renew rigging, and in general overhaul her gear. This could be a very anxious time for a corsair captain since with the gear out and the ship careened on one side, he was a vulnerable target for his enemies. Hence the importance of the fairly easily defended Greek islands. Indeed, even though the corsairs posted guards on the peaks of the islands and sent the felluccas out to keep watch on shipping in the neighbourhood, the Turks made most of their captures of corsair ships while they were in harbour. In the early 1730s, for instance, the spies of the Maltese inquisitors reported on the activities of six ships fitted out in Malta but flying the Tuscan and Spanish flags. Two of these were captured in the Archipelago; the crew of one escaped in the boats, but the crew of the other were all enslaved.[44]

Apart from the reasons considered above, another factor tending to keep the corsairs in harbour was the winter. The Mediterranean winter is a dangerous time for sailing ships, and much paper has been covered by historians trying to assess the degree to which both trade and maritime warfare tended to drop off during the winter. The main conclusion is that winter meant an almost complete halt to the pursuit of maritime warfare, but that trade did not cease as completely as was once thought. If it was possible merchants and shipowners would defer their voyages till the spring, but the timing of harvests and the problems of surviving with a dwindling food store often meant that it was imperative for some trade to continue. Those Maltese corsairs whose licences lasted for longer than the short summer fighting season had therefore a choice of returning to Malta for the winter or of remaining in the Levant. Although the former might be the more attractive alternative, the latter was for business reasons the most sensible. Since some trade continued, and since the Turkish navy was normally in harbour, the winter might in fact give an opportunity for a really worthwhile prize. Also, of course, by staying in the Levant they were on the spot to start work the next spring. And so the corsairs normally spent the months of November, December, and January in their havens in the Greek islands, maintaining a constant lookout for potential prizes, and sending the felluccas out now and then to see what shipping was about. The weather was often very bad in the winter and this could be a dreary time, enlivened however by the fact that other corsairs and merchantmen also wintered in the Aegean, so that visits could be made from ship to ship to exchange news and entertain each other.

Such then was the Maltese corsair in action. Most of the summer was spent chasing defenceless Greek shipping. Most of the winter was spent in harbour in the Aegean playing cards and carousing. But every now and then such a leisurely life was rudely interrupted and the manhood of the corsairs was put to the test. The arrival of a Turkish galley while the corsair lay becalmed; a raid on a defenceless Turkish village turned into a nightmare fight for survival by the arrival of Turkish cavalry; a potential prize with somewhat better defensive resources than the corsair had thought. Such events made the corsairs really work for their living.

CHAPTER 8

The Maltese Prize Market

What happened to the actual prizes captured by the corsairs?
As we have seen, a high proportion of all prizes were never
brought home. Cargoes of foodstuffs and naval stores were often
taken straight into the corsair ship for its own consumption.
Ships, slaves, and cargoes could be sold or ransomed in the ports
of the Levant, or even in Barbary, and this practice often made
much better business sense than bringing them back, at considerable expense, to Malta. It was the proceeds from such
transactions that provided most of the working capital of the
corsair.[1]

But many prizes were of course brought back to Malta and
there were sold, normally by public auction. An incomplete
prize register of the *Tribunale degli Armamenti* has survived for
the years 1659–61 and this gives a good idea of what happened
to the various goods as they were sold in the public auction.[2]
The register records the sale of some twenty ships, 500 slaves,
and a vast assortment of cargoes. Amongst the last the goods
recurring most frequently are rice, coffee, cotton, flax, sugar,
beans, and grain – the staples of Levantine and North African
shipping. A large number of individuals and the Common
Treasury of the Order appear as buyers of these goods. But
amongst this crowd of purchasers a few merchants emerge as
large-scale participants in the prize market.

Such were Balthazar Alard and Marcel Reverst, both French
merchants living in Malta.[3] These were the sort of men who

kept the whole, rather strange, economy of Malta going. At every stage of the *corso* we can see their business interests. Both had shares in corsair ships and both made loans to finance other corsairs. If a corsair needed a ship, guns, wax, sails or biscuit they would sell them to him. And they provided the same services to the galleys of the Order. When the prizes came in they were ready at the auction. Ships, slaves or goods – they dealt in everything. But prize-goods did not remain long in their warehouses. The coffee was sold to a Maltese sea-captain, flax to an Italian, rope to the Galleys of the Order, a ship to a Frenchman. Ships were chartered and insured to carry goods to Marseilles, Leghorn, Messina, Scanderoon, Smyrna or Constantinople. And so the prize-goods were fed into more straightforward commerce. Back from France came a cargo of cloth to be distributed in Sicily and the Levant. Back from the Levant came a cargo of hides to be distributed in Sicily and France. But the Sicilians were slow in paying. A power of attorney was given to another Frenchman to speed up payment. With their commercial network set up they could provide other services. A Knight needed cash? Payment was made on bills of exchange and letters of credit from Lisbon, Leghorn or Marseilles. The Order wanted to receive the income from its estates in France? The money was paid to André Alard in Lyons, and Balthazar made payment in Malta. A slave arranged his ransom? The money was paid to his master, payment to be made to Marcel Reverst in six months. Everywhere we can see the busy hand of capital helping the corsair to dispose of his booty.

And the human prizes, what happened to them? What was the fate of Mohamet, son of Musa, of Algiers, twenty-seven years old; or Riheu, Negro eunuch, twelve years old, slaves unloaded from the corsair ship of Captain Carlo Juvara on 10 December 1661? [4] The story is indeed much the same as that we have already seen in Barbary. The slaves were landed, went through quarantine and then were sold. As we have seen, the Order was entitled to one in ten, and they could buy others at a fixed price. Many of the Order's slaves were destined to a hard life on the galleys – in 1632 there were 1,284 slaves employed on the Order's six galleys. [5] Others were employed on public works, building and repairing the enormous fortifications, or in the hospital, bakery or workshops of the Order. Others, perhaps more fortunate, worked as servants in the Magisterial Palace or the Auberges of the Knights. Some, indeed, were given away as presents to other courts.[6] But, although the Order itself was the biggest buyer in the slave-market there were many others. In the third quarter of the seventeenth century one of the most important buyers was the French agent in Malta, buying slaves for the galleys of France.[7] Experts considered the Turks, and especially the North Africans, to have no equal as rowers, and it was felt essential to have at least one Moslem slave per bench. In the eighteenth century the galleys of France declined in importance until the Corps de Galères was abolished in 1748, but as Bamford has said: 'The Infidel Turk, with his distinctive clothing, moustache and reputation for physical strength, was a symbol of the old fighting galley.'[8] As late as 1712 there were over 1000 Turks in the galleys. Spanish, Neapolitan, and Papal galleys were also destinations for slaves sold in Malta.

Not all slaves, nor even a majority, were however bought for the Order or for Mediterranean galley-fleets. Quite a number were bought by the corsair captains themselves. Captain Agostino Vial, for instance, bought nine out of a batch of twenty-three slaves which he had himself captured.[9] Some of the slaves purchased by corsairs were clearly destined to work on their own ships, such as Achmet bin Mohamet of Algiers bought by Captain Fra Carlo Labartes specifically 'for the ship'.[10] But others were no doubt bought as a speculation. No one had a better opportunity of ascertaining the possible ransom value of a slave than his capturer. But many slaves were bought by private individuals, for Malta, like Barbary, was a country permeated by slavery. Dumont commented at the end of the seventeenth century that 'almost all the Maltese are served by slaves, who are suffer'd to walk freely about the streets all day.'[11] Although Dumont was prone to exaggerate what he saw on his travels, on this occasion the prize register bears him out quite well. Knights, priests, and commoners were all present as buyers of slaves. Just as in Barbary such slaves were employed as domestic servants, as clerks, and in shops. Many buyers of slaves were mainly interested in the possibilities of making a good profit on a future ransom, and we find merchants buying slaves and letting them out to others while a ransom is being negotiated. An active internal market in slaves also existed and an individual might change hands many times before being ransomed.[12]

Most slaves could expect to be ransomed eventually but this might be a very long time after their original capture. Godfrey Wettinger has examined the fate of a group of slaves captured by the Galleys of the Order in a raid on the town of Coron in southern Greece in 1685.[13] Some of these slaves left Malta with their ransoms paid in just over a year. A group of Jews were particularly fortunate in this respect, though they had to pay high ransoms. In twenty years over half the slaves had taken out safe-conducts to leave Malta and it is more than likely that several more had left on the well-armed Dutch and English ships, thus avoiding the expense of a safe conduct. But a few were still negotiating their ransoms in the early eighteenth century. And some probably never left Malta, but were either baptized or died. For Christendom made its converts from slaves, just as Islam did, though the renegade rarely played a very distinguished role in Christian society.

Of all slaves, the galley-slaves found it most difficult to organize their ransoms. States which ran galley-fleets had a constant preoccupation with trying to keep their rowing benches manned and were extremely reluctant to let a fit young man go. When the slaves were old or sick it was a different matter of course. Now they were just an unnecessary charge on the establishment, and so we find the Order giving their freedom to nineteen useless (*disutili*) slaves in 1679.[14] The only payment that the slaves had to make was their fare and their keep on a tartan which was sailing to Tripoli. A fit man, however, might spend thirty years or more on a galley bench.[15] A particularly harsh case was that of a slave from Damiatta who petitioned for his freedom in 1682. He said that he had been a slave for fifty-four years, fifty of which he had spent as an oarsman in the galleys. On two occasions he had been promised his liberty for special services. The first was at the Battle of the Dardanelles in 1656. Twenty years later he was again promised his liberty for his services in burying infected slaves during the plague of 1676. Neither of these promises had been honoured, however, and 'now the poor supplicant is over eighty years old and desires to finish his life in his

own country'. For which reason he begged that 'he could be
placed in the number of old slaves who are being sent to
liberty as a result of alms sent from Barbary'.[16] The experience
of this slave was no doubt exceptional, and there are numerous
examples of young men being ransomed from the galley
benches. But, in nearly all cases, it was necessary to purchase a
substitute. Thus, in 1681, Fra Francesco Ralli promised to provide two slaves for the galley *San Luigi* to be exchanged for a
slave already serving. The man released from the oar was to be
exchanged in turn with Fra Francesco's nephew, a slave in
Tripoli.[17] Even if the Order did not demand a substitute they
always required full payment, however moving a plaintiff's
story. In 1682 a baptized Moslem woman offered all she had –
200 piastres gathered together after selling all her possessions and
borrowing – to purchase Ali, a one-eared galley slave, whose
exchange she had arranged with her daughter, Nicola, a slave
in Tunis. Ali was released, but the officials of the Treasury
decreed that they would retain the woman's salary until she had
paid the normal ransom price of 300 piastres. And if she died?
There was always the salary of her son, Antonio, a sailor on the
Grand Master's personal galley! [18]

Malta, like Barbary, had professional ransom agents. We
have already quoted the safe-conduct of a Greek sea-captain
who wished 'to deal both in Islam and Christendom in the
ransom of slaves, Christians as well as Moslems'.[19] There were
many like him, such as Joseph Cohen, Jew of Algiers, who got
leave to go to Tunis and Algiers 'taking with him some Turkish
slaves whom he has bought from our Holy Religion, and who
must bring back in exchange for them as many Christians, our
vassals, who are slaves in those parts'.[20] Another was Francesco
Mainero, a merchant of Chios, who declared his desire to enter
into the business of ransoming slaves belonging to the Order,
and to private individuals, and who was given a safe-conduct
to carry Moslem goods on his ship for this purpose.[21]

Like Barbary again, the Maltese authorities often allowed
slaves to return home to fix up their own ransoms. In 1633 a
sixty-year-old Turk from Cairo was given a safe-conduct to go to
Alexandria to collect the ransoms of his wife and children and
other Moslems who were slaves in Malta, and to return within a
year with merchandise and money on any Christian ship.[22] The

will of a freed slave, drawn up in 1666, shows this process at a later stage.[23] Ali, son of Ahmed, of Alexandria first of all declared his debts. He owed small amounts of money to five other slaves and 120 pieces of eight to the Signora Anna for the ransom of one of her slaves. To his former master Aloisio Violardi he owed 17¾ pieces of eight, the balance of 738½ piastres that Violardi had lent him to pay the freight on goods that he had brought from Alexandria. He also owed Violardi 300 pieces of eight for his own ransom and small sums for quarantine expenses and the cost of his safe-conduct. Finally he owed the Maltese customs some money for import duty on his goods. His assets included flax, cloth, turbans, carpets, and musk – the remainder of the goods that he had brought from Alexandria to sell in order to pay his own and other Moslems' ransoms. In his will he instructed his former master to pay his debts, and to use any balance for the ransom of other slaves.

Normally there were two stages in the freeing of a slave. First he was given a conditional freedom which then became absolute when his ransom had been paid. The notarial records of Malta have hundreds of declarations of such conditional freedom for slaves who promise to pay their ransom, or the balance owing, within a certain period, or within such and such a time after their arrival at a stated Moslem port. A good example concerns thirty-one slaves who were given their freedom in March 1662, on condition that they paid 22,000 pieces of eight to the officials of the Common Treasury within the space of three years. It was agreed that two of the slaves could go to Cairo to collect ransoms on behalf of the whole group, while the rest stayed in Malta until payment had been made. But if these two did not return, then the ransom of the remainder was to rise by a further 3,000 pieces of eight. The only exception to this clause was if the two agents should die a natural death, or if their ship should sink. No other form of violent death would prevent the ransom of the rest being increased. Furthermore it was stipulated that the ransom covered the whole group. If all should die but one, he would still be obliged to pay the whole of the 22,000 pieces of eight if he wished to receive his absolute freedom.[24] Leaving a hostage behind was quite a normal practice but sometimes slaves were allowed to leave Malta to fix up their ransoms with only the flimsiest of securities. As in the similar case of Christian slaves making such declarations in Barbary, one is amazed at the few cases of outright refusal to pay. One or two refusals of this kind can be found in the records at Tunis. In 1689, for instance, Lazzaro dell'Arbori, a Maltese merchant and ship-owner, whose family were prominent in the ransom and exchange of slaves throughout the second half of the seventeenth century, had brought three Moslem slaves to Tunis after paying their ransoms in Malta. But on arrival the slaves fled without repaying their debt, and one had since died. Dell'Arbori appealed to the Bey of Tunis, and this worthy, himself extremely interested in the smooth running of the ransom business, paid over fifty pieces of eight as some small token of regret at the bad faith of his co-religionaries. [25]

Although ransom could often be a long drawn out and tire-some affair for both owner and slave, it was often a very profit-able business for the former. In the seventeenth century the average price paid for the ransom of a Moslem slave was about three times the price that could be expected from his sale as a galley slave. With the decline in demand for galley slaves in the following century the differential became even greater. [26] Such an average naturally conceals a very wide range of actual ransoms paid. As in Barbary it was necessary to take into con-sideration the supposed wealth of the slave, the desire of his family to have him (or her) back at home, and his qualifica-tions, before fixing a price. In Malta the highest prices were normally paid for ships' captains and merchants. But perhaps the highest prices of all would be paid for the renegade captain of a Barbary corsair ship. The ransom of renegades, however, posed problems. If brought back to Malta they were supposed to be delivered up immediately to the Maltese Inquisitor, so the only chance for the Maltese corsair was to ransom them (ille-gally) in their place of capture. [27] Naturally, if this could be arranged the renegade would pay handsomely since he was quite likely to be purchasing his life as well as his liberty. But any Barbary corsair who was captured could expect to pay a very big ransom. In 1674, for instance, an enormous ransom was paid on behalf of Mehmet Rais, the corsair son of the Dey of Algiers. The sum, equal to more than 300 times the normal ransom price, was paid almost entirely in grain, and it is probable that it was only the shortage of bread in Malta at that time which allowed such a useful bargaining piece to be ransomed at all.[28]

The life of the Moslem or Jewish slave in Malta must have been very similar to that of Christian slaves in Barbary. In both places the authorities had a major preoccupation with security. Unless they had special permission from the Treasury, all slaves over the age of fifteen, whether belonging to the Order or to private individuals, were locked up at night in vast slave prisons.[29] The two biggest were in Valletta and Vittoriosa, and a third was built in Senglea in 1629. Provision was also made for the confinement of slaves whose work kept them in the countryside or in the inland city of Mdina. During the day all slaves had to wear an iron ring on their leg as a distinguishing mark,* and were never allowed outside the gates of Valletta or the Three Cities without an escort. To prevent escape by water an armed guard-boat was constantly on duty in the harbours, and no more than thirty slaves could be kept on each galley when it was in port. Despite these and other precautions there were a number of successful escapes by slaves who managed to get hold of a boat and flee the island. In 1737, for instance, a Provençal renegade managed to give his guards the slip, and forced a boatman and his son from the village of Zabbar to take him to Tripoli.[30]

Inside the prisons the slaves of the Order were issued with food and clothing. A constant preoccupation of the Treasury was that these issues were being made to slaves who were not entitled to them. New orders were issued in 1647 to try to keep down the costs of running the slave prisons.[31] First of all slaves that were no longer fit to work must be sold. For the rest clothes were only to be given in return for work done, and bread was to be issued only to those who were employed in the various workshops of the Order, on public works and fortifications, and to the ill and convalescent. All other slaves were to be fed and clothed by their employers, and the great army of slaves who were busy building Malta's splendid baroque village churches were to be fed by the parishes.

* Other such marks included close-cropped hair and a prohibition on the wearing of Christian clothes.

We do not have any descriptions of life as a slave in Malta by anyone who actually suffered captivity there, and Christian visitors were remarkably reticent about the whole institution of slavery in Malta. Even D'Arvieux, one of the best-informed writers on the seventeenth-century Mediterranean, has little to say on the Maltese *bagno*, though he did visit it. His main interest was to report the amazement of the slaves at his command of oriental languages![32] However, it seems that the slaves were quite well treated in the prisons. They had their own mosques and priests, and their own judges to try disputes. Adequate provision was made for the care of the sick by the Order in its nursing rather than fighting role. Stalls could be set up, and freedom of movement within the prisons was considerable. Punishments for any transgression of the rules were, of course, very severe, normally a public beating in Valletta. On the other hand, arbitrary ill-treatment was unusual, but was sometimes applied as a reprisal against similar ill-treatment to Christian slaves in Barbary.[33] It was in this way that the treatment of slaves in both territories was kept very much the same.

Slaves in Malta had provision to earn money as did their fellows in Barbary. Certain jobs on board galleys, such as stroke oarsman, carried the right to a small salary,[34] but more profitable was the running of a small business in Malta itself. Though such occupations were never on the scale of businesses run by Christian slaves in Barbary, they played an important part in the life of a slave. Stalls, taverns, and barber-shops were the commonest businesses run by slaves. Occasionally a petition to the Treasury throws a little more light on these occupations. In 1680 some galley slaves, who had rented shops belonging to the Order in Vittoriosa and Senglea, declared that, because the last voyage of the galleys had been longer than usual, they had not made sufficient profit to pay their rent.[35] In 1740 an Ethiopian slave complained that, since he was in the prison in Vittoriosa, he was unable to make a success of his trade as barber, and asked to be transferred to the prison in Valletta.[36] Such requests were often granted, but from time to time it is clear that the authorities felt that the businesses run by slaves were getting out of hand. New rules then had to be established or old ones were re-affirmed. No slaves were allowed to rent shops belonging to private individuals. No stall was to be opened except in the main square in Valletta. One means of making money which the authorities were always trying to prevent was the custom of the warders of the prisons to let out slaves to work for private individuals, when they were not being employed by the Order. The warder and the slave shared the slave's wages, but the Order got nothing!

Malta was markedly different from Barbary in its treatment of baptized slaves and free Moslems. There was no honoured place for the renegade in Maltese society. Baptized slaves continued to row in the galleys and, when in Malta, had to sleep in the slave prisons, as indeed did free Moslems. Permission to sleep outside was slightly easier for these two categories than for Moslem slaves, but was by no means common. Even if a baptized slave should manage to free himself, his life was still restricted, and it was very rare that he should receive permission to leave the island. Restrictions also surrounded the life of the Moslem slave during the period of conditional freedom normally granted during the collection of a ransom. Although allowed to enter into contracts – essential if he was ever to raise his ransom – all such contractual obligations had to be approved by his former master. Despite the fact that they were technically free, the former slaves were still employed on the galleys, and, as we have seen, had to sleep in the slave prisons.

The first half of the eighteenth century saw a considerable relaxation in attitudes towards slaves in Malta. Many of the old regulations were allowed to lapse, and much greater freedom of movement was given to slaves. All this changed, however, in 1749 when a talkative slave gave away details of a widespread plot, in which the Grand Master and most of the Knights were to be murdered, the slaves freed and armed, and the forts guarding Valletta seized until the arrival of the Turkish navy.[37] This so-called Rebellion of the Slaves was followed by a considerable tightening of discipline. The ringleaders were executed in various unpleasant ways, and a much stricter control was kept on the rest of the slaves, and indeed on the whole Moslem and Levantine population in Malta.[38] No slaves were to leave the prison unless chained in pairs, and the chains were to be kept on during work if the nature of the work permitted it. No slaves were allowed to keep shops or stalls except under the walls of the slave prison itself. In addition to these new regulations all the old ones were re-affirmed. How long the tight control of slaves was continued is unknown, but it is probable that time once again worked towards a relaxation of the rules. But over twenty years later, Patrick Brydone noted that the slaves were more strictly watched and had less liberty than before the revolt.[39]

From the point of view of the corsairs the life of the slaves was of little interest. What mattered to them was the fact that they knew they could dispose of their slaves and other prizes in the island. As a correspondent of the Chambre de Commerce at Marseilles wrote in the late 1720s: 'The great advantage of Malta is that the Maltese have an outlet for slaves.'[40] An advantage indeed! Only Leghorn in the Christian Mediterranean had a prize and slave market that could rival Malta.

CHAPTER 9

The Corsairs

Most people will no doubt have in their mind some stereotype of the sort of person who would choose to earn his living by attacking defenceless shipping, robbing the owners of their goods and ships, and selling the passengers and crews into slavery. Epithets such as ruthless, cruel, debauched or sadistic are commonplace in the descriptions of pirates or corsairs in popular novels. Clearly such epithets must have fitted some of the men engaged in the Maltese *corso*. A French consul in Cyprus, for instance, described two French corsairs as 'those bandits, who have made of their ships floating dens of debauchery and trickery'.[1] But it seems unlikely that all corsairs were blackguards. Here one has to remember the enormous strides that attitudes to various activities have taken in the past two hundred years. We are often prepared to blind ourselves to the things we do in the name of our strange ideologies of the twentieth century, and yet to condemn our forefathers for what they did in the name of theirs. The point is that in the seventeenth and eighteenth centuries institutions such as slavery, privateering, and the worship of God were institutions that existed, and as such were accepted, with little thought of change, by the vast majority of people.

The corsair was a gambler, and he presumably had more taste for adventure than the majority of his contemporaries, but these are not necessarily attributes to be condemned. In his own world he was no outlaw. In fact, if anything, he was to

be envied and admired, for there were few other activities in
which the poor man could feel that he had a chance of becoming
rich so quickly. Winning at cards, a good marriage, flattery of
the great, commerce and industry – other means of getting
rich – all needed capital, embodied either in education, good
looks or money, things not easily acquired by the poor.

What sort of people were they then who served in the Maltese
corso? Where did they come from? What was their background?
How did they behave? Such questions are, of course, extremely
difficult to answer. It is one of the tragedies of history that we
know so little about the poor, and what we do know is handed
down to us from the comfortable moral position of the rich.
Nevertheless, a few insights into the origins and character of the
Maltese corsairs can be gained. By far the best source is the
evidence supplied by the cross-examination of sailors that
formed a large part of the numerous lawsuits. Such questions
as 'how old are you?', 'how long have you been in the corsair
business?', 'what is your trade?', 'do you frequent gambling
dens, brothels or taverns?', 'have you ever been in prison?',
or 'when did you last go to confession?' formed a common part
of interrogation. The answers, even when they adopt the
defence mechanism, so common in modern questionnaires, of
'I don't know' are quite illuminating.

As far as the geographical origins of the officers and crews
are concerned, we do not have enough evidence to give a
detailed breakdown. Only one completed crew list has been
found[2] but scattered evidence elsewhere enables some conclu-
sions on the subject to be made. The best information is on the
captains. There were three main sources for these. In the seventeenth century the main source tended to be the Knights and
Sergeants of the Order of St John themselves. And of the
Knights it was the representatives of the three French Tongues
who were predominant. But as the century progressed, and in
the eighteenth century, most corsair captains were Maltese or
French laymen. Very few knights were corsair captains in the
eighteenth century, maybe reflecting the fact that fewer knights
made a career in Malta as the significance of the Order declined.
Apart from the French and Maltese, captains of other nations
were occasionally licensed by the Grand Master. Prominent
amongst these were the Corsicans, a people whose function, like

the Swiss, appears throughout history to have been to provide men to fight for other lands.

The previous experience of corsair captains was very varied. One very common training-ground for the *corso* was the navy of the Order, and a considerable number of captains, especially in the seventeenth century, had previously been galley commanders or had held other positions in the galleys and ships of the Order. But there were other training grounds. The navies and corsair ships of other princes could provide the same sort of education as those of Malta. A career in merchant ships would teach the future corsair his way round the Mediterranean even if it should give him little experience of fighting. Nor, indeed, was it essential for the corsair to be a seaman at all. Since all corsair ships carried pilots and ships' officers experienced in the ways of the sea, and since much of the actual fighting might well be hand to hand action on board an enemy ship, the dash and bravery of a soldier could well be as effective as that of a sailor.

Just as navies could train men for the *corso*, so could the reverse be true. Indeed, it was the fact that it provided an ever active school for seamen that was one of the justifications of the *corso* in the eyes of contemporaries. As the Grand Master wrote to King Louis XIV, 'the corsair vessels of the Religion . . . provide the subjects of the Crown with experience at sea, and indeed captains and sailors of fame and valour have always graduated from this school to the service of France.'[3] This was certainly true, and a long line of distinguished French seventeenth-century sailors spent some of their youth as Maltese corsairs. One such was the man known to history as Le Chevalier Paul.[4] Born in 1597, the illegitimate son of a washerwoman and the Governor of the Chateau d'If, he ran away to sea as a boy. After killing his corporal in a duel in Malta, he was made to embark on a corsair brigantine. Paul distinguished himself so well that when his captain was killed in action he was put in his place. Henceforth, he never looked back. His exploits attracted the attention of the Grand Master who made him a Sergeant of Arms and gave him command of one of the Order's ships. Richelieu, with the permission of the Grand Master, made him captain of a French ship-of-war. Nearly always successful, he was still in command of the Toulon fleet when he died of gout at the age of seventy!

The knightly corsairs of the seventeenth century had a different approach to the job of the *corso* than their secular successors of the following century. Although all were at least partly motivated by the desire to make good prizes, there was certainly a far greater desire for glory and adventure amongst the Knights of the earlier period. They often attacked ships greatly superior in strength to their own, and engaged in other such heroics.[5] By the eighteenth century the corsair was interested in profit with the minimum of risk. The change in attitude was reflected in a very high survival rate for eighteenth-century corsairs. In the two volumes of applications for a licence to sail as a corsair which cover the years 1704–34 there is only one case where it can be clearly seen that a captain had to be replaced because he had been killed in action, though many were wounded.[6]

Such talent for keeping out of trouble meant that many corsairs in the eighteenth century had very long careers, sometimes lasting for thirty or forty years. Such corsairs naturally became very well known in Malta and formed a small community within the merchant and seafaring class of the island. Some were successful enough to form a dynasty of corsairs. Such were the family of Preziosi. The first member of the family arrived in Malta in the early years of the eighteenth century. From then until near the eclipse of the *corso* there was nearly always a Preziosi at sea as a corsair. But the family did not limit their activities to the *corso*. They intermarried with another corsair family, the Camilleri. They invested their profits in commerce, in the ransom business and in property. They were indeed a shining example of the fact that privateering was just another kind of business.

It would be difficult to analyse systematically the origins of anyone on board apart from the captains. There was a tendency for officers to be of the same nationality as their captains, but this was by no means a firm rule. Pilots were very often Greeks, familiar with the operating area of the corsairs. The crews were a heterogeneous collection drawn from all over the Mediterranean, but certainly the largest single element was the Maltese themselves. These were drawn not only from the ports but also from the agricultural communities. Other main groups, by reason of propinquity rather than anything else, were Frenchmen, Sicilians, Italians, and Greeks. An interesting example of the wheel of chance that operated in the Mediterranean at this time were the number of sailors described as Russians. These arrived in Malta almost certainly as the result of slaving activity by peoples such as the Crim Tartars to the north of the Black Sea. The Tartars would then have sold the Russians to the Turks, and some of these would have ended up on the galleys of the Turkish navy. On such occasions as the galleys of the Order or a Christian corsair vessel managed to capture a Turkish ship, these galley-slaves would be released. This happened, for instance, in 1661 when seven galleys of the Order captured four Turkish galleys in a battle near the island of Milo. Of the 251 galley-slaves released, 128 were Russian, 37 Muscovite, 25 Hungarian, and 10 Polish.[7] Free, but at a loose end in Malta, what more natural than to enlist on a Maltese corsair ship? Whether they ever got back to Russia is, of course, another matter. One European group that is hardly ever found on Maltese ships are the sailors from the Protestant countries of northern Europe. In fact only one English sailor has been found at all, Thomas Robinson of London, and he deserted after three months.[8] Whether the Protestants were frightened of the Inquisition or felt they would be more profitably employed on the ships of their own countries is not clear, but one major factor involved is that the shipping of Protestant Europe rarely called at Malta. Leghorn in Tuscany was to the English and Dutch what Malta was to the French, and it seems likely that, if English or Dutch sailors were to enlist on any Catholic corsair ship, they would enlist on those that operated from Leghorn.

The previous trades of crew members clearly indicate that it was not necessary to have a maritime background to engage on a Maltese ship. Though more corsairs gave their trade as sailor or corsair (*corsale*) than any other, a great variety of trades is represented. The collective trades of a single ship were considerable, but except for such as carpenters, coopers, caulkers, sailmakers, and cooks, most of these landsmen would have engaged as soldiers and so would not be practising their trades while on board. There were few slaves employed on board

Maltese corsair ships, and in fact the great majority of the crew signed on as volunteers with an understanding that they could leave the service of the ship either when the ship had been cleared of debt, or when they had made three cruises. Captains were often reluctant to release their officers and crew outside Malta, and there are several court cases referring to the captain forcing men to stay on the ship by one means or another. Whether empressment was common is difficult to say, though captains were certainly prepared to go to considerable lengths to enlist key men such as in the case of the unfortunate Stafraci in 1661.[9] His wife gave evidence that two brothers, Fra Francesco and Fra Ernesto de Noylant, followed her husband around for a month, 'praying him and persuading him and tempting him with offers to sign on as their pilot'. Stafraci had always refused to join the corsairs saying that the business was too dangerous, and that he could in other ways, and with less risk, get what he needed to live. The brothers said on their word as knights that they would give him 100 scudi on signing on and would give 500 piastres to his wife in the event of his being made a slave, if only he would serve them. Stafraci was tempted, and either his wife was a liar or a knight's word was not as good as one might think, since Stafraci had been enslaved and his wife was suing for the 500 piastres which should have been sufficient for his ransom. However, even if Stafraci did not like it, there were clearly plenty of people in Malta who felt that the *corso* was a worthwhile activity. Although some of the crew only did one voyage, many remained in the *corso* as a life-long occupation, slowly working their way up from a position as a common soldier or seaman to much more profitable occupations such as boatswain, captain of prize crew or head gunner.

What sort of people were these sailors? After a survey of what evidence there is, one comes to the conclusion that they were much like other sailors. They fought, drank, swore, stole, deserted, and went to brothels and confession. Some did more of some things and some of another. Perhaps because of the nature of their trade they were slightly tougher and more reckless than other sailors, but there is little evidence to prove it. One does not get the impression in Malta that there were gangs of corsairs whooping it up in the streets of Valletta as the buccaneers were supposed to do in Port Royal. Rather one gets the impression of behaviour similar to what one might expect in any other large seaport. At one end of a scale of self-confession is a soldier who informed the court, 'I have no trade nor profession, and when I have money I gamble and go to bars, and sometimes to whores'.[10] At the other was the temperate or hypocritical witness who said 'every now and then I drink in a tavern, but I never gamble or go to brothels'.[11] In other words the corsairs were much like other people.

Discipline on board Maltese corsair ships seems to have been incredibly weak. There appears to have been no formal structure of punishment on board ship to match the lashes of an eighteenth-century British boatswain. One is struck immediately by the attitude of equality before the law assumed by all men on board ship. Suits against superiors, especially the captain, were commonplace, and a captain must have been well aware that he might have to answer for his actions against any of his subordinates at some later date before the courts of Malta. The captain and the officers appear to have drunk and played cards regularly with the lowliest members of the crew. Such informality would have been unheard of on a British naval ship, and probably even on a British merchant ship. There appear to have been only two ways in which the captain could at once maintain order and the respect of the crew. The most successful way was to be lucky and to take plenty of prizes. Otherwise the captain had to rely on his personality and his sheer physical strength. An item in the indictment of Captain Aloisio Gamarra is illuminating on the score of discipline: 'that having an argument with some of the sailors, one of them hit Captain Aloisio in the face with a club, but he was not a man who cared to avenge himself . . . '[12] In other words the indictment was one of his honour and not of his ability to enforce discipline on board ship. Indeed the Captain makes no reference to discipline in his defence saying only that 'in the whole time that he had been a corsair, he had always treated his crew well, giving them food and drink according to need . . . and treating them equally or according to their rank . . .' and on the score of his honour that he was 'a man of good behaviour and reputation, and brave, and as such he was and had always been held by those who knew him . . .'[13]

Where discipline was enforced the results could be disastrous.

The crew of the ship commanded by Captain Martin in the early 1670s decided that they had had enough of the severe discipline he imposed. They waited till the fellucca had left to collect wood and water, and then attacked the men who were faithful to the captain. They knifed fourteen and threw them in the sea half-alive. They then went for Captain Martin, who tried to defend himself with the arms in his cabin. Unfortunately the mutineers had taken the precaution of unloading them. The captain then burst out of his cabin, flung himself through his attackers, and, despite receiving three sword cuts, managed to get down to the bottom of the hold, where he thought he could defend himself until the fellucca returned. The rebels promised him his life if he surrendered. Believing them, he climbed on deck, and was immediately cut to pieces with hatchets and thrown into the sea. The mutineers then set sail for Saida and gave their ship to the local Pasha. The leaders turned Moslem, those who had been on their side were declared free, and those who had supported the captain were enslaved.[14]

The nature of the corsair's job naturally conditioned his behaviour to a considerable extent. As we have seen, months might go by without his having to fight at all, and then suddenly one morning he might find himself involved in a battle in which the penalty of failure was death or slavery. Even so apparently commonplace a chore as collecting wood from a deserted shore might quite easily end in a fight for his life, should he be attacked by such people as the inhabitants of the Peloponnese, many of them brigands happy to sell their captives to Moslem or Christian alike. To maintain the pitch of fitness and fighting ability needed to cope with this sort of emergency must have been extremely difficult, especially in view of the weak discipline on board most corsair ships. Indeed almost certainly the major problem on board any corsair ship was the need to combat boredom. Month after month of cruising round the eastern Mediterranean with the occasional seizure of a small prize must soon have palled as an exciting way of life.

Given the likelihood of boredom on board ship and the willingness to take risks implicit in the decision to become a corsair, it is hardly surprising that gambling appears to have been the major occupation of the Maltese corsair. Whether at cards or dice, gambling is a constant theme in almost any court-case which involves much description of life aboard ship. From the captain to the cabin-boy there seem to have been few corsairs who could resist the temptation to add to their earnings from the *corso* some trifle won on the turn of a card in the card schools that would almost certainly develop in some part of the ship. A court-case which gives interesting information on gambling at sea is briefly outlined below.

The case concerns Paolo del Zante, who was engaged as *algozino*, or warden of slaves, on a corsair ship fitted out in 1660.[15] When the ship was ready to sail he had brought on board a quantity of tobacco in leaf, a keg of brandy, and a large number of packs of playing cards. Most of these stores he placed in his cabin and almost immediately after they sailed, he began a card school. As Lorenzo Zanin, a Venetian soldier, put it, Zante, his mate Publio Pullicino, and the Quartermaster 'during the whole voyage did nothing else . . . but sell tobacco and brandy, and with cards earn a great quantity of money'. Del Zante and his two colleagues not only sold the cards to potential players, but also took a commission from the winners. There was a limit, of course, to the time that the game could go on, as more and more of the revolving gaming fund of the crew ended up in Del Zante's pockets. As Salvo Borg of Siggiewi in Malta said, 'the game of cards . . . lasted about two months continuously, but afterwards the crew began to lack money and did not play every day, but only every now and then. . . .' There were two different ways of renewing the stock of cash on board, and both these were employed to keep the game going. If the ship met another corsair vessel, the crew was inevitably attracted to what had by now become the most renowned card school in the Levant, and as long as they lost this would of course add to the revolving fund. Probably a more profitable way was to plunder the prizes that the ship itself, during short lulls in the card game, was able to make. Much of the case turned in fact on the origins of a certain quantity of goats' hair cloth, copper, and carpets which Del Zante had bought from the lieutenant and other members of the crew. His accusers were convinced that these had been broken out of bales of prize goods in the hold, though none of the witnesses would admit that this was true.

A witness in another case gives a list of the games that they played on board, 'zechinetta, cartella, quaranta, primiera, tre sette, scoperta, maniglia, and paria'.[16] Most of these are well-known Italian card games and one of the most popular was the vicious *zechinetta*, a game banned by Italian law. Introduced into the Mediterranean by the hated Lanzichenecchi, Charles V's German mercenaries, it is a very simple game. The banker states the sum that he is prepared to gamble, and either one or a number of other players agree to play for that sum. The banker then deals out two cards, one for himself and one for his opponents. He then continues to deal, one to himself, one to his opponents. The first player to receive a card of the same value as the first card dealt wins. A remarkably simple game – and one that was obviously very attractive to the Maltese corsair as a means of disposing of his booty.

There is not very much evidence of other shipboard vices in the records at Malta. Most ships carried considerable quantities of alcohol, mainly brandy and wine, but there does not appear to have been very much drunkenness on board. Generally men of the Mediterranean appear to be more temperate than their brethren in the north of Europe, and probably drink was less of a problem in Maltese ships than it was in contemporary English ships. Apart from the kind of informal bar run by a crew member, as described in the case of del Zante above, the crew would bring drink on board in their own equipment.

Neither is there at Malta much evidence of the wholesale rape of slaves that makes such salacious subject-matter in most stories about corsairs. The Inquisitor Fabrizio Serbelloni reports in his memoirs the violence of the corsairs who 'without thought of their honour allow deflorations, rapes, and adulteries to be committed with scandalous publicity'.[17] He may be right but there is little evidence to support him, and by law 'the corsair or his crew who failed to respect the honour of these defenceless women [captured slaves] forfeited all rights of property over them and the outraged slave became a free woman'.[18] Women, or the absence of them, do not in fact seem to have been a serious problem. There were brothels in Malta and there were others in the Greek islands. The traveller, Dumont, reported that the population of Argentiera, one of the main corsair hide-outs in the Aegean, was composed of seven or eight priests and about five hundred women who 'live purely on the

work of Nature; so that all merchants and corsairs, who come
to the island, choose a Female companion, according to each
Man's particular fancy'.[19] On board, however, women other
than slaves were forbidden by a special order of the Maltese
Council of State in 1679.[20] The fact that this order was made at
this time, and that the prohibition was not included in the
original rules for the *corso*, may be an indication of the infiltration of camp-followers on board corsair ships. But the only
reference to women on ships at all, apart from a bare note of
the capture of female slaves, concerns two captains. Both were
accused amongst other things of keeping slave-girls in their
cabins 'to the great scandal of the crew'. A witness in one of
these cases said that 'the difference between the Captain and
the Chaplain was born because the Captain took a female slave
into his cabin with scandal, and the Chaplain took her out again,
and the Captain did not want her taken away'.[21] But the
woman troubles of most of the crew probably did not begin
till they returned to Malta. As Alonso de Contreras writes 'we
returned to Malta with contentment, and I squandered the
little that I had won. For the wenches of that land are so fair
and so wily that they are mistresses of all that belongs to both
gentlemen and soldiers'.[22]

If the corsair should have trouble with his conscience there
was often an opportunity for him to confess his sins. For nearly
all large corsair ships carried a chaplain. The chaplain often
doubled as medical officer and was normally paid a salary as
well as having a share in the prizes taken.[23] Sometimes there
could be a clash between spiritual and temporal authority on
board, as on the ship captained by Carlo Guevarra where
matters got to such a pitch that the captain threatened to strike
his chaplain and threw some of his belongings into the sea.[24]
But more often there was a sensible working arrangement.
The best example of the use of the spiritual arm to forward
temporal aims comes from a conversation quoted as evidence
in 1713. 'Captain,' said the chaplain, 'this evening I will make a
special devotion to the Holy Souls in Purgatory, and will
continue for seven days.' The Captain replied: 'Father, if we
make a prize within this period of seven days, I promise you a
coat of whatever cloth you wish, provided that it is of a black

cloth suitable to your station.' On the fifth day the captain took two prizes![25]

The problem of the alleviation of boredom, referred to above, was not the only one on board ship. An unsuccessful voyage and a bad captain could turn what was potentially a pleasant enough cruise into an extremely unpleasant experience. The first problem that an unlucky corsair was likely to incur was to run out of food. The provisions listed in the armament of the *Santissimo Crocefisso e Sant'Anna* in 1706 sound quite plentiful:[26] biscuit, cheese, wine, vinegar, oil, olives, salt herrings, sardines and cod, beans, lentils and peas, pasta, salted meat, dried fruit and nuts, eggs as well as live chickens, and sheep. But this could soon run out when shared amongst one or two hundred men, if no prizes had been taken. This could lead to a similar condition to that which occurred on the ship of Captain Guevarra.[27] This ship had been sailing for four years, and had made very few prizes so that eventually, as a French witness describes: 'We suffered hunger, thirst and cold, and were in extreme necessity. We had eighty people sick without provisions or medicine, and we did not have more than two sacks of biscuit left.' Captain Guevarra was nearly forced to abandon the ship and his crew, but was saved by a timely loan It was this sort of situation that could bring out the worst in the corsairs. When men were starving the rules of the game were forgotten and anybody was likely to be attacked by the hungry crew.

The corsair was not only quite likely to find himself starving but he also, of course, shared the common lot of sailors in having to face the normal risks of navigation. Louis Des Hayes describes well the problems of sailing in Greek waters. 'As for the sea, this navigation is very dangerous, especially in the Archipelago, where there are nearly 300 islands, which in some places are so near the one to another, that it is necessary to be very right to pass them; for if whilst one is in the middle of these islands, some gale gets up, the ships . . . are forced to go up close to the rocks, and when night takes them, which removes the sight of these islands and rocks, and the means of avoiding them, it is a miracle when they save themselves from them.'[28] We have already seen how bad the weather could be in winter, but in summer too the Mediterranean is liable to sudden storms. The normal reaction of shipping to a storm was, of course, to try to get to a safe harbour. As the storm got worse less and less sail would be carried until eventually the ship would be racing along with bare masts. The next stage would be to start jettisoning gear and cargo. One of the first things to go were normally a number of the guns, these tending to make most ships rather top heavy. Finally, if none of these measures had enabled the ship to get to safety, and the gale was continuing to threaten the ship, there was no other recourse but prayer. The Frenchman, Du Loir, gives a vivid description of a seventeenth-century storm at sea when he was travelling with a Venetian ship off the coast of Anatolia. When finally the captain gave up all hope he sat with his face covered by his hands, and when the storm had abated, and the ship was within easy reach of the harbour of Lemnos, a member of the crew had forcibly to remove his hands to convince him that they were saved. At the height of the storm a number of passengers and crew crowded round a priest to make their confessions. Whenever anyone accused himself of a sin, 'the others did not give him time to finish, but cried in a louder voice, "Me too, Father; me too, Father", each avowing himself guilty of all faults in the fear of forgetting one of them'.[29]

To the dangers of starvation and shipwreck should be added the wheel of fortune that turned in the Mediterranean during this period. A possible outcome of any voyage was to end up a slave of the Moslems. Many an eminent corsair finished his career chained to an oar in a galley commanded by his rivals, or in the *bagnos* of Algiers or Tripoli. And the fate of a captured corsair was normally much worse than that of a civilian.

A strange life, then, that of the corsair. Months of uneventful cruising, of card playing, and the capture of insignificant prizes might be interrupted with little warning by a sudden storm, a lucky card at *zecchinetta* or a battle – the outcome of which could be death, slavery, or sudden riches. No wonder that the motto of Captain di Natale's purser inscribed on the title page of his log-book[30] was '*Fortuna fammi fà felice fine*'.* In five words this motto summarizes both the motivation and the career of the corsair.

* Roughly: 'Fortune make me have a happy end.'

PART FOUR

Five Corsairs

Introduction

In this part of the book we will move from the general to the particular, and describe the activities of five rather different corsairs. Three were Christian, one a Moslem, and the story of the fifth describes the process by which he became a renegade. Our knowledge of each is based on different types of source material, a fact which enables an extremely broad picture of the realities of life amongst the corsairs to be built up from these case studies.

The first corsair, Alonso de Contreras, belongs to the heroic age of the Holy War in the early seventeenth century. A picaresque and braggadocio Spanish soldier of fortune, our knowledge of him depends entirely on his autobiography. Naturally this is likely to exaggerate his prowess, but nevertheless his description of his activities agrees remarkably well with what one can learn about the corsairs of this period from other sources.

Most of what we know of the second corsair, Aloisio Gamarra, comes from a lawsuit of 1661 in which he was sued by his employers. By this date the Maltese *corso* was at its peak as a business organization, and the lawsuit illustrates well the problems likely to arise in the relationship between investors in Malta and corsair at sea, as well as providing interesting details about life at sea.

The story of the Gaoler-Captain, the subject of the third study, is a unique description of life amongst the corsairs as seen by a Moslem. The story was originally written by a Moslem slave in the form of a letter to his master. It describes a mutiny led by the French gaoler of a corsair ship in the 1670s, his subsequent apostasy and capture of three Maltese corsair ships. Although it has, as yet, been impossible to check the facts of the story, it seems very likely that this letter was based on a true sequence of events. Despite the extremely fast movement of the narrative, there is nothing in it which is impossible within the circumstances of the story, and the detail provides an extremely convincing record of life at sea in the second half of the seventeenth century.

The fourth corsair provides a strong contrast to the adventures of the Gaoler-Captain. Francesco di Natale was active in Malta during the years 1739–46, a period when the *corso* was rapidly declining in significance. Most of what we know of his activities comes from two log-books kept by his purser. These tell us what can be discovered from no other source – the day to day routine of a corsair at sea. Whether the log-book of a voyage undertaken a century before would present such an uneventful picture as that of Captain Natale is difficult to say. One gets the impression from other sources that the seventeenth century was a more adventurous period for the corsairs. But there are no log-books which describe seventeenth-century corsair voyages, and the sources we have to use for this earlier period are biased towards the dramatic. Captain Natale fought only two real battles in four years which hardly fits the popular image of the corsair. But as has been explained before, although many hotheads were attracted to the *corso*, it was a business, and there was no sense in risking one's investment unnecessarily.

This part ends with a description of the successful life of the last great corsair to sail from Algiers. The career of Rais Hamidou was built up by his biographer, Albert Devoulx, from the prize registers which have survived in Algiers. To this bald statement of his successes it has been possible to add a little more description from the accounts of some of his Christian contemporaries.

Where lengthy quotations have been made from the original documents, an attempt has been made to capture some of the spirit of the original rather than to translate into good modern English.

CHAPTER 10

Alonso de Contreras

Alonso de Contreras[1] was a Spanish soldier-of-fortune who served in Malta in various capacities during the first two decades of the seventeenth century. All that we know of him comes from his autobiography which was written some time between 1630 and 1650. Much of his story reads like a 'romance of roguery', but there is documentary evidence of Alonso's real existence, and indeed one of Lope de Vega's plays is dedicated to this colourful adventurer.

He was born in Madrid in 1582, one of seventeen children of poor parents. While still a boy he stabbed one of his schoolfellows who later died, and soon after this incident he left home and went to the wars. On his very first day as a soldier he lost all his money, his new shirt, and his new shoes gambling. The pattern of his adult life was already taking shape. Working in camp kitchens, he followed the Spanish army to Italy, Burgundy, and Flanders where he deserted and made his way in the company of his corporal to Sicily. In Palermo he was engaged as page to Captain Felipe de Menargas and sailed with the galleys of Naples and Sicily to the Morea where he came under fire for the first time. On his return to Sicily he heard that the galleys of the Religion were in port and sailed with them to Malta. His first stay in Malta was made in the service of the Grand Master's Receiver of Rents and lasted a year. Then back in Sicily again he went on several expeditions with Sicilian galleots and galleons against the Turks and

Barbary corsairs. During this period he gained precious experience of fighting and seamanship for his future career. In his own words he 'went mad on navigation, and was always instructing myself in the company of the pilots, watching them make charts, and getting to know about the lands which we passed, with their ports and capes'. This period of his career was brought to an end by a series of bar-room brawls in Palermo and Naples. The murder of an innkeeper by one of his colleagues caused a hue and cry to be set up for Alonso and his friends. Alonso was fortunate enough to find a Knight of St John in Naples who hid him until the galleon which he was fitting out was ready to sail. But two of Alonso's colleagues were less fortunate – they were caught by the authorities and hanged.

It is now that Alonso's career as a Maltese corsair begins. After a few days in Malta he sailed for the Levant with his rescuer's galleon and a frigate.

The following is Alonso's own account.

'We spent more than two months without making a prize. But one day, as we were about to put into Port at Cape Silidonia we found inside a fine-looking caramusal, which was like a galleon. We attacked it and the Turks flung themselves in the boat to save their freedom. The captain ordered us to go after them, offering ten *scudi* for each slave. There was a big pine-wood there, and I was one of the soldiers who jumped ashore in pursuit of the Turks. I carried my sword and my shield, but of beard not a hair. I lay in ambush in the pine-wood and ran up against a Turk like a Philistine with a pike in his hand, from which was flying a flag of orange and white, who was calling to his comrades. I went up to him and said to him "Down on the ground". The Turk looked at me and laughed, saying *"bremaneur casaca cacomiz"*, (which means bumboy, your arse stinks like a dead dog). I was furious and gripping my shield went straight for him. Dodging the point of his pike I gave him a stab in the chest that sent him to the ground. I took the flag from the pike and girt it round me.

'I was stripping him when two French soldiers came up saying, "Shares". I got up from over the Turk and gripping my shield told them to leave him alone, that he was mine, and that if they did not I would kill them. They thought it was a joke and we began to give it to each other in good style, when four other soldiers came up with three Turks that they had taken and made peace between us. On which we all went together to the galleon without despoiling the wounded men of anything.

'We told the captain everything, who, having questioned the Turk, said that I alone was the owner of all. The Frenchmen nearly mutinied because I was the only Spaniard in all that galleon, and there were more than a hundred Frenchmen. There was so much trouble that the captain had to send the case to Malta, before the lords of the *Tribunale degli Armamenti*. The Turk had more than 400 golden sequins. The caramusal was laden with soap from Cyprus. We put some men on board and sent her to Malta.

'We remained to seek more prizes and we headed for the *crocieri* of Alexandria. Towards nightfall we saw a ship which seemed to be very big, which indeed it was. We followed in her wake so as not to lose her and at midnight we caught up with her, and with the guns run out we hailed her: "What ship?" She replied: "A sea-going ship". As she had also made ready, she thought nothing of a single ship since she had more than 400 Turks on board and was well equipped with artillery. She fired a volley at us that took seventeen men into the other world, not counting the wounded. We fired one back which was as good as hers. They boarded us, and there was a stiff fight, for they managed to gain our forecastle, and it was tough work forcing them back on to their own ship. Thus we stayed all that night until day. But as day broke we went for her and she did not run away. However, our captain made use of a stratagem which stood us in good stead, for he left on deck no more men than necessary, and closed down all the hatches so that we had to fight or jump in the sea. The battle was hard; we carried their forecastle and held it for a long time till they threw us out. Then we drew apart and fought it out with the guns for we were better sailors and had more guns. And here I saw two miracles that day which are worth telling.

'A Dutch gunner was loading a gun without protection, and they shot at him with another, and hit him right in the middle of his head, blowing it to smithereens and showering those around with his brains. And a bone from his head struck a sailor on his nose, which had been crooked from birth; but this

cured him and his nose remained as straight as mine, with only
a scar from the wound. There was another soldier in such pain
that he would let no one sleep in his mess, with his blaspheming
and cursing; but that day he was shot at by a cannon, and the
ball shaved his two buttocks. And never again during the whole
voyage did he complain of his pains. He used to say that he had
never sweated better than in the draught from a cannon-ball.

'We continued our fight that day on the high seas, and, as
night came, the enemy tried to reach land which was close to.
We followed and at daybreak we all found ourselves becalmed
quite near the land. It was the day of Our Lady of the Concep-
tion. The captain ordered that all the wounded should come on
deck to die, for he said: "Gentlemen, either we dine with Christ
or at Constantinople." Up they all came, and I amongst them,
for I had a thigh pierced by a musket shot and a great wound on
the head which I had got from a halberd the day before as I
was boarding the enemy's ship, when we captured their forecastle. We had on board a monk, a Calced Carmelite, as chaplain, and the captain said to him: "Father give us a blessing,
for this is our last day." The good monk did so, and that done
the Captain ordered the frigate to tow us up to the other ship
which was very close.

'We drew alongside, and so great was the battle between us
that however much we might have wished to get away from
them, it was impossible; for they had thrown over us from the
other ship a big anchor with a great chain lest we cast loose. It
lasted more than three hours, and at the end of that time it was
recognized that victory was ours. For the Turks, seeing that
they were near the land, began throwing themselves into the
sea, not noticing that our frigate was going round fishing them
out. Our victory was complete, so after securing the slaves, we
gave ourselves over to sacking the ship; and the booty was rich
and great. There were so many dead that there were more than
250 below, whom they had not wished to throw into the sea
lest we might see them. We threw them overboard. And that
day I saw something which shows what it is to be a Christian.
For among the numbers of dead whom we threw into the sea,
there was one who remained face upwards, unlike the Moors
and Turks, who when you throw their corpses into the sea,
at once turn face and body downwards, but the Christians turn

upwards. We asked the Turks whom we had taken prisoner how it was that this man remained face uppermost, and they said that they had always suspected him of a being a Christian, and that he was a baptized renegade, and at the time when he renounced his Faith he was a man of French nationality.

'We repaired our ship and the prize – and they both needed it – and we set our course for Malta, where we arrived shortly after. And since the prize was so rich, the captain ordered that no one should gamble, so that every man should come rich to Malta. He gave orders to throw dice and cards into the sea, and laid a heavy penalty on anyone who should play. And so they arranged a game, in the following manner; they made a circle on a table as big as the palm of one's hand, and in the middle of it, another circle as small as a piece of eight, and into this little circle each player put a louse. Each man kept his eye on his own, and they laid very heavy wagers on them. The first louse to leave the big circle took all the stakes, and I vow they ran as high as eighty sequins. When the captain saw how determined we were, he allowed any man to play who would. So great is the vice of gambling in the soldier!

'At Malta I bought a lawsuit about my slave whom I captured on land at Cape Silidonia. And when I had done what was necessary in every quarter, the Lords of the Tribunal gave judgement that the 400 sequins should be counted as part of the prize-money, and that a bounty of a hundred ducats should be given me for the prisoner and the flag, with the privilege of bearing it on my arms as a trophy if I wished; which I did with much content, and bestowed the flag upon the church of Our Lady of Grace. What with my prize-money and the bounty, there fell to my share more than 1500 ducats, which I squandered in a short time.'

His money having run out, Alonso was soon off again, this time with the galleys of the Order, with whom he sailed for two short expeditions. He soon returned to Malta where he 'squandered the trifle that he had won. For the wenches of that land are so fair and so wily that they are mistresses of all that belong to both gentlemen and soldiers.' In fact Alonso retained the same wench during most of his stay in Malta who relieved him of the lion's share of his prizes every time he returned to the island, and who was soon beginning to invest her gains in real estate.

For most of the rest of his lengthy stay in Malta, Alonso de Contreras was in command of frigates commissioned by the Grand Master to gain information about the movements of Turkish and Barbary shipping. This was a very common type of commission and the corsairs who were entrusted with this task were usually able to combine fighting and prize-taking with their spying activities. Alonso's voyages took him all round the Levant and the Barbary coast. Although he is too successful to be entirely credible, his numerous adventures give a good idea of the life of the corsair, as well as of the movements of Turkish and Barbary shipping which he had to report. Whatever the situation Alonso always wins. Prizes are taken, powerful ships are tricked by Alonso's stratagems, potential disaster is averted by his dash and bravery, hidden slaves or booty are soon discovered.

The events following the capture of a small dismasted brigantine manned by Greeks provide an illustration of his ruthlessness and his coarse irony. Alonso, certain that there were Turks hidden aboard, asked where they were, but the Greeks denied their existence. Alonso, however, had noticed Turkish eating utensils on board, and so 'began to put them to the torture, and not in play either. They all stood it except a boy of fifteen, whom I had stripped and bound and set upon a low stone. "Tell me the truth", I said. "If not, I will cut off your head with this knife". When he saw that I meant it, the father of the boy came and threw himself at my feet, and said to me, 'Ah, captain, do not kill my son, for I will tell you where the Turks are." And this very man had befouled himself under the torment. See what the love of children can do!' Alonso's ruthlessness paid off well, since the hidden Turk turned out to be a wealthy gentleman who provided a good ransom.

Sometimes Alonso can be extremely eloquent, as in his description of the island of Estampalia (Astypalea, some 100 miles west of Rhodes). 'It was a feast-day; and so soon as they knew that it was I, they took counsel together, and at once there came out almost all the people, with Captain George (for that was the Governor's name) calling upon me as "*O morfo pulicato*", which means, "Young Gallant". There came many mar-

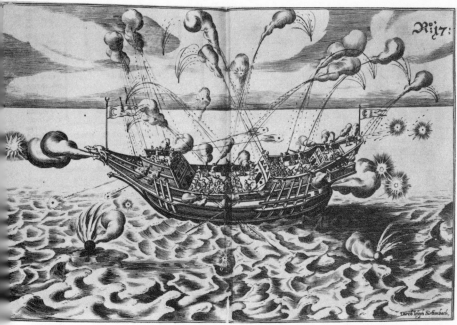

'A fine-looking caramusal, which was like a galleon.' The caramusal
was one of the commonest Turkish ships employed in the Levant.

ried women and maidens, in bodices with skirts falling to the
knees, and coloured jackets, having the upper half of the sleeve
almost tight to the arm, but flowing out in a rounded cuff
half across the body. They wore coloured stockings and shoes,
and some of them had pattens open at the toe. Some wear them
of velvet the same colour as their dress; those who can of silk,
and those who cannot of scarlet. Their beads, which among us
are worn round the throat, are here round the brow; and whoso
can wears ear-rings and bracelets of gold on their wrists. Among
them were many of the gossips, whose children I had held at the
font.'

However, leisurely description soon turns to action.

'They all came sad and weeping, and begging me with much
clamour to be their judge; for a frigate of the Christians had
carried off by guile their *papaz* – that is their priest – and had
asked for him 2000 sequins. I asked where he was, and when he

had been captured. They said that very morning, and they had not heard mass, and the hour was then two in the afternoon.'

Finding out where the corsairs had gone Captain Alonso set sail and when he found the frigate ordered her captain to come on board. It turned out that he was carrying a forged commission from the Viceroy of Sicily. He ordered the crew to be put in irons but they began to protest, 'saying that it was not their fault; that Giacomo Panaro – for that was their captain's name – had deceived them saying that he had a commission from the Viceroy; and they would go to the end of the world to serve me, but that they would not go an inch for the other'. Alonso relented, but he 'set the captain on shore on the island, naked and with no provisions, so that he should pay for his sin there by dying of hunger'. Back in Estampalia Captain Alonso was made much of by the Greeks and was kissed on the cheek, first by the men and then by the women, 'and sure it is that there were some right comely women, whose kisses grieved me not at all, for they were some antidote to all those given me by so many bearded men – and great beards they had, too'.

Indeed the Greeks were so impressed by Alonso that the priest begged him to stay in the island and marry the Governor's daughter, 'a virgin both lovely and well attired'. Such a powerful protector would clearly be a great asset to an isolated Greek island and the priest said that he could get Alonso a commission from the Turks. But Alonso said that this was not possible; he had to return to Malta, and 'besides which, it would bring reproach on my name; for it would be said that I had not remained behind to marry in a Christian land and with a Christian, but in Turkey, denying the Faith which I hold so high'. The Greeks were insistent and said that he must stay and closed the gates. Alonso sent a messenger to the frigates who 'related what had happened, at which they all marvelled. But if they loved me up yonder, how much more did my men!' The crews of the frigates threatened to force the gates and sack the town if their captain was not released. This persuaded the Greeks to let Alonso go, but as he took his leave 'there was weeping and gnashing of teeth as if it had been the Last Day'.

On his next visit to the island Alonso discovered that after he had left, the Greeks had gone with a boat to the island where he had left the pirate captain 'and had brought him back and

Early seventeenth-century galleon. The words galleon, vessel, and nef were virtually synonymous in describing large fighting or trading ships in the Mediterranean.

feasted him till a French tartan arrived, coming from Alexandria, and they handed him over to be taken to a Christian land having given him good refreshment and ten sequins for his journey'. Captain Alonso makes no comment on this display of Christian forgiveness.

In his travels Alonso does not always meet Greeks who are so nice as those on Estampalia. One place he visits is the Arm of Mayna, a peninsula in the Peloponnese. Here lived Greek Christians whom many seventeenth-century travellers described as bandits and robbers. Alonso remarks that the Turks have never been able to subdue them, although they live in the heart of the Turkish lands. The purpose of this visit to the peninsula was to sell a caramusal full of grain to his friend Antonaque, the Captain of Porto delle Quaglie (Port of the Quails). Antonaque came on board and after much bargaining a price of 800 sequins was agreed on. He then went ashore, promising to return with the money the next day. During the night, however, the cable of the caramusal was cut and the boat was taken away and unloaded. Alonso's revenge was typical. Tricking Antonaque into coming on board he weighed anchor and once out of the harbour ordered him to strip. 'He stripped to the skin, and they stretched him out, held down by four strong lads, and they gave him more than a hundred strokes with a tarred rope's end. Next I had him washed with vinegar and salt, as the custom is in the galleys, and said, "Send for the 800 sequins or I shall surely hang you". In less than an hour the money was brought by a swimmer in the skin of a kid.'

On his last voyage to the Levant as a Maltese corsair Alonso had an adventure which is thoroughly in character. Meeting a Greek boat from Chios, he heard that Soliman of Catania, Bey of Chios, had gone off in his galley, and had left his wife behind in Chios. Hearing this, Alonso's pilot exclaims, 'I swear to God, we must carry her off to Malta! For I know her house as well as if it were my own; and since Soliman went off last night in the galley, they will be off their guard.' Alonso hesitates as he has not many men but eventually agrees. 'And indeed it was even easier than he had told me. We waited for night; and on the stroke of midnight we landed with ten men. The pilot went up to the house as if it were his own, and knocked, speaking of Soliman like one new come from Chios. They opened to him. We went in and captured without resistance the renegade Turkish woman, who was Hungarian by race, and the loveliest I ever saw. We took two boys and a renegade and two Christian slaves, one a Corsican by birth and the other an Albanian. We took the bed and furnishings, with nobody to say us nay. We went on board and sailed off with the utmost speed, until we got outside the Archipelago, for God sent us good weather. The Hungarian was no wife, but a mistress. I gave her the highest marks of honour, for she was worthy of them; though I found out that Soliman of Catania had sworn in my absence that he was going to look for me; and if he took me, he would have me outraged by six negroes – for he thought I had lain with his mistress – and then I would have been impaled. He was not lucky enough to take me, though he had my portrait drawn and posted in different parts of the Levant and Barbary, so that if I were taken, these portraits should tell them who I was.'

If Alonso was lucky, his pilot who suggested the whole scheme, was not. Four months later he was captured in the Levant. 'And they flayed him alive, and stuffed his skin with straw, and it is over the gates of Rhodes to this day. He was a Greek, a native of Rhodes, and the most skilful of all the pilots who were in those lands.'

This was nearly the end of Captain Alonso's long stay in Malta. But he was not to leave without having trouble with the wench who had helped him to get rid of his prize money so fast during his career in Malta. One day he found her with someone else. 'And I had been so good to her! I ran him through twice with my sword, so that he lay at death's door. And when he was recovering he left Malta, for fear I might kill him, and the wench fled.'

Captain Alonso's own motive for leaving Malta is in the classic tradition of the hard man with a heart of gold. One day he remembered his old mother to whom he had never written in all these years, and so taking leave of the Grand Master he set sail in a Spanish galleon for Barcelona. The rest of his life continued to be a series of adventures – in Spain, Italy, Flanders, and the West Indies – and he made two more visits to Malta. On the second of these visits, which must have been in about 1626, Captain Alonso was on his way to Pantellaria. He had been appointed Governor of the small island which served as a staging post for corsairs operating in Barbary waters. He held the job for sixteen months during which time he repaired the church. At the end of this period he got the permission of his employer, the Viceroy of Sicily, to go to Rome. And here we find Alonso managing to obtain an audience with the Pope. 'I gave him an account of my services, and said that the treasure of the Church was for men like me, who had had their fill of serving in defence of the Catholic Faith.' Persuaded by Alonso's plea, the Pope issued him a brief in which the Order of Malta was commanded to admit him to the rank of Knight of Justice, and Alonso returned once more to Malta to present his briefs. 'They were instantly obeyed, and they armed me as Knight with all the necessary ceremonies, and gave me a Bull which I

esteem more highly than if I had been born of the Infante Carlos.'

Here Captain Alonso's connection with Malta ends and we will leave him. He represents to a considerable extent the corsair of fiction, the bold buccaneer. As such he makes a strong comparison with the corsair considered in the next chapter, Aloisio Gamarra, who was indicted by his employers for cowardice.

CHAPTER 11

Aloisio Gamarra

Captain Gamarra is the only one of the three 'Maltese' corsairs considered in this part who was in fact Maltese. Practically all that we know of him comes from a lawsuit of 1661 which is the subject of this chapter.[1] From his own evidence we are told that he had served for several years on merchantmen, and had gained sufficient experience to be engaged as pilot on the flagship of the Order's navy.[2] His first appointment on a corsair ship was as lieutenant and pilot on the vessel of a successful privateering Knight, Fra Ector Giannettines.[3] In 1659 he got an independent command when he was licensed as captain of an 11-bench brigantine for a summer cruise in Barbary.[4] This was a successful expedition and in the next year he was licensed as captain of a tartan for the waters of Barbary and Levant.[5] It is this last voyage which is the subject of the lawsuit.

The tartan had a crew of about seventy soldiers and sailors, and was financed by a syndicate of seven merchants from Valletta. It is clear that most of these merchants were representatives of Maltese 'big business'. Nearly all of them were leading underwriters in the island's thriving marine insurance business. One of them, Placido Lo Duca, was an important slave merchant. Another, Marcel Reverst, a merchant born in Marseilles, had trading interests throughout the Mediterranean.[6] Investment in the *corso* was thus only a part of their financial interests, but it could be imagined that they would be hard bargainers who would expect to see a handsome return on any investment that they should make. Their total investment in Captain Gamarra's tartan was 13,000 *scudi*, and a contract was made with the captain and crew that the expedition should be *alla fratesca*. This was a realistic type of contract that gave the crew specific permission to retain anything that they plundered from the personnel of captured ships or anything found on the decks. All other booty, however, was to be shared in common between investors and crew, after all expenses had been paid off. This contract, which was submitted as evidence in the lawsuit, was signed by all the officers of the tartan.[7] Captain Gamarra's cruise started in August 1660. He first sailed to Barbary, then to the Levant where he wintered. After cruises in the Levant and Barbary he returned to Malta in the summer of 1661. On his return he was sued by his employers.

The main reason for the indictment of Captain Gamarra was his employers' disappointment at the poor results of his voyage. They were not prepared to attribute this to bad luck, and in the case that they brought against the captain they did all they could to blacken his character and to demonstrate his incompetence as a corsair. Their objective was to get the court to order the captain to repay the whole cost of the expedition. Their indictment reads: [8]

'Since, after having sailed for many months with the said tartan in Barbary and Levant, the said Captain, by reason of his bad behaviour and negligence and his divers notorious and fraudulent defects, has never made a prize worth any consideration; on the contrary, on several occasions being presented with the chance of making good prizes, the said Captain through terror and bad orders has lost them; whence he had to return to port to the grave damage of the interests of the above shareholders and investors. Therefore, they make humble instance that the said Captain Aloisio Gamarra be constrained and condemned to pay and restore to the said plaintiffs all that sum of money spent by them in the service of the said *armamento** not only in the pay distributed to the crew, but also in the provisioning of the ship's company and in the fitting out of the tartan and every other expense that

---

* *Armamento* means the total investment in a voyage, i.e. rather more than a synonym for ship.

must be made, together with all damages and interest suffered
or to be suffered in said *armamento*.'

In support of their statement that the captain missed
chances of making prizes they submitted that 'the same Captain
Aloisio sailing with the flower of Maltese youth, valorous
soldiers and sailors, met many times with enemy ships, and
contrary to the will of the officers and crew gave orders not to
board with various excuses, not having courage . . .' . They also
said that the captain spent far too much time in the ports of the
Levant at times 'when he could have been sailing to look for
prizes'. While in port 'he never lost a chance of attracting
foreigners in conversation, of going aboard other vessels continuously to play cards, eat and drink, abandoning the *armamento* of the said tartan and his crew, consuming the company's
provisions in said conversations and feasts'. While he remained
on board these other ships 'he kept the crew of his skiff alongside these vessels for days and nights at a time in the cold, making them suffer through hunger, while he was playing cards and
drinking'.[9]

The plaintiffs brought very little further evidence to support
their case. Most of what they did bring was hearsay resulting
from the visit of a group of officials to the ship while it was lying
in quarantine. Four witnesses, none of them sailors, said that
during this visit a majority of the crew had told them that they
did not wish to sail for another voyage with Captain Gamarra.
The evidence of Antonio Cutaiar of Valletta was the most
specific. He said that the captain was not respected by any of
the soldiers or sailors, that he was timid, and that since the
crew saw that he was not experienced in the corsair business
they did not obey him. When Gamarra was captain things did
not go as they should. He deported himself like a coward and
always liked to stay in the ports.[10]

For his defence against these accusations the captain relied
mainly on the evidence of his crew. He stated only 'that in the
whole time that he was cruising with the said tartan, he stayed
with the ship and tried as far as possible to remain in the *crucieri**
and other good places for making prizes, without having ever
entered port unless to careen or to water, for bad weather and

* Areas where various trade routes cross, i.e. areas good for prizes.

for other similar reasons, as do all the other corsairs ... That
in the whole time that he had been a corsair, he had always
treated his crew well, giving them food and drink according to
need ... and treating them equally or according to rank ...
That he had always shown himself desirous of making prizes,
with the determined intention of boarding any ship, even more
powerful than his own, as in fact he did on some occasions, as
witnesses will shortly say ... That the defendant with his ship
has made certain prizes as witnesses will say ...'. [11]

Fifteen members of the crew and the purser were called to
give evidence. Not one of them spoke against the captain. All
were prepared to say on oath that they considered him to be a
brave man of good reputation, and that if they had to sail for a
second voyage, they wanted no other captain. Referring to the
evidence of the group of officials who visited the ship while in
quarantine, they said that only three or four of the crew, who
had a grudge against the captain and wished him ill, had said
he was a bad captain and that they no longer wished to sail
with him. Others had said that they did not want to go on a
second voyage, but this was because they felt that they had
already fulfilled their obligations and not because they did not
respect Captain Gamarra. [12]

Many were prepared to support their bald statement of the
captain's bravery by quoting an incident that had occurred on
the voyage. Sailing in *conserva* with Captain Re in the waters of
Barbary, Captain Gamarra had sighted a well-armed pink
which was much more powerful than his tartan. He had lent
fifty of his men to Captain Re, and then with a skeleton crew
of twenty had run past the pink to draw her fire and force her to
unload her guns. Captain Re had then been able to close and
board before the pink could reload. Ironically the whole exercise was a wasted effort since the pink was Dutch and thus not a
good prize. [13]

All the sailors stated that the captain was conscientious in his
search for prizes, and did not hang about in the ports as his
accusers stated. Whether he had ever made a prize 'worth any
consideration', however, is a matter of judgement. Witnesses
listed his prizes, and for a year's voyage they can hardly be
called impressive. [14] On his own he took a *carobo*, with four slaves,
and two pollaccas, which were sent to Malta. In *conserva* with

Captain Lahe he forced a galleot to run aground in Cyprus. The cargo of timber and carpets was brought to Malta, but the crew had fled, and no slaves were taken. Also with Lahe he forced a *petacchio* to run aground near Alexandria. Five slaves were taken off this, two women being Gamarra's share. In *conserva* with Captain Re he took a *saicotta* laden with rice which was sold in Scanderoon (Alexandretta) for 800 pieces of eight, three Negroes captured ashore, and a *sambecchino* laden with rice which was bartered on the spot for ship's biscuit. Since Captain Gamarra's ship was the weaker in each of these two *conserve* his share was much less than half, and the proceeds of the voyage could have done little to repay the 13,000 *scudi* invested by the merchants in the ship, let alone provide any profit. This, of course, was what really worried the merchants and much of the case hangs on two factors.

First, did the captain do all that he could to refloat the *petacchio* run aground in the Levant? This was the most valuable prize taken in the whole voyage.* The plaintiffs said that 'being able to get the said *petacchio* afloat he had not wanted to do so, to the grave prejudice of their interests'.[15] However, it seems very unlikely that the captain was, in fact, at fault. The purser stated that several days were spent trying to refloat the ship. But the ship had gone aground under full sail and was well up on the land. The sea was rough which made the exercise very difficult and, furthermore, Captain Lahe, who had the more powerful ship, refused to help.[16]

The second major factor in the case relates to the sacking of prize-goods by members of the crew. The plaintiffs stated that after the capture of the two pollaccas in the waters of Barbary, Captain Aloisio 'by his negligence and bad government let his crew sack things from the hold of these prizes, and in particular some bales of barracans† (more than five of them) . . .'. Later in the voyage when the *petacchio* was run aground, 'the crew of

---

* Some idea of the relative value of these different kinds of ship can be had from the only surviving prize register of the *Tribunale degli Armamenti* which records the sales of prizes in the years 1660/2.[17]

Galleon	– 5,550 *scudi*	Galleot (plus cargo) – 550 *scudi*
Pink	– 4,800	Pollaque	– 450; 226
Pettachio	– 2,152	Carabo	– 306; 210
Saique	– 1,500; 1,000; 856		

† A North African cloth, normally made of goat's hair.

the tartan jumped on board the *petacchio* from which they took divers sums of money and goods . . . The said Captain Aloisio, not caring at all, had not made (as he should) a visit to the vessel, nor had he searched the crew.'[18]

In reply to these points the captain said, 'that having captured the two Turkish pollaccas . . . , the soldiers and sailors of the tartan had only sacked those goods that were on the decks of the said pollaccas, as is the custom observed amongst corsairs on similar occasions: he, the defendant, had locked and sealed the hatch to the hold, and had taken the greatest possible care to save the cargo from being ransacked by the crew . . .'. Also 'in the capture and ransack made by the crew on the *petacchio*, he had gone on board and made the usual search of the crew'.[19]

The evidence of the sailors regarding the ransacking of prizes was an aspect of the case that dragged on for a long time. They all supported the captain's evidence relative to the sacking of barracans from the two pollaccas. One witness was more specific and said that 'the crew ransacked only the deck where there was nothing except an open bale of barracans which the Turks had cut open to throw into the sea'.[20] But barracans were of little value, and it was the plundering of the *petacchio* run aground in the Levant that really interested the plaintiffs. It is clear from the purser's evidence that the crew made a good haul.[21] Three of the sailors found purses each containing 1,500 *piastre* (equal to about 1,500 *scudi* in all). Another 300 or 400 *scudi* in loose cash was also found, as well as silks, velvet, cloth of gold and brocade, and gold and silver bullion. The total value of this haul from the decks was almost certainly higher than the value of the ship itself and the five slaves captured, so it can be understood how keen the plaintiffs were to have this booty included in the general account to be shared between investors and crew, rather than that it should be kept by the finders alone.* Whether Captain Gamarra searched the crew as he should have done is not clear from the evidence. In his own defence he stated 'that he had gone on board and made the usual search of the crew', but Francesco Morello, normally a

* Actually not by the finders *alone*, since most sailors on corsair ships worked in syndicates and shared their finds with two or three comrades. A syndicate would normally have a man in each of the boat crews.

Trading tartan. Captain Gamarra's ship was a larger and better-armed version of this.

favourable witness, said that Gamarra did not make the search since Captain Lahe 'was on the prize with his cutlass drawn and made us go back to our ship without any of us being able to touch anything on the prize, and thus there was no need for a search'.[22] This, however, conflicts directly with the purser's evidence, and, since no one else mentions the incident, it is possible that Morello was thinking of the Turkish galleot which had also been run aground a few days previously. On the whole it seems extremely unlikely that all this was legitimate booty for the crew, and in fact the court later ordered that although the barracans were '*robba tagliata*' and thus could be retained by the plunderers, the velvet and brocade taken off the *pettachio* were not, and should enter into the *communità* or general account of prizes to be shared in common between investors and crew.[23]

One other specific accusation of incompetence relates to the capture of the *carobo* near the beginning of the voyage. The plaintiffs said that one of the four slaves captured, who was the captain of the *carobo*, 'escaped to land by swimming, the said Aloisio Gamarra not having secured him as he should'.[24] The captain's defence to this was that the captain of the *carobo* had promised to help him make a good prize near the island of Gerba in exchange for his liberty. Captain Gamarra had agreed to this, and had kept him unchained in his cabin. However, when they drew near the place suggested by his prisoner, the latter jumped overboard and began to swim for land. Seeing that he had been tricked, Captain Gamarra immediately sent his skiff after him, but 'with all their diligence they were not able to find him'.[25] The crew supported the captain's story and most presumed that the prisoner had drowned.

Captain Gamarra, as we can see, was quite capable of defending himself against the accusers. But perhaps his most telling piece of evidence is his defence of the accusation that his officers deserted him because of his incompetence. The plaintiffs stated that 'the senior officers, i.e. lieutenant, sergeant, pilot and boatswain, seeing the bad government and squandering of the said captain, and realizing that as a result of his incompetence there was no hope of making prizes, deserted, staying in Crete or joining other ships, and the junior officers resigned in disgust'.[26] Gamarra's defence, which was supported in detail by his crew, tears this charge to shreds and underlines the plaintiff's reliance on people with a grudge against the captain to support their case. The captain said that he had 'dismissed his lieutenant, who was once his sergeant, for having abandoned the guard while the ship was aground to be careened. He had fallen asleep, and as a result two men were lost. He had dismissed the sergeant because, as a result of his failings (which witnesses will describe), two men from the tartan were killed. He had dismissed the pilot because of the grave scandal he had caused through the relations that he had with the cabin-boy of the tartan (for which reason he had also dismissed the cabin-boy). He had dismissed the boatswain because when he, the defendant, had inspected the cannon and perrier-guns, he had found them unloaded, and also because he had been negligent in his duties.' [27] The sergeant's failings were that while in command of an expedition to get water 'he had allowed two men to be killed by the Turks, whom he could have saved'.[28]

The plaintiffs' case against Captain Gamarra includes, besides these major accusations of incompetence and cowardice, many smaller charges which are intended to blacken the captain's character and to make him out to be a coward, a gambler, and a libertine. The captain's defence and the supporting evidence of his crew make most of these smaller charges seem rather ridiculous. The implication that the captain would rather play cards in port than hunt for prizes has already been mentioned. Another factor made much of by the plaintiffs was the captain's treatment of the two female slaves, who were Gamarra's share of the slaves captured from the *petacchio*. The charge was that 'having taken from the said *petacchio* two women, one Turkish and one Russian, the captain had kept them all the time in the cabin of the tartan with him, scandalizing the whole crew; he treated them very well, giving them food and drink, and from then on he did not attend to the government of the ship and the crew, unless specifically asked'. [29] The captain replied, 'that there was no other place than in the cabin where the two women could be kept safe from the crew, in order to avoid any inconvenience'. He himself 'remained in sight day and night, without scandal, and that is the truth'. [30] All the witnesses supported the captain and swore that the captain's cabin was the only place on the ship where the two female slaves could be safely held, and that the captain himself always slept on deck. The suggestion of delectable banquets in the plaintiff's statement – 'he treated them very well, giving them food and drink' – is brought down to earth by the evidence of Angelo Grech of Valletta. 'The Captain sent the women a little soup, bread and cheese, and no more.' [31]

The implication of cowardice in another charge that one of the sailors, having had an argument with the captain hit him in the face with a club, but the captain 'was not a man who cared to avenge himself' is also not proven. [32] The evidence relating to this episode shows that the captain was tolerant, but not necessarily dishonourable or a coward. While they were anchored off southern Anatolia the officers and crew bought a barrel of wine. The drunken party that followed ended in a noisy argument, and the captain went below to see what was happening. It was dark and one of the crew hit him, not knowing who it was. When they saw it was the captain 'everyone excused themselves and asked him to pardon them since they

did not know it was him'.[33] Drunkenness seems to have been
quite a problem on board Captain Gamarra's ship since a
steward whom the plaintiffs stated had thrown the crew's water-
butt into the sea 'in disgust and rage' also turned out to be
drunk.[34]

We shall, almost certainly, never know whether the almost
universally favourable evidence given by his sailors and purser
was sufficient to clear Captain Gamarra of the charges brought
against him. For the sentence of the court no longer exists. It
seems probable, however, that the court decided for Gamarra.
It hardly seems likely that the captain would have been able to
bribe sixteen witnesses into giving evidence favourable to him.
If anyone was able to bribe witnesses one would have thought
it would be the seven merchants with their far greater resources.
Some indication that the decision did go for Gamarra is the
fact that in December 1661 the Grand Master ordered that the
shareholders should restore to Captain Gamarra the goods and
money that they had sequestrated when he consigned the prize-
goods to them.[35] In the following month the plaintiffs announced
that all differences between themselves and Captain Gamarra
had now been settled.[36] But implications of cowardice once
made, even if not proven, are likely to stick. The reader may
agree with Captain Gamarra's assessment of himself as 'a man
of good behaviour and reputation, and brave', but the suspicion
remains. There must be something wrong with a captain who
has to dismiss all his senior officers, however good his reasons.
And what is more, Captain Gamarra had committed a cardinal
sin. He had been unlucky. Whether they won the case or not
his employers had obviously lost confidence in him, for they
transferred the command of the tartan to the Cavalier Fra
Constantino,[37] and Aloisio Gamarra never sailed as a corsair
again.

CHAPTER 12

The Gaoler-Captain

The story of 'The Gaoler-Captain and his Fight with the Hell-bound Maltese Corsair Ship' is told in a letter[1] written by a slave and starts with the narrator, the slave, Jussuf, travelling on a French merchantman from Alexandria to Constantinople.

'On the first day we had a favourable wind and made good progress, but towards evening the wind dropped and all around us the sky clouded over; it was still and very dark. A storm was obviously on the way, and everyone on the ship, from captain to passengers, was gripped with fear, each praying to his own God for safety . . . Then in the fourth hour of the night a tremendous storm, coming from the east, swept over us, getting worse all the time. The waves were like mountains, and an unparalleled storm of rain and wind broke out. When our captain saw the waves come straight across and break over the ship he was forced to heave to and parry the waves by movements of his tiller. In this way we went along with cries of "Allah".

'At dawn, the wind, at God's command, veered to the west and became even fiercer. Until the time for the midday prayer a storm raged which surpassed even the earlier one in intensity. Again we hove to and allowed ourselves to be driven before the storm. By the time for the afternoon prayer it had become so frightful, as to be beyond words. From both sides mountainous waves flooded over the ship. At the time for the evening prayer the storm, the lightning and the rivers of rain made it

impossible for the sailors to grip anything, their hands were so
affected by cold, rain, hail, and the rough wind. The hatch
which led into the hold was firmly closed, because the sea had
driven it in. The passengers in the belly of the ship rolled over
one another, groaned, prayed, shrieked and wept, each in his
own way.

'Then God willed that lightning should strike the mainmast;
both it and the yard were shattered to bits. Also one of the
infidel sailors and a Moslem passenger who was in his cabin
were burned and died. Thanks to the grace of the Just One
the hold was not touched, but in the interior of the ship there
arose an indescribable wailing. . . . Soon after a wave rolled over
the flagstaff on to the poop, and took a Moslem passenger and
the ship's notary with it, washing the compass case away as
well. Since the ship had no other compass, the captain went out
of his mind about this loss, for the compass is a ship's eye; it
was like riding a blind horse. . . . They were travelling aim-
lessly, when, about the fourth hour of the night, there was a
flash of lightning, and in this light they saw a distant dark object
before them. The captain said it was land; others took it for
clouds. The darkness was incredible. But, after a while, thanks
to the Just One's grace, a second flash came, and it was clear
that it was land. They wished to approach the coast and anchor;
but because the mainmast was gone, and it was difficult to come
close to the shore with the aid of the foresail alone, they decided
that it was more sensible to go out to sea again, and then in the
morning, when it was light, to steer towards land.

'So they headed out to sea. But the captain did not know that
stormy weather produces many currents in those waters. While
he, in the pitch blackness, believed that the ship was moving
out to sea, they saw in the morning that the ship had been
carried by a current around the cape of an island, and had come
close inshore. So, for good or ill, they dropped two anchors,
and anchored in the fashion known as "oxenhorn". But in this
place they were still at the mercy of the waves which pulled the
ship to and fro, and often swept over the deck. . . . In the clear
light of morning they saw that they were in front of a deserted
island. But what could be done? The storm had not abated for
twenty-four hours, had perhaps got even worse, and the
dismasted ship was shaken from bow to stern by the assaults of

the waves. It was impossible to lower a boat in order to land and fix the cable.

'They stayed there, swept up high and then plunged down again. Evening, and the time for the night prayer came, and the storm got worse again. . . . Then one of the two anchor cables parted. The captain, who knew that the last hope for the ship had gone, lost his head. He went to the opening of the hold and called: "Travellers, don't be idle! Our main cable has gone, we now have just the one. Woe to our position! But be on the alert, perhaps we will be cast up on the shore!"

'When they heard the captain yelling like that, the passengers also lost their heads; each of them thought "Every man for himself". Some got undressed, others wept or howled, and those sorely tried in the ship turned their faces to the throne of the Just One and cried: "O Lord be our protector!" In the fifth hour of the night a great wave came, the ship heaved, the second cable parted and, amid din and uproar, the ship was beached and broken up. With cries of "Allah! Allah!" they made for the shore. Some were drowned, others broke an arm or a leg, others were wounded. Most were naked and wet through. In the cold and pitch blackness their position was so bad that a miserable clamour went up to Heaven.'

Altogether twenty-one of the seventy-three people on board the ship were killed or drowned in the storm and shipwreck, and another ten were hurt. The position of the remainder on the deserted island would have been hopeless had not one of the Christian sailors recognized where they were: 'Near here there is a cave, let us take shelter there,' he cried. Each clinging to the man in front they moved off in the darkness. They found the cave, and inside there was some wood, but nothing to light it with. But amongst the travellers there was a dervish who, feeling about in the darkness with his hands, found a piece of dry wood. He split it in two and rubbed the two pieces together until he got a fire. Then he found some dry earth in a corner of the cave, kneaded it with urine and attended to the wounded with this substance. The bleeding was stopped and the pain eased. Once more God had been bountiful. 'If the infidel and the dervish had not been there they would have had to spend the night out and would certainly have died from lightning, rain, cold, and injuries.'

Later the shipwrecked crew made a great bonfire to attract the attention of passing shipping, and on the fifth day their efforts were rewarded. A galleon was sighted. Although the French merchant captain concealed it, she was assumed, rightly, to be a French corsair. This posed a problem to the Moslems. Either they stayed on the island and starved; or they went on the corsair galleon and were enslaved. In the end everyone went on board the corsair ship, and those who were uninjured were chained up in the hold.

Five or six days later the galleon captured a barque in Cypriot waters. Loaded with hides, vinegar, wool, and cotton she had a crew of seven Greek Christians. The French corsair captain made a deal with the captain of the barque, who in return for his liberty and his cargo, showed the corsair where he could make a great haul of booty by telling him: 'On Cyprus, an hour's journey inland, is my village, and there lives a great Moslem landowner. He has prepared a great celebration on the occasion of his son's circumcision. He has invited fifteen or twenty dignitaries and rich Aghas from town, and they have already promised to be there on the fifteenth of this month.' The corsair captain considered this and they agreed that the barque skipper should land one of his men to act as a spy, and, when the Aghas had arrived, to light two fires on a hill visible from the galleon. . . . The barque skipper's slave thought there were still three or four days to go before the guests arrived. So that evening after sunset the Christians landed and sent out the spy. Then the galleon took the barque in tow, and began to tack to and fro between the coast and the open sea.

But the captain was not the only person making plans. His gaoler had for some time nursed a grievance against the captain and now saw a chance to avenge himself. If the captain and his best fighters went ashore in Cyprus, then he would have a great opportunity to lead a mutiny and seize the ship. He took his Moslem prisoners into his confidence. On the sixth night the captain received the signal and the raiding party left the ship. Altogether he took 140 'soldiers of evil', leaving seventy remaining on the ship under the gaoler's command. Ten of these supported the gaoler.

Jussuf continues: 'After the captain and his evil band had gone, the gaoler found some excuse to go down into the hold and bring the good news to the prisoners. Then he opened a cask and distributed wine to the remainder of the crew. . . . The infidels, having free wine, drank until they were all drunk and lay about on the floor unconscious. When the time came, the gaoler came down and freed the prisoners from their chains. He gave them instructions and urged them on. "The chief gunner, the steersman, the sailmaster, and the chief boatswain are now in the cabin. I myself, with fifteen men, will break in." He picked out fifteen men to follow him and enjoined them thus. "Take care not to wound the four I named. Capture them alive and bind them. Strike down all the rest without giving them time to resist."

'Then he took three brave men and ordered them to see that no one set fire to the ammunition and powder. Ten more he directed to deal with the infidels on the after deck; the rest were to take on the infidels on deck and in the forepart of the ship. He tied bands round the heads of the ten loyal to him, who were on watch, and he ordered them to take care not to attack these men. When they had all received their orders, they crawled up to the arms store and armed themselves with what they found there and in the magazine, sabres, muskets, swords, pikes, etc. Now they were ready. But the gaoler had warned them: "Be careful, don't move before I let you know when." With the cry, "O key of the gates, open the best gate for us", the whole band climbed up. Then when the gaoler with his bold men entered the cabin and everyone else had reached his post, and stood armed and ready, the gaoler gave a great shout: "Get them!", and the fight began.

'The infidels did not have the strength to move from the spots where they lay drunk. Only a few, cursed warriors, were seized by blind zeal and, thinking the galleon had been attacked from outside, some looked for matches in order to fire the cannon, and others shot their lead out to sea. On the ship an indescribable noise and chaos broke out. Twice infidels came with matches in order to set fire to the powder magazine. It would have gone ill if the gaoler had not prepared for this and placed his men at the entrance.

'Meanwhile the gaoler had captured and bound the four

named infidels in the cabin; the rest had been cut down. Then when he had taken the cabin, the gaoler came out and saw that only four of the Moslems were still fighting; the others stood confused. . . . When the gaoler saw that the ship was still not won, he seized a long iron hook . . . and hit the infidels, who were still alive and fighting, so fiercely over the head, yelling the while, "Get them! Get them!", that he filled the others with new zeal. Thus, thank God, they seized the galleon, with His help, after a battle of 1½ hours.'

The gaoler then prepared for the return of the raiding party. He loaded the guns and armed his men with the weapons of the dead Christians. In the morning they heard shots and saw the captain's party running towards the sea. Lookouts had been posted at the circumcision party who had given warning as soon as they saw the corsairs coming. When the captain realized what had happened, he turned back and managed to get to his boats.

'As they pushed off from the land they believed they were safe and steered towards the galleon. They had no idea what was about to hit them. It was something over three miles from the shore to the galleon. As they rowed nearer, the men on the galleon stood ready with matches. The moment the boats came to the right place, with the cry "O Opener!" and with one match-strike they opened up such a tremendous fire that one boat sank at once and another was damaged. But the third boat was still all right and the most experienced fighters were in it, so they darkened their eyes and stormed the galleon from the foredeck. About thirty godless Giaurs forced their way aboard. When the men in the damaged fellucca saw this, a blind enthusiasm seized them and they also wanted to storm the ship. But Kara Weli, the standard-bearer, fired a great gun from the after deck, and another of the Faithful followed this up with a whiff of grapeshot, so that on the fellucca the infidels lay around like logs.

'Meanwhile the gaoler had matched thirty men with guns against the thirty infidels from the boat, and he had them all fire at once so that almost half the attackers were killed or wounded. They fell upon the rest with sabres and after a long

Barque. A very common trading ship in the Mediterranean.

fight they slew them all with God's help. Then they cheered and ran up the flag of Tunis. . . .

'When the Moslem soldiers on the shore saw these events, of which they did not know the cause, they were amazed. The gaoler now had a boat manned and sent ashore to get water, and to explain to the Moslems what was behind this religious war. . . . Then the brothers, Mohammed's people, were full of joy, and in order to show their pleasure and thankfulness, they fired a salvo from their guns.'

The Gaoler-Captain now sailed off to refit at a harbour two or three hours from the fortress of Famagusta. The next day, safe in port, he held a meeting on the after deck. He persuaded the four key members of the original Christian crew to join him. They agreed, and to show his pleasure, 'he had banners, flags and bunting hoisted, and shots of joy fired. Without these there can be no galleon, for they are her spirit, her eye.' He then divided all the booty among his crew of fifty-three Moslems and seventeen Christians.

While they were refitting and buying provisions, an Agha arrived with an invitation from the Pasha of Cyprus. He had heard of the great victory and wished that the galleon should sail to Famagusta, where a great feast would be held to celebrate the triumph over the enemies of the faith and of the Empire. But the Gaoler-Captain was suspicious of this invitation and made excuses, saying that he and his men were too dirty and too poor to appear before such distinguished persons. 'But if the merciful God wills it, and if our Lord will show us the grace and favour of his kindness, we will set sail, and as soon as we have been lucky enough to capture a rich prize, we will return loaded down with treasure and we will cast ourselves down in the dust at his feet.' After these words he gave the Agha a suitable gift, and sent him away with a salute from the guns.

Then he assembled the chief crew members to a council and spoke to them thus: 'O brothers! We must join some lordship or an Odjak.* To go on on our own is hopeless. If we go to Constantinople and fall into the claws of the Ottomans, they, as is well known, will take our galleon and our goods, and make us slaves; so long as our lives lasted we would be in their hands. And if we join the Odjak of Algiers? That is an energetic but also a greedy Odjak; probably our ship would be confiscated, for at the moment there is no ship in the Odjak of Algiers so smart or so racy as ours. (If ours was now decently equipped it could carry fifty guns.) Or shall we join the Odjak of Tripoli? But that is an impoverished Odjak, and not very helpful either. Compared with the others the Odjak of Tunis is rich, and as right at the start we hoisted a flag of Tunis which just happened to be there, it is a good omen. . . . What do you think? What is the most sensible?'

When he had finished, they all spoke as though from one mouth: 'You are our captain, and your opinion is worth more and is better than all ours together. What you think most sensible will be our wish and will.' So they decided for the Odjak of Tunis.

The Pasha of Cyprus was very angry when he heard that his invitation had been refused and he sent his Agha back to arrest

* See p. 26.

the Gaoler-Captain. This the Agha managed to do while the gaoler was ashore with a few of his men, but the gaoler managed to slip a message to the men aboard ship, telling them to leave port and sail around for a few days near Famagusta. On their way they encountered a pink on which they saw some Moslems in white turbans. Realizing that the pink was heading for Famagusta they closed in, fired a shot, hoisted the flag of Tunis and ordered the pink to heave to. The pink lowered its sails and the galleon came alongside.

'Where do you sail from?'

'From Constantinople,' came the answer.

'And the passengers, are they soldiers or merchants?'

'They are the son and the consort and the people of the Pasha of Cyprus; also the son and the consort of the Cadi of Cyprus.'

When the men on the galleon heard this, they cried: 'Our business is now in order,' and were pleased. They captured the pink and took from it the son of the Cadi, and the younger and elder sons of the Pasha, as well as his steward and his minister.

Then they wrote a letter to the Pasha: 'You have taken five of our people and thrown them into prison without cause; so we have taken five of yours and imprisoned them. If you release ours in good shape and send them to us, then we will free yours. If you do not we will leave and take them with us. If you kill ours, we will kill yours.'

They took nothing else from the pink and let it go, with the letter, while they themselves returned to their former harbour. But the Pasha's advisers reckoned that without their captain and the chief crew members the galleon would be disorganized. They knew that the seventeen Christians on board were outnumbered by forty-five Moslems, and hoped that the latter would not fight against their brothers in faith. So they thought they would be able to take the galleon in a night attack with the pink and a three-masted tschember then in Famagusta harbour. From the land 200 men ought to be able to control the neck of the galleon's harbour to prevent the ship leaving. But the Pasha did not know that the galleon was recruiting more men and that there would be about 110 fighting heroes.

Against much advice he carried on with his plans to attack the galleon.

'But aboard the galleon they were not idle. All through the night men took it in turns to keep watch, both on shore and on the ship (both on the fore and after decks), while the matches lay ready in the gun ports. The land watch reported the approach of the troops, so the galleon prepared to leave harbour. It was midnight. There was no wind, so they wanted to man the fellucca and take the galleon in tow. But the men in the fellucca would have been exposed to fire from the shore, so they waited for an off-shore wind. An hour before dawn the watch saw two sails. At this moment they got a little wind and steered towards the harbour entrance. They were nearly there when a volley from the shore troops greeted them. They replied with a match strike which took at least twenty men, some killed, some wounded. The rest scattered among the stones and rocks. Immediately the galleon left the harbour.

'The tschember was rowed and came up first. It intended to fire off a salvo and then run alongside the galleon and board. But its salvo was returned by a broadside from the galleon which hit it on the water line, as did one or two chainshots. The holes were very big and the tschember could not survive this blow. With difficulty it got near the harbour entrance, and there, in shallow water, it sank. Some of the crew were killed, others wounded, and the rest made for land, most of them leaving their guns behind, and fled towards Famagusta.

'The pink had the same plan as the tschember. She too fired a volley. But the galleon's broadside pruned back its masts and yards, leaving just bare stumps. Since it was packed with men, many were slain or wounded. The others, who had never seen such a sea battle, lost their heads, and were like men stunned. But the galleon did not let the pink escape and wanted to set it afire. . . . The men on the pink begged for mercy, and the galleon's Moslems took pity on them. But, if it had not been for the slave Jussuf [the narrator] and the standard-bearer Kara Weli, the others would not have been restrained from setting the whole thing ablaze, in revenge for the damage done to the galleon – the bowsprit shattered, a sailyard damaged, two men killed and some wounded, including the chief boatswain.

'The crew of the pink were forced to drop their weapons and guns, and then allowed to take to the boats, row to shore and make off towards Famagusta. The galleon put a crew aboard the pink, towed it into harbour and again dropped anchor. It turned out that the Pasha's elder son, Ali Bey, was a hero like a royal falcon. He had a black moustache, was keen on wine and music, and for this reason his father did not like him, but only the younger son. So as his father had nothing for him, and he had for a long time been mad about the life of a seaman, he had said on his very first day aboard the galleon: "I don't want to be a Bey or a Pasha. I am a corsair like you." So he changed his clothes and, in the events just narrated, he had done more than anyone.

'When the Pasha heard of the defeat he lost his mind, held his handkerchief in front of his face and, sobbing loudly, began to weep. And all the Aghas wept with him. Those who had advised the attack fled to distant regions for fear that the Pasha would kill them. The gaoler-captain was released and was persuaded by the French Consul not to press charges against the Pasha for his wrongful arrest. Finally he was escorted with great honour to the galleon. The corsairs returned the pink, but not the guns and ammunition which custom allowed them to keep, at any rate until they had captured enough of their own, when they would, they said, return them. Then, firing off salvoes, they sailed to Famagusta, where the Pasha, when he saw how well his younger son had been treated, gave them rich presents, especially ship's gear. When he heard of his elder son's decision to become a corsair he exclaimed: "That's very wise. Piracy is a coat made to measure for drunkards like him!"'

Now at last the Gaoler-Captain was free to go on his cruise. With all the guns and gear taken from the pink, and the extra crew he had recruited ashore he now had an extremely well-armed corsair galleon. Altogether he had forty-two guns and a crew of 250 men. He set sail and was given a three-volley salute from the Pasha. After three or four days they saw a sail in the waters of Damiatta. Through the telescope it could be seen to be a galleon.

'In these waters no galleon sails alone – unless it's a corsair,' said the Gaoler-Captain.

When they came closer he looked through a good telescope and recognized the ship.

'It's a Maltese galleon name so and so [sic]. It has twenty-four cannon and a crew of 110.'

The chief boatswain and the gunner also recognized the ship, and reckoned that, with God's help, they could capture it. So they made for it, and when they were near enough fired a shot and showed their colours.

But, shortly before this, some Algerine ships had met a Dutch galleon in the Straits of Gibraltar, captured it and put a crew aboard to take it to Algiers. This in its turn had been taken by the Maltese, who acquired twelve more cannon, that is, they now had thirty-six, and other weapons. Then they put a crew on the Dutch galleon and sent it to Malta. Later the Maltese galleon had sailed round the islands and picked up more crew, so that they had at present a total of nearly 200.

'They challenged each other, and made their preparations for the fight. Then they opened fire. The Gaoler-Captain urged his men on. "My falcons! Keep at it boldly! If the most high God wishes it and gives us his help we will not come empty-handed to the Odjak." Full of fiery zeal and devotion they began at once. The fight thickened more and more. That day from late morning to the evening at least 300 shots were fired on each side. But neither succeeded in overcoming the other.

'When evening came the wind rose, the waves got higher, the sea came overboard and swept through into the ammunition room. Besides, it was evening, so they postponed battle till the next day and separated. They worked through the night at repairing the damage. But they did not leave those waters.

'When night fell the Gaoler-Captain held a council and spoke: "Brothers! This ship is not what we expected; it is much better equipped, with many cannon and soldiers. The best thing to do is to board it, for it will not be beaten in an exchange of cannon shot. What do you say to that." They all answered: "We are ready; whatever you think is best."

'Before dawn broke the Gaoler-Captain selected eighty heroes and had them stand ready with bare sabres. According to custom he promised the first man to jump into the enemy ship 100 gold pieces and a boy, and 100 gold pieces to the second.

He, himself, took command, and nominated another man to take his place as captain. Then he had the cannon and other guns properly loaded, and everything else that was necessary to make ready for battle was done.

'When morning came the Gaoler-Captain found that he had the wind, and at once took his chance. But the enemy had already realized that the galleon was to come alongside and board, and they had also loaded every gun, and stood ready with matches in their hands. When they were at the right range they both fired broadsides, so that the sea trembled and both ships were hidden in blue smoke.

'The Gaoler-Captain came alongside the galleon's foredeck and when he gave his heroic cry, "Storm them, my brave ones", they went over with cries of "Allah! Allah!" Then God opened the gate of grace to the Gaoler-Captain for he was worthy of the attention of the Guiding One. He raised a finger and spoke the word of a witness.

' "People of Mohammed, brothers!" he shouted, "My name is Mahmud!"

'Then an enthusiasm and a cheering broke out at this news, as though the angels in heaven and the fish in the sea had become our helpers. The fighters for the Faith surged on with zeal for Islam and struck out with their sabres at the damned-to-hell enemies with an indescribable fervour. The hell-inhabiting Giaurs barricaded themselves at the foot of the mast and on the afterdeck, and turned the afterdeck cannon against the Moslem soldiers. The faithful warriors piled up various cases, spars, rigging, buoys, and anything else they found as a barricade on the foredeck before the foremast. They had boarded in the first hour of the day. The fight now lasted until the third hour. Three or four times they attacked the afterdeck, but without success. They could not do it because the enemies of the Faith had too many guns on the deck.

'Then they tried something else. Through a tiny hole which led from the foredeck to the powder-room thirty or forty heroes got into the powder-room. Their leader was the Pasha's son, Ali Bey. They did such good work with their sabres that the infidels there could not hold out, and some fled up on deck, others jumped into the sea in their confusion, and the rest were put to the sword. So, thanks to God, they took the gun-room of the galleon. Then they pulled the cannons backwards out of the gun-ports, took the wedges behind them out, and turned the mouths up towards the deck. The balls bored through the deck and went as far as the poop and into the cabin. But despite so much hard fighting, and despite the fall of the gun-room, the enemy resisted stubbornly. From that one can see how obstinate the enemy was. The Gaoler-Captain was happy, especially when they had got control of the entrance to the powder-room, for he had been worried in case they set light to the ammunition.

'Meanwhile, from the open sea, the galleon saw that the ship had not yet been conquered. Because they could not keep patient any longer they loaded the cannon and other guns, and, from close to, fired such a broadside that the sea shook. With God's help the chain-shot hit the mainmast about a fathom beneath the crow's nest, so that the mast with all its gear, sails, yards, and tackle fell down on the enemy on the afterdeck with a great din. The enemy soldiers were buried under mast, yards, and sails. The Moslem army took its chance, and fell upon the enemy with cries of "Allah! Allah!" and with indescribable sabre blows. The captain barred himself in the little cabin and shouted: "Set fire to the powder room." The Pasha's son, Ali Bey, seized the notary of the galleon and, thinking it was the captain, lifted him angrily up high and then dashed him against the deck so that he was smashed.

'Thanks be to God, with His help, they captured the galleon. Then their own galleon came alongside and the surviving infidels were put in chains. Thirteen Moslem prisoners were freed from the prison. And eleven of them were comrades from Tunis!'

All but twenty-seven of the Maltese crew were killed in the battle, as were forty-two of the Moslems.

The freed Moslems told the victors that thirty days previously two ships bearing presents had left Tunis for Chios. The eleven Tunisians should have sailed with them, but had had permission to visit their relations in the Levant and had shipped on a tschember, which had been captured by the Maltese corsair. The Maltese had taken the tschember to Patmos and had sold it to a Christian there. So the Gaoler-Captain, now Captain Mahmud, sailed to Patmos to recapture the tschember, and to have the two galleons caulked and repaired. This was all successful, and they then sailed to Scalanova where they had a great feast and recruited another 400 men, some of whom were put in the recaptured tschember. They then sailed to Chios, where after three days the two Tunisian present-ships arrived.

The Tunisians were astounded to find two other galleons flying the Tunisian flag, but Captain Mahmud had the fellucca manned and sent it ahead with one of the freed Tunisians, a former corsair captain called Mehmed, to explain everything.

'The four galleons fired so many thunderous salvoes that the whole population of Chios and the outer villages came to the seashore to watch the show. The next day they started a celebration which lasted for three days and nights in a garden, eating, drinking, and pleasures of all kinds. This was the occasion of the circumcision of the Gaoler-Captain. Then they all set sail for Tunis. Near the island "Messina" they sighted two galleons. Were they French, Dutch, English, or Algerine? With the help of a telescope Captains Mehmed and Mahmud established that they were Maltese.

'The Maltese general, when he heard that the Gaoler-Captain had mutinied and had taken over as a corsair, had sent these two galleons out to find him. He had also sent the same orders in writing to the corsair galleon which the corsair had already taken, but the news of this capture had not yet reached the Maltese. The Maltese, therefore, took the four ships to be a four-galleon Dutch convoy which was expected on its way from Smyrna. They knew that none of the Odjaks had four galleons out, and hoped that they would receive news of the Gaoler-Captain from the Dutchmen.

'But Captain Mahmud realized what they would think, and he sent his fellucca to explain the situation to the two Tunisian ships. The Maltese approached, fired a greeting shot and hoisted the Maltese flag. The Tunisians had put their soldiers below decks; only a few, disguised and wearing hats, were to be seen. They hoisted the Dutch flag. And so the two Maltese galleons came closer. One was right big and had forty cannon; the other thirty. The damned had equipped them excellently.

'They noticed bronze cannon on Mahmud's galleon and immediately fired a signal shot and made to turn. But the Moslem ships had the wind. At once they hoisted their own flag, blew the trumpet and with the cry, "Where are you going, cursed one?", the vice-admiral and Mahmud took on the big ship; the flagship and the captured galleon the small one. The first broadside hit the smaller ship's powder-room, and the ship went up in flames. So the larger one also furled its sails, one against four is too much; but the captain grabbed a match and went into the powder-room. "Let me go, or I will set it alight." "They are pig-headed, these infidels," said the Moslem captains and they agreed to give them pardon and freedom, according to the old custom.'

They continued their voyage towards Tunis. It turned out that the captain of the Maltese galleon had long been joined in brotherhood with the Gaoler-Captain. When he saw that the latter had gone over to Islam, he followed suit and took the name of Ahmed. Forty or fifty miles from Tunis the vice-admiral manned a fellucca and sent it ahead to give the joyful news to the Dey so that he could prepare a welcome. When the five galleons arrived, covered over with trimmings and decoration, countless shots of pleasure were fired from the bastions and ships, and with cheer upon cheer, and parade upon parade they were welcomed.

Ali Bey was made captain of the first captured galleon, and Mehmed was made his chief boatswain. Ali Bey was given instructions to follow Mehmed's advice on seafaring matters, for although he was a Pasha's son and a brave hero, he had no idea, as yet, of seamanship. The second captured ship was returned to Captain Ahmed, and Mahmud stood surety for him. These three galleons kept together in friendship and did very well as corsairs. The other odjaks envied Tunis for these fine ships.

But then the Dey of Tunis died, and a new one succeeded who became jealous of Mahmud, though he owed his position to him. He planned to poison him, but Mahmud's friends warned him, and his love for the Odjak cooled a bit. From Algiers he received friendly letters and gifts, and invitations. So secretly he planned to go. He had the three galleons made ready and loaded up with his cash and valuables, bit by bit and secretly. The empty trunks in his room he locked up and left two slaves to guard them, just as he always did. Then on the pretence of a corsair trip he left, with half the naval strength of Tunis. The three galleons each had forty to forty-five cannon and about 250 picked fighting men. When out to sea they put all their Tunisian colours in a fellucca and sent it back with a few men aboard. When the people of Tunis learned what had happened they began to weep and mourn. But the Dey of Algiers gave them a tremendous welcome. After a few days he appointed Mahmud admiral in charge of his whole fleet. And thus the gaoler of a French corsair ship became the Admiral of Algiers.

'May God, the glorious, blessed and sublime, ever make the people of Mohammed victorious and triumphant through his goodness, favour and grace; and may he destroy and crush his evil enemies. Amen.'

CHAPTER 13

Francesco di Natale

Captain Giovan Francesco di Natale was a Corsican, and from 1739 to 1746 he operated as a Maltese corsair in command of a ship called *The Blessed Virgin of the Rosary*. Little is known about his career prior to this period, but in 1738 he was lieutenant on the same ship under the command of his uncle, Captain Giacomo di Natale. At this time the ship was flying the flag of the King of Spain and his uncle was sued in Malta by the Greek captain of a *sambecchino* which he had captured in the waters of southern Anatolia. The Greek claimed that his ship and its cargo of coffee, rice, and flax belonged to Greek Christians and that the depredation was therefore illegal. The case was heard before the Minister for Spain in Malta who, having heard the evidence, observed that the ship had sailed with the Turkish flag which had been thrown into the sea by one of the crew when the ship was boarded, that the entire cargo belonged to Turks or to Greeks subject to the Turk, that it was loaded in Alexandria and was going to Smyrna, both of which places belonged to the Turk, and that therefore it was a good prize.[1]

By the next year Francesco had been promoted and had also changed his flag. On 19 April 1739 he was issued a five-year patent by the Grand Master of Malta to fight the eternal war against the enemies of the Faith, in the waters of Barbary and Levant, under the flag of the Holy Religion.[2] His uncle had retired to devote himself to business, though he retained a majority share in the ship. We know nothing about the ship itself except that it was a *nave*, that is a big, probably three-masted vessel armed with about twenty-four cannon. Two felluccas and a caique were also part of its armament. Most ships of this kind carried a crew of well over 100 men and it is possible to identify 46 of these.[3] They were a very mixed bunch indeed, including 16 Maltese, 8 Greeks (all from the islands), 6 Sicilians, 6 Corsicans, 5 Italians, 3 Dalmatians, a Spaniard (who later deserted), and a Frenchman. Some of them had already served on the same ship for many years under the command of Francesco's uncle, such as the pilot, Gio Battista Rossi of Senglea in Malta, the boatswain, Vittorio d'Angelo of Messina, and the master gunner, Jean Jacques Ciprian of Marseilles, but most of the crew had been recruited in 1739 for this particular voyage.[4]

A lawsuit of 1742–3 throws a certain amount of light on the character of Captain Francesco himself, and of his Maltese pilot, Rossi.[5] Captain Francesco was clearly a compulsive gambler, and Rossi, who was suing him, declared that he had made a wager with his captain during their last voyage. The terms of the wager were that if Captain di Natale should play games '*di resto*' before the ship had been cleared at Malta, he should give Rossi two coats, of a value of eighty *scudi* each, and that if he did not play such games then Rossi was to give the captain one such coat. Almost immediately after making the wager the captain started gambling again, and Rossi was suing for his coats. Much of the evidence given to the court involved the definition of the expression '*di resto*'. Most witnesses agreed that games '*di resto*' were games played for cash rather than for drinks or other trifles which were known as games '*di passatempo*'. One witness gave evidence that he had won ten or fifteen *zecchini* from the captain, but that the captain 'continued to play every sort of game, all over the ship, with whoever he happened to meet . . . and that he even gave orders to people to play with him'. The captain's defence was quite amusing. He first stated that he had never made the wager, and then went on to say that it was an unlikely story since Rossi had never worn a coat worth eighty *scudi* in his life, but at the most thirty-five or forty. Rossi indignantly replied 'that there was a time when I had some substance and dressed in coats richer than eighty *scudi*, and although at present the public does not see me well dressed, the reason is because I am troubled with a family, and the most I can do is to find their daily bread . . . I always dress according to the profit I have made . . . and when I got married on this island, I wore a coat of *"del beuf"*cloth which cost me 125 *scudi.*' Whether Rossi got his coats or not we do not know, but this was not the only time that Rossi sued his captain, and it is possible that there was little love lost between them. Rossi had been a corsair for twenty-four years at the start of this voyage and may well have preferred the old days under Francesco's uncle. As for the captain's proclivity for gambling, there is little evidence that it affected his judgement as a corsair. Indeed he was rather cautious than otherwise.

The two log-books which tell us what happened during Captain Francesco's career as a Maltese corsair were both written up by his purser, Angelo Ferrandini, a fellow Corsican.[6] The first one describes a cruise to the Levant which lasted from April 1739 to July 1741, and the second a cruise to Barbary in the summer of 1742. Most of the matter in the log-books describes the ordinary routine of the voyage, and I have summarized the material to give a general account of the voyages, only quoting *verbatim* when something of particular interest occurred. Ferrandini had a vivid way of describing dramatic events, as will be seen below, but his normal style reflected the fact that most of a corsair voyage was not very exciting. The normal information given is the position of the ship, its route, the direction of the wind and brief descriptions of what other ships were seen. When another ship is hailed any important news is entered in the log-book, but far more common is the remark that there was no news (*senza novità*). Much of the voyage was spent at anchor and here we learn what other ships visited or were seen from the anchorage, and a brief account of the business of unloading, careening, and waxing the ship which had to be done at frequent intervals to maintain its efficiency. The log-books give virtually no information about life on board ship, but on the other hand the regular appearance in the books of death and bad weather, as well as the long periods when nothing whatsoever of interest happens, gives the reader a very good idea of what life as a corsair was really like.

The first few pages of the first log-book are missing, and we first meet Captain Natale on 14 June 1739 sailing west from

Crete in company with a prize he had taken. He sails past Cape Matapan, Coron, and Paxos, south of Malta past the islands of Linosa and Lampedusa, and then into the strait between Malta and Gozo. On the morning of 2 July he is just outside St Paul's Bay and he sends the prize ahead to Grand Harbour. He himself spends the night at the mouth of Marsamxett and the next day sails into Grand Harbour. Little of interest occurs on his trip from Crete except an encounter with a strange ship on the 29 June. This ship on seeing Natale raised the Maltese flag. Suspecting a trick Natale raised the Turkish flag, but when at last they came near enough to hail each other, it turned out to be a Swedish ship four days out of Tripoli with wool for Leghorn.

After two days in Malta taking on water and provisions, Captain Natale set sail again. He was not to return for over two years. These two years are broken up into three summers spent cruising in the eastern Mediterranean and two winters spent in his winter-quarters in the Cyclades. There is very great similarity in the Captain's activities during each of these campaigns. Every summer he sailed via Crete and Rhodes to Cyprus. Most of the summer was spent cruising round Cyprus and in the waters between Cyprus, Syria, and southern Anatolia. And in the course of each summer a cruise was made to Damiatta in Egypt, either direct from Cyprus or along the Syrian coast.

Until the very end of this period of two years Captain Natale never fired a shot in anger. All the fighting and capturing of prizes was done by his felluccas. These were often away from the parent ship for weeks at a time, coming back at intervals with prizes or potential prizes. Although some two dozen ships were captured and prize goods taken off several others in the three summers covered by the log-book, none of these were really significant prizes, and the general results of Captain Natale's cruise were rather disappointing. Not all the prizes accrued to Natale either, since for a considerable proportion of the time he was in *conserva* with other corsairs.

In addition to their activities in bringing in a stream of potential prizes to the parent ship the crews of the felluccas also made many raids ashore in Cyprus, Anatolia, and Syria. These were not all successful, however. In June 1740, for instance, the crew of one of the felluccas landed in Syria. They marched inland until midnight, and then raided a village where they took many Turks. But on their way back to the boat they were attacked by superior forces of Turkish cavalry. Four men were killed and six wounded in the fight that followed and the corsairs had to leave their prisoners behind. Suspecting that they had been led into a trap they killed the Arab guide who they had engaged to lead them to the village. Another two men were killed in an unsuccessful raid on a Turkish village on the mainland opposite Rhodes. The total booty from these two raids was one Turkish girl captured in the second raid. A more successful raid was made in May 1740 in Cyprus. Here, after a short exchange of fire with some cavalry, they raided a village and captured twenty-five women and children, the men having taken flight on hearing the musket fire.

Captain Natale himself spent more than half of each summer at anchor – maintaining his ship, taking on water, organizing ransoms, receiving news, or just resting. There was a constant need to clean and wax the wooden bottom of his ship and the captain spent much time with his ship careened and all the gear unladen on shore. This was clearly a dangerous operation since Turkish naval ships were in the habit of swooping down on corsairs while they were being careened, and he normally went to the same places to maintain his ship. These were presumably selected for their ease of defence, and the two favourite were the island of Chalki off the west coast of Rhodes and Provençal Island to the north of Cyprus, a notorious hangout of corsairs. He spent a week in the latter place in the summer of 1740 replacing his damaged mainmast with a mast taken from a prize *sambecchino*. The job finished, there was a little ceremony as 'with the name of God and the Virgin Mary' the new mast was raised.

Practically all of Natale's prizes – except for some of the slaves – were ransomed or sold on the spot in the Levant. Often this was done at Turkish ports in Cyprus and Syria. The captain would sail up flying a white flag and would then salute with a single cannon-shot. If the fortress was also flying the white flag and returned his salute, then it was safe for him to sail in. Negotiations would then begin, often with the Turkish governor or the French consul acting as a ransom agent. The ports of

Brig careening. Corsair ships had to be careened at least every two months to maintain their efficiency.

Larnaka in southern Cyprus, Scanderoon in Syria, Beirut in the Lebanon, and the island of Kastelorizo off southern Anataolia seem to have acted as general ransoming centres for Maltese prize-goods and slaves in the Levant. Slaves would often leave their families aboard as hostages while they went ashore to arrange their ransoms. On one occasion two Turkish women came up to the ship and voluntarily offered themselves as hostages so that their enslaved husbands could fix up their ransoms. Apart from ransoms, many of Captain Natale's prize-goods were sold to traders in the ports or other ships at sea.

The receipt of news was vital for the corsair, and Captain Natale hailed practically every ship he saw, Christian or not, for an exchange of information. It was particularly important to know the whereabouts of the Turkish navy and of the ships of provincial governors who spent most of the summer looking for corsairs and protecting Turkish shipping. During the period that Natale was in the Levant there were at least eight powerful caravels sailing in the same waters, as well as galleys and galleots. It is some measure of the efficiency of his information service that, although the log-books are full of reports of the movement of these ships, they only came within striking distance of the corsairs twice during the whole two years. Significantly, the weather was calm on both occasions. The first time Natale was chased for a whole day by a big Turkish naval ship, but was fortunate enough to have the two felluccas close at hand. These were able to tow him clear of his pursuers until the wind freshened and he was able to get away. The second episode ended in the battle which will be described later in this chapter. Apart from news of enemy shipping Captain Natale learnt much about potential prizes, the activities of his fellow corsairs as well as general information. On 17 September 1739, for instance, he heard that war had been declared between Spain and England.

By mid-October it was time for the captain to be thinking about moving to his winter-quarters in the Cyclades. Each year, cruising slowly via Rhodes and Crete he reached the Aegean in early November and then settled down for the winter. His favourite winter anchorage was at the island of Antiparos, but occasionally he would vary the scenery by weighing anchor and moving a few miles to Delos or Argentiera (Kimolos). During the whole winter he never moved any further. The felluccas continued to be sent out at intervals, and occasionally took a prize or a slave, but the level of activity was minimal compared with the summer. Turkish naval activity also stopped during the winter. In early December 1739, for instance, a French pollacca reported the good news that the Turkish navy were on their way home. The three caravels based on Tenedos were headed for Constantinople, and all the galleys had been laid up.

The islands of the Cyclades seem to have been like a second home to the corsairs, and the Turks left them well alone in the winter, though in the summer they might make sudden raids. The winters in the Aegean were cold, and the log-book provides a grim record of gales, snow, rain, thunder and lightning. The winters of this period are known to have been particularly bad in the Mediterranean, and the log-book records that it was still snowing on 30 March 1740. Each winter some of the crew and slaves died, and many of these men were buried in the churchyards of the Cyclades. Bad weather and death were relieved by the fact that most of the other Maltese corsairs licensed for the Levant and several French merchantmen also wintered in the Cyclades. Visits were made from ship to ship and news was exchanged. News of prizes, news from home, as when Captain Geronimo Preziosi turned up on 30 December 1739, twenty-eight days out of Malta. No doubt Captain Natale was also able to indulge his passion for gambling during this period of inactivity. By late February Turks and corsairs were beginning to think about next year's season. News would arrive that caravels were being fitted out against the corsairs. A shepherd from Delos reported the caravels sailing towards Andros. It was time to be moving.

In 1740 Captain Natale did not leave his winter-quarters till early April. The next year, the weather was better and he was on the move by late January, but although the period till April was spent cruising he did not leave the Aegean till 2 April. While Captain Natale was cruising in the Aegean, his felluccas were once again cruising on their own. One of them, com-manded by the veteran Lieutenant Rossi, who had just com-pleted twenty-five years as a corsair, sailed into the harbour of Santorino on 18 March and attacked a caique belonging to the Monastery of St John the Evangelist at Patmos.[7] The caique, which was loading wine and other provisions for the monastery, was sacked and when its captain demanded to be taken to Captain Natale's ship to make a protest, Rossi threatened to kill him. While in Santorino Rossi also went ashore, broke into some warehouses and took cheeses and wine, and then waylaid two merchantmen sailing into the harbour with cargoes of grain. He seized the cargoes, 200 piastres in cash, the anchors, sails, and other gear, together with the belongings, clothes, and sleeping gear of the crew. Probably the first that Captain Natale knew of this was when he sailed to Santorino on 29 March and met the fellucca. But for all that, Rossi was almost certainly under his captain's orders, and it is probable that the motive behind this raid on an island which was specifically protected by letters patent issued by the Grand Master, was that Natale had run out of both food and money. In any case he made no attempt to deny the facts of this raid when he was later sued by representatives of both the Università of the island of Santorino and of the Monastery of Patmos. His only interest was to keep the damages as low as possible.

Natale made no further prizes during his cruise in the Aegean and on 2 April he sailed for Cyprus. This was his last summer in the Levant as a Maltese corsair and his activities were as usual. While he was cruising Natale's information service continued to feed him with news of Turkish naval operations. On 9 June, whilst anchored at Larnaka, he heard that three Turkish caravels had gone to Alexandria with soldiers for the garrison, and that they were due to sail via Damiatta to Alexandretta; another four were at Adalia and also due to sail to Alexandretta, two along the north coast and two along the south coast of Cyprus. On Sunday 25 June he heard that the Mufti would be arriving in Jaffa with a galley of 26 benches with 300 men and a galleot of 18 benches with 130 men. As we can see Captain Natale's information service was very good, but he saw none of these ships until suddenly on 9 July he saw the two galleys from Jaffa in the waters of Finika Bay and shortly after was involved in a ferocious battle. It was the first time that Natale had had to fire a shot in anger since he left Malta over two years previously. I will leave the purser to describe what happened.

Waters of La Fenica

Day of the Battle with the Galley and the Galleot of the Pasha Mustafa called Musta

Sunday 9 July 1741: We are east of the Caccamo and south of La Fenica, the weather is calm. At two bells* of the first watch we saw two ships to the north-east and they seem to be the galley and the galleot and they are coming towards us. At seven bells of the first watch the galleot is fairly close and we have raised the pennant and the standard, and fired a cannon-shot. Now the galley is drawing near and the galleot is nearer still, and has fired a shot at us but it fell short. At eight bells the galley has drawn near and fired five shots but they fell short. At the first bell of the second watch, being still nearer, she discharged all her bow guns with ten shots, and struck us in the

* *Ampollette*, literally two hourglasses.

mainsail and the foresail and in the other sails. We replied with four cannon and broke many oars and cut away the fellucca. The battle continued, with the galley as much as with the galleot, and we had to fight to starboard and to port. The galley always kept astern of us, and drew nearer still, firing fiercely with the galleot in support. The second time she struck us on the mainmast near to its foot, doing much damage to it. The third time, having come still closer, she struck the foremast with three cannon shots, two passed right through and one parted the foremast and spritsail yards and hit the bowsprit. The fourth time they cut the stays, counterstays and hoops of the mainmast, mizzen and foresail, and all the sails were ruined by cannon-balls, angel-shot,* chains and grapeshot, and one ball broke the starboard port of Santa Barbara,† and one cannon-shot level with the water on the port side of the poop entered the food store, but was at once satisfactorily dealt with. The fifth time they broke the topsail yard and the whole sail was wrecked and fell down, and they broke the flagstaff in three pieces and the standard was torn to shreds, and also the mizzen and mizzen topsail, and another broke the starboard mainsail yard. And one of them shouted and said, 'Captain Cicco,‡ you wretch, strike your colours', and he replied to them, 'come on board you old whore'. They grappled us on the port side and then drew away. The sixth time we blew off all their parapet and catwalk and it fell down, and the mainsail and mainsail yards fell down too, their cannon were dismounted, and the big bow cannon was struck in the mouth, and their foresail was wrecked by the balls and the grapeshot, as was a cannon in the poop and others that we could not see, and they came to grapple us on the starboard side but then drew away, not being able to endure the damage from the cannon and the muskets. The seventh time they came and grappled us and rammed us aft near the starboard port of Santa Barbara, but with fire grenades, *trombette* and musket fire they drew away and we smashed their catwalk. But on board us the *canavette di foco* caught fire, and also the discarded *canavette*, and burnt the

* A kind of chain-shot, made of the segments of a bullet, attached by chains to a disk. (O.E.D.)
† The patron saint of arsenals and powder magazines, hence the magazine.
‡ Diminutive of Francesco, i.e. Captain Francesco di Natale.

members of the crew that were on the *cassara*, and many other things, and the mizzen. And the galley, after it had drawn away, turned and set its course for La Fenica with the galleot. The battle lasted seven hours* and we fired eighty-eight cannon at them.

Dead, wounded and burnt

Killed in action. Constantine of Crete, ensign; Nicoletto Sirgetto; Pietro Schiavinetto, caulker; the lieutenant, Piero Domerghi; Giuseppe Falzon was burnt and threw himself into the sea, he died soon after; Antonio Dingli. On the 10th the black Turk died and was baptized at his request; also Nicolo of Crete died of burns. On the 11th Saverio Ruggieri of Naples died of burns. On the 13th Salvo, known as Zenzo, of Casal Ghaxaq died of burns; also died Janni Scurianotto, Stieni Rumeo, Michel Angelo, Maltese; Maestro Francesco, Sicilian; Giacomo Miraglia, watchkeeper; Gianni Carbati, Maltese; Pasquale Ricardi of Lipari; wounded: Aloisi Camilleri, steward; Girolamo Camarotto; Antonio Loi; Vincenzo Schiavone; Paolo Zuave. In all 22.

After the battle Captain Natale limped home. His route was south of Crete to the waters of Barbary and then past Linosa and Gozo to Malta where he anchored in Marsamxett on 31 July. On the way one of the slaves managed to escape by jumping overboard. As he approached the east end of Crete Natale received some more bad news. A Turkish caravel had surprised the corsair Paolo Spiteri while he was anchored at Santorino. Although Spiteri himself had got away with many of the crew in his fellucca, his ship had been captured. Altogether July 1741 must have been a better month than most for the long-suffering protectors of Levantine shipping. As for Captain Francesco, he can hardly have been too happy about the results of his two-year voyage. Although he had captured some twenty-five ships altogether, not one of them was a really significant prize and it is doubtful whether the proceeds from the whole lot would more than cover his expenses. On the debit side his ship was badly damaged and he had lost thirty-eight men, fifteen as a result of the battle and the fire which arose from it, six deserters,

* Literally fourteen hourglasses.

Saique. The commonest Moslem or Greek trading ship. Used for the carriage of goods and pilgrims.

six killed ashore in raids, and the rest apparently from natural causes.

We lose touch with Captain Natale after his return to Malta but it is unlikely that he went to sea again that year. He had plenty of business to attend to. First of all his ship was in a very bad condition after the battle with the Turks and he would have had to supervise the repairs. Then he would be busy disposing of his slaves and arranging for the distribution of the proceeds, as well as of the ransom and prize money which he had acquired in the Levant. He was also engaged in a considerable amount of litigation. On 4 September the Rev. Don Luca Barbarigo, on behalf of the island of Santorino, opened his suit against Natale for the recovery of the prizes seized by Lieutenant Rossi in Santorino harbour last March.[8] The Maltese courts ordered the sequestration of the prizes until the case was settled.[9] On 20 September Magdalena 'Ancona opened a suit for arrears of prize money owed to her son who had died the previous November.[10] In February 1742 Lieutenant Rossi was suing for his prize money and also for the two coats he claimed as a result of the wager he had made with Natale.[11] In all these cases Captain Natale and his uncle can clearly be seen playing for time and it is obvious that the generally poor results of the last voyage and the expenses of repairing the ship were making a big hole in their resources. In fact the winter of 1741–2 was a very bad one for nearly all the Maltese corsair captains. Three of Captain Natale's brother captains spent the winter in gaol while their various cases were being heard in the courts.[12] Captain Cristoforo di Giovanni in fact spent over a year in gaol accused of seizing a Venetian ship.[13] Complaining that he and his wife were perishing of hunger he managed to get the Grand Master to order that an allowance of four tari a day be made to him from his sequestrated effects. Later his creditors agreed to raise this to six and a half tari a day.[14] It was not till 1743 that he was again at sea. Captain Paolo Spiteri, whose ship was seized by the Turks at about the same time that Captain Natale was fighting his battle, was also in prison, as was Captain Geronimo Preziosi. He was being sued by Captain Francesco and his uncle, who had a financial interest in his ship, as well as by other creditors, and eventually his ship was put up to auction by order of the courts to clear his debts.[15] Altogether rather a different winter than the one spent by all these captains the year before in the Cyclades! Captain Natale must have been looking forward to getting to sea again as he fitted out his ship for a summer cruise to Barbary.

He eventually set sail for Barbary on 10 June 1742.[16] A week later he was cruising near the Kerkennah Islands. On the 19th three ships were sighted coming towards them; they were his own two felluccas which had been sent out hunting and a sendale which had been made a prize. The sendale's cargo of oil and barracans was taken on board, also seven slaves (a man, a woman, four boys, and a girl). The sendale itself was sunk as being too much trouble to take back. The corsairs now headed back for Malta where they arrived on 27 June. On their way they met a French ship headed from Algiers to Tripoli whose captain and two members of the crew had died of the plague. Back in Malta the prize cargo was unloaded and the ship was careened. Then having taken on fresh water Captain Natale set off again on 29 June to the north-west. Passing Gozo and Pantellaria, where he sent a fellucca for news, he was off Cap Bon on 10 July. The next day a ship was seen headed for Kelibia and the felluccas were sent in pursuit. By late afternoon they had caught and captured the ship which was a Turkish scampania with seventeen Turkish corsairs aboard, two of whom had been wounded in the fight. The prisoners told Natale that there were another thirteen corsair galleots at sea.

Taking his prize in tow Captain Natale headed north and then turned west past Bizerta to the Galita Islands. Sighting a large ship he prepared to defend himself but it turned out to be a false alarm. It was a Dutch merchantmen headed for Tripoli from Algiers, carrying Turkish passengers. That night Captain Natale headed once more for home, and having saluted the Madonna of Pantellaria* on 17 July, anchored in Marsamxett the next day.

Once again he careened and watered, and then on 27 July he put to sea again, this time south-west towards the island of Gerba. For several days he cruised in the sea area between Gerba, the Kerkennah Islands, Pantellaria, and Lampedusa where he met several ships, including two flying the English flag from Port Mahon in Minorca.† On 13 August he was anchored in 6 *brachia*‡ of water near Gerba. Just before dawn a ship was seen anchored nearby and the felluccas were sent off. By daybreak the ship could be identified as a Turkish volicchio.§ By this time 'the felluccas were fairly close. The volicchio opened fire and raised the red flag. The felluccas came astern and attacked the volicchio with a great weight of fire. The volicchio replied with cannon and musket fire. At two bells of the first watch the felluccas went to the poop of the volicchio and fought fiercely. . . . . Then the men from the felluccas boarded and we sent the caique to help them. At four bells the felluccas drew away, so we ourselves weighed anchor and went towards

* The islands of Pantellaria, Lampedusa, and Linosa lying in the centre of the narrow sea area between Islam and Christendom, were used by both Maltese and Barbary corsairs as anchorages. Pantellaria numbered amongst its population Christian and Moslem hermits.
† Minorca was a British possession from 1708–56, 1763–83, and 1798–1802.
‡ About 18 feet.
§ A fairly large trading ship.

them. We sounded continuously and found 4 or 5 *brachia* of water. The volicchio then set sail and at five bells her caique drew away loaded with people. The felluccas set out in pursuit. When they came up to the volicchio they found that it had run aground. One of the felluccas followed the caique [laden with the fleeing Turks] and, coming close, fired at it with muskets and pistols. Then the caique too ran aground . . . At eight bells one of the felluccas returned. The sergeant major, a Greek from Cephalonia, and Innocente, a Corsican, had been wounded. Sergeant Alessandro and Janni, a Greek, were dead. As the volicchio was aground, the captain went aboard her [i.e. to try to refloat her]. At four bells of the second watch the other fellucca arrived bringing two wounded Turks. All the others had fled. One man was wounded in the foot and Biagio the Slav was wounded. At two bells of the fourth watch we got the volicchio under sail, and it was anchored at our bow. This evening we took four cannon off the prize. We also buried Sergeant Alessandro in the sea. The other dead man, Janni, had been thrown off the volicchio by the Turks.'

The prize was placed under the command of Antonio Rizzo with a crew of ten of the corsairs and five Greek sailors who had remained on board when the Turks fled. Then late that evening corsairs and prize set sail. The voyage back to Malta took a long time as winds were contrary and very light, but finally after running along the north coast of Malta, past St Paul's Bay and St Julians they anchored in Grand Harbour on 24 August.

On 5 September they set sail, this time towards Cap Bon again. A ship from Port Mahon carrying wheat and barley was stopped for news, and they heard that a few days previously a French corsair had been wrecked off the Galita Islands with great loss of life. On the 13th the felluccas brought back a sendale as a prize. They had taken it the night before after a long chase which ended by the sendale running aground and most of those aboard escaping ashore. However six men, a little boy, and four women remained as slaves. In the evening Captain Natale was able to do a satisfactory piece of business by ransoming the sendale itself and its cargo of empty wine-jars to a Turk who was a passenger on the ship from Port Mahon.

The next day Captain Natale caught up with three other Maltese ships, two galleots and a barque, and for the next week all four cruised together in the neighbourhood of Sfax and the Kerkennah Islands, but without making any further prizes. On 26 September all the ships set off towards Lampedusa where they anchored two days later and took on fresh water and wood. On 2 October they set off for Malta but the weather was very bad and they had to reef. On the 3rd they were still only in the vicinity of Linosa and 'the wind was getting stronger, it was raining hard and we were sailing with the foresail alone. At five bells of the first night watch we bore up to the north-north-west. The weather was getting worse. At seven bells of the second night watch it was blowing a gale with thunder, lightning, hail and rain, the wind west-south-west gale force. We threw . . . four cannon, and other gear into the sea. We broke up the fellucca and threw that in too. We were in great danger and making much water.' But next morning it was calmer and they sighted the Sicilian coast near Sciacca. Finally, after anchoring in Sicily for a few days they set sail for Malta. And, after another very bad day of thunder and lightning, they sighted Cape San Dimitri of Gozo on 8 October and that night were safely anchored in Grand Harbour.

No more log-books of Captain Natale's voyages survive, but he definitely made a cruise in 1743 to complete his five-year patent as a Maltese corsair.[18] On 10 April 1744 he was issued with a new patent for one and a half years to operate in the waters of Barbary from Cape Misurata to the Straits of Gibraltar and the Kingdom of Morocco.[19] This may have been his last voyage flying the Maltese flag, but not the end of his career as a corsair. For, five years later in 1749 we hear of him again in the Levant. He was then captain of a corsair ship flying the flag of the King of Sardinia.[20] In the 1750s he was once again operating from Malta, but this time with the flag of the Prince of Monaco. This was just one more move by the corsairs in a long diplomatic game that they played to get round the new regulations that forbade them to cruise in the Levant.[21] Francesco di Natale was a professional, and it would take more than regulations to keep him from his favourite hunting grounds in the waters of Cyprus and Southern Anatolia.

CHAPTER 14

Rais Hamidou

Flee, unbelievers, flee! Hamidou rides the seas as master.
The regions through which he has passed remain devoid of foes.
Flee, infidels! May your warships quickly take refuge in their ports:
Or they will become the prey of the champion of the Holy War![1]

The last corsair whom we will consider was probably the best known to his contemporaries. Rais Hamidou became Admiral of the Algerine fleet in a period of corsair renaissance which spanned the confused era of the French Revolutionary and Napoleonic Wars. Not for half a century had the Algerians had so large or so powerful a fleet. This renaissance was to be the last really successful period for the Algerian corsairs. After Hamidou's death their power and influence continued to decline for the last fifteen years of their existence.

Hamidou's origins were strange for a Barbary corsair. He was neither a Turk, nor the son of a Turk, nor a renegade, but a native Algerian, a Moor. Such was a disadvantage in the social, political, and religious structure of North Africa, and Hamidou's successes were to arouse considerable envy and mistrust amongst his Turkish co-religionaries. The son of a tailor, he was apprenticed to his father's trade at the age of eleven. But like many another small boy the smell of the sea and the tales of the corsairs enticed him away from such an unexciting calling and he embarked as a cabin-boy on a corsair ship. 'By climbing in the rigging,' he said, 'he hoped to stretch his legs, cramped by the awkward posture of the tailor.'

Little is known of his early career as a corsair. Legend has it that he served for some time at least on a Portuguese merchant-man, acquiring useful knowledge for his later career. What is certain is that his promotion was fairly rapid from cabin-boy to sailor, and from sailor to officer, until eventually at some date around 1790 he was given his first independent command of a xebec belonging to the Bey of Oran. Later he took command of the Bey's whole fleet, two or three xebecs and as many felluccas. News of his exploits and of his great courage soon reached the Dey of Algiers, Hassan, and he was summoned to the capital city. Such a summons could not be refused and Hamidou was given command of a twelve-gun xebec with a crew of sixty men. Although this was somewhat of a come-down after commanding a whole fleet, it was clearly a great honour to be given a command by the Dey himself.

After a few early successes Hamidou nearly wrecked his whole career by an error in seamanship. He was anchored on a lee shore at La Calle, near the eastern border of Algeria, when the wind got up. Despite his efforts with extra anchors and extra cables the xebec was blown ashore and broken up on the rocks. Rather than face the Dey's anger Hamidou fled to Tunis. Later, hoping that the affair might have blown over, he returned to Constantine, within the boundaries of the Dey's dominions. But orders were sent for his despatch to Algiers and he returned to the scene of his earlier successes as a prisoner. His biographer, Albert Devoulx, reports his interview with his master.[2] As Hamidou bent to kiss the Dey's hand, the latter pushed him back and cried: 'Back, wretch! What have you done with my xebec, you son of a dog.' Hamidou replies: 'My Lord, it was the will of God that it should perish. I could do nothing about it.' The Dey, remembering his youth at sea, was not convinced and asked him what he was doing at La Calle at all, since it was not a recognized anchorage. Here, however, the Dey was on weak ground, since La Calle was marked as an anchorage on all contemporary portulans, and Hamidou was able to point triumphantly to the anchor illustrating this fact on a chart which was brought in. Beaten in the argument the Dey eventually pardoned his captain and Hamidou was given command of a new xebec. A year or two later, in 1797, Hamidou was given an even better ship, a corvette, whose captain had deserted to the Emperor of Morocco. This was the largest ship in the Algerian fleet at that time and carried thirty-six guns.

From this date it is possible to follow Hamidou's career in some detail as his prizes can be found in a register kept by the officials in Algiers. Whether this document registered all prizes taken by the Algerians is unknown, but even if it is incomplete, the three years during which Hamidou was in command of this corvette were successful ones for the corsair. The register records his capture of nineteen ships during this period.* Hamidou operated for the most part on his own or in the company of one xebec, but occasionally he joined in a combination of several corsairs for a particular exploit such as the capture in 1798 of a large Greek ship loaded with soap, paper, and corn. The corsairs' proceeds from the sale of the cargo of this prize came to more than a quarter of a million francs.

Hamidou's success was making him a rich and powerful man. While some of his wealth was expended in establishing his new status he was also ploughing back a portion of his profits. For while he completed his last campaigns in the corvette (and in a pollacca which he used while the corvette was damaged) a Spanish carpenter was building him a forty-four gun frigate. Built to Hamidou's specifications the new ship was ready in 1801. It was the finest ship seen in Algiers for many years, very fast and extremely seaworthy. Even in 1815, after fourteen years of almost constant privateering, the ship could be described as 'uncommonly fast'. When fully armed the frigate carried over 400 men, and thus with its speed and its fighting strength was likely to be a real menace, not only in the Mediterranean but in the Atlantic as well. Since Algiers was at peace with England, France, and Spain who indeed could check the corsair's career?

Soon after Hamidou acquired his new ship, he performed his most famous exploit. This was the capture in 1802 of a forty-four gun Portuguese frigate in single combat with the loss of hardly a single man. This was clearly a piece of bravado rather than good business since the warship carried little cargo and the ship itself, by Algerian prize rules, would accrue to the Dey rather than

* 14 Neapolitan, 3 Genoese, 1 Venetian, and 1 Greek.

Hamidou's first command was a xebec. Used by both Maltese and Barbary corsairs in the eighteenth century.

to the corsair. The ruse by which the ship was captured is typical of the tactics of the Barbary corsairs. Flying English colours Hamidou completely fooled the Portuguese and when the latter realized their mistake it was too late. Already close, Hamidou ran alongside, grappled the Portuguese frigate, and his janissaries poured over the bulwarks. Confused and ill-organized, the Portuguese offered little resistance and the frigate, together with 282 prisoners, was soon captured. The prize was the greatest seen in Algiers for a very long time and Hamidou's reception as he sailed into the port was tumultuous. For the Portuguese it was the beginning of nine years' slavery, their release only coming in 1811 with the signing of peace between Algiers and Portugal, a treaty largely promoted by Portugal's English allies.[3] A few years after their capture some news of the fate of the Portuguese officers is contained in the diary of the wife of the English consul:[4]

' . . . we ventured as far as the Swedish consul's, where we were invited to a ball. I danced with the unfortunate Captain of the Portuguese frigate, taken by the Algerines a few years ago . . . The hapless Portuguese officers are, by the yearly payment of a certain sum, exempted from labouring at the Marina like beasts of burden – the dreadful lot of their companions in slavery.'

As recompense for his poor reward for the risks he had taken, Hamidou was given a gratuity of over 100,000 francs to share with his crew. The Portuguese frigate was converted into a corsair, named *El Portekiza* and took a rich haul of prizes before she was destroyed by Lord Exmouth's expedition against Algiers in 1816.

From 1802 to 1808 Hamidou continued his career of taking prizes. There is an element of unreality in the Barbary corsairs' activities during these years as England and France continued to fight out their war. But general warfare meant general confusion and Hamidou was under no illusions as to its effects. 'God save Napoleon!' he said, 'as long as nations do business with him, they will be beaten and will not dream of bothering us.'[5] Algiers was determined to keep on good terms with both the main belligerents, despite France's conquest of the Ottoman

province of Egypt. Although the Sultan gave orders to the Dey
to declare war on France, this came to very little. The French
Consul and other French nationals were thrown into prison but
were released after a month. A few French prizes were taken
but it did not take the Algerians long to see where good sense
lay. If war against France was taken seriously, reprisals would
be rapid and little help could be expected from the Turks. So
Algiers remained at peace with both France and England,
and the corsairs concentrated their attention against the ships
of weaker nations. The main sufferers were Portugal, Sicily,
Naples, Genoa, Hamburg, and later Holland, Denmark, and
Sweden. One problem was that, as these small states came under
the rule or became allied to one or other of the main belligerents, so the pressures for the corsairs to cease their attacks
became stronger. England was particularly strong in her
protests against the seizure of Sicilian and Portuguese shipping,
while Napoleon, of course, became the protector of Italy. One
other potential victim was protected by neither power. This
was the United States. A treaty was made in 1795 between
the U.S.A. and Algiers, and a regular tribute was paid by the
Americans until 1810. But America was a long way away and the
Algerians saw little danger in seizing the occasional American
merchantman.

And so Hamidou continued his career. Often sailing in company with his brother, Hamdan, the captain of a xebec, he
made numerous prizes, mainly Portuguese and Neapolitan,
but including an American schooner with a cargo of beans
captured in the year of Trafalgar. Many raids ashore were
made during these years as well and the prize register records
the proceeds realized by the sale of the slaves captured during
these raids. But in 1808 there was a check in Hamidou's career.
Despite the envy and jealousy felt by many in Algiers at his
success, and despite the dislike felt by others of his non-Turkish
origins, he had successfully weathered the rise and fall of
several rulers. But at last he slipped, and a new pasha exiled
him to Beirut. Not for long, however. A year later there was
yet another palace revolution and Hamidou was back again,
more powerful than ever.

From now until his death in 1815 he was commander-in-
chief of the Algerian navy. This meant that from now onwards

he rarely operated on his own, but normally with a powerful squadron. In 1809, for instance, he commanded three forty-four gun frigates (his own, *El Portekiza*, and *El Merikana*) and a twenty-gun brig on a voyage through the Straits of Gibraltar. It must have been a very long time since the Algerians had been able to put such a force to sea and they made some good prizes, including a magnificent Portuguese brig with a cargo of tobacco on its way back from Havana. Returning to the Straits he found his way barred by the Portuguese navy – a ship-of-war and three frigates. Hamidou's courage did not desert him. He gave orders to his squadron to bear straight down on the Portuguese. Just as he was about to run their flagship down, the Portuguese lost their nerve and put their ship on the other tack, enabling Hamidou to lead his squadron through and safely back to Algiers.

From 1810 to 1812 Algiers was at war, not for the first time, with Tunis. This gave the Algerians a whole new source of prizes and Hamidou joined the rest of the corsairs in their search for Tunisian shipping. One of the few real naval combats of this war resolved itself into single combat between Hamidou and a personal rival commanding the Tunisian flagship, also a frigate. This battle, which seems to have been watched by the rest of the Algerian and Tunisian fleets, was very bloody and lasted over six hours. Only after she had lost 230 men did the Tunisian strike her flag. Once again Hamidou was able to return to Algiers in triumph, leading in a frigate that he had captured single-handed.

What sort of man was this Algerian corsair who seems to have been so continuously successful? All reports say that he was extremely brave, while his detractors comment that his successes were due more to his courage than his skill. His biographer, who spoke to people who had known him, describes him as of medium build with a fair complexion and blue eyes, though another man who knew him says he was swarthy. All agree that following the custom of the corsairs he shaved his beard, but grew his moustaches to an enormous length. One person who knew him and was very impressed was the daughter of the English Consul:[6]

'The Rais was an Algerine, (not a Turk), and a very

distinguished commander, although not the most rigid observer
of the Alcoran, as he sometimes chanced to drop in when my
father was at the dessert, and never was so bigoted and un-
social as to refuse to pledge him in a few glasses of Madeira.
He was one of the finest-looking men I ever saw, and was as
bold as one of his native lions. He was one of our nearest
neighbours in the country; his house and garden were kept
up in the greatest order and beauty.'

Clearly Hamidou was an impressive man, and not by reason of
his success alone.

An interesting sidelight on his character and on life on his
ship is given by the Tuscan poet, Filippo Pananti, who was
captured by Rais Hamidou whilst travelling on a Sicilian brig
bound from London to Palermo.[7] His capture seems to have
been entirely unnecessary and resulted from the stubbornness
and incompetence of the brig's captain. 'Even the barbarians
after our capture said that we had a bad Rais; as, if we had made
the slightest movement towards reaching the shore, they would
not have attempted to follow us; but seeing our total inactivity,
and a seeming disposition to approach, rather than get away,
they thought us enchanted. . . .' So while the brig made no
effort to escape, Hamidou's turbaned soldiers with their
scimitars flashing boarded, searched the ship and took the
passengers off to the frigate.

Pananti's first impressions of life on board Hamidou's ship
were naturally not very favourable. Shut up in the cable locker
with his frightened and miserable companions he spent a most
uncomfortable night, and he was much disgusted at having to
jostle with the frigate's crew to get his share of what looked a
revolting mess from a common pot. Nor was he much impressed
with 'the filthy Algerine ship' or the crew 'composed of almost
every race sent forth by the African continent, with the addition
of several of the Levantine banditti'. All were covered in vermin,
many had skin diseases and all seemed to spend most of the
time smoking their pipes. But after a few days he made a
reassessment. 'It is true, our diet was not of the finest quality;
but hunger, the best of all sauces, made us eat; and though our
bed was not of down, yet habit enabled us to sleep.' Furthermore, despite his forebodings, they were left unchained. Nor

were the crew all barbarians. 'On a more intimate acquaintance, we discovered some very honourable exceptions to the
general character of the Algerines.' In particular he found the
purser and the Agha of the janissaries to be extremely cultivated
men. 'It would be deviating from the strict impartiality of my
views, were I not to declare that there was no personal insult
offered to our party.' None of the women were bothered by the
crew and the Turks were particularly kind to two children who
were amongst the prisoners. Nor was life dull. Apart from having a ringside seat at the capture of a Greek merchantman and
at a battle between the frigate and a Tunisian corvette, Pananti
was also entertained by the crew. He enjoyed their songs and
dances, and indeed the captives recovered their good spirits
sufficiently to sing songs of their own lands when called on to
do so by the Turks.

As for Hamidou he 'began to invite us into his cabin where
an Arab tale was recited, and what was still better, a cup of good
Yemen coffee handed round, followed by a small glass of rum,
that is to say, of our own, which had been taken out of the brig.
Those are not the worst species of robbers, who take with one
hand, and return a little of the stolen property with the other.'*
Of Hamidou himself, he said that 'though possessing rather a
fierce physiognomy, his manners were by no means repulsive'.
His main fault was his arrogance. 'The Rais was fond of depre-
cating the merits of others, by attributing every success to his
own bravery and talents.' Another fault was his failure to
control the plundering of his crew. Hamidou dismissed such
trifles as 'below the attention of a good general'. Indeed it
would have taken a very good general to stop the crew of any
corsair ship from plundering! Regarding his actual running
of the ship the Rais 'scarcely ever walked about the ship, but
seated cross-legged on a conspicuous part of the deck, he
generally passed three or four hours of the day, occupying himself between the intervals of giving orders, in smoking, and
smoothing down his moustachios'. Back in Algiers Hamidou,
like most corsairs, liked the populace to admire his success.
Forming his captives up into a line he ordered them to form a

---

* Hamidou obviously had a good reputation as a host. Some years earlier he
invited some Englishmen on board 'and to their unexpected gratification, gave
them some excellent tea!' [8]

procession in his rear, as he strolled by a circuitous route to the palace where new prisoners were examined.

The liberal Italian's description of life on the frigate acts as a fairly convincing antidote to the normal accounts of unmitigated horror. No doubt Hamidou could be as bloodthirsty as anyone else on occasion, but there seems no reason why corsairs should not have been civil to their prisoners. Pananti's meeting with Hamidou comes at the height of the latter's success in the middle of the war between Tunis and Algiers. After the war Hamidou continued his operations, as successful as ever. During these last years he rarely cruised with squadrons of less than five ships. The Algerian squadron with four frigates and two corvettes was now really dangerous and made a big haul of prizes. In 1814 for instance six Algerines led by Hamidou went out after Danish and Swedish shipping and brought back six Swedish, three Dutch, and two Danish ships with cargoes ranging from cochineal to coffee and sugar to salt and cod.

But the long career of Hamidou was drawing to a close. In January 1815 be brought in his last prize, a Dutch ship laden with salt, and seven Christians. Five months later he was dead. His end was a fitting piece of irony. The United States, humiliated for so many years by the payment of an annual tribute which was still no protection for their shipping, declared war on Algiers barely a fortnight after the end of their War of 1812 with England. A squadron of three frigates, two sloops, three brigs, and two schooners – all battle hardened and experienced – were sent to the Mediterranean under the command of Commodore Stephen Decatur, one of the great heroes of the young American navy. After a passage of twenty-six days they arrived at Gibraltar on 15 June 1815. Receiving news that the Algerian fleet was at sea they set out in search of the enemy.

By an unusual coincidence Hamidou was at sea in his frigate without his normal supporting squadron. Mordecai M. Noah, the American Consul in Tunis gives a description of what happened:[9]

'The squadron left Gibraltar and near Cape de Gatt, fell in with an Algerine frigate. She was then under English colours, and our squadron carried the same flag. Not suspecting the approach of an enemy, the Algerine continued under easy sail, but the interchange of signals and suspicious movements of our squadron alarmed her, and setting all sail, she bore away with the utmost expedition . . . Our squadron pursued her, the *Constellation*, Captain Gordon, being the headmost ship, first fired into her, the *Guerrier*, one of our best and swiftest vessels, came up and brought her to close action; the Algerine had maintained a running fight for 25 minutes, principally with musketry, as her large guns were awkwardly managed, and after a few broadsides, she struck, with the loss of 30 killed and many wounded. Among the former was the Admiral, Rais Hamida, who was cut in two by a round shot. She was boarded and taken possession of – the prisoners, amounting to four hundred, were exceedingly alarmed at their fate, calculating to meet with the same treatment as they were accustomed to afford their captives . . . After the battle, in which they had exhibited their usual bravery, they were quietly seated on the cabin floor, smoking their long pipes with their accustomed gravity.'

The Americans captured another Algerine ship and then sailed for Algiers where the Dey immediately made peace, only forty days after the squadron had left the United States. But to Consul Noah's disgust the Americans restored both the captured ships to the Algerians, and it needed Lord Exmouth's expedition in the following year to do real damage to the corsairs.

And so Rais Hamidou was at last defeated, falling for the same trick that had fooled the Portuguese frigate thirteen years previously. By his own orders his body was thrown into the sea to avoid falling into the hands of his enemies. He was the last great Algerian corsair.

PART FIVE

Epilogue

CHAPTER 15

The Last Years of the Eternal War

Earlier in this book we have seen how the extremely powerful and virtually unchallenged position of both the Maltese and the Barbary corsairs had been much circumscribed in the century between 1650 and 1750.[1] The growth of French, English, and Dutch trade in the Mediterranean and the simultaneous development of their naval strength had provided both the motivation and the means for a check on the free-for-all that had existed in the early years of the seventeenth century. By 1700 the pride of Barbary had been sufficiently humbled by the attentions of both French and British navies to ensure that the merchant shipping of both these nations was fairly safe from attack by the corsairs in the century that followed. Once the example of treaty relationships with the Barbary powers had been established smaller maritime nations were keen to follow it. By 1750 many new treaties had been made. Such treaties normally involved the payment of tribute, often in naval stores, in return for a guarantee by the corsairs not to attack the shipping of that particular nation.[2] In other words these small nations provided the means for the Barbary corsairs to attack other Christians in return for the safety of their own nationals. A useful form of blackmail for Barbary! And, in fact, since the treaties were not backed by much force on the Christian side, they were often not fully observed or else were unilaterally broken by the corsairs. A nineteenth-century historian of Algiers writes: 'when too long a peace had made the Treasury empty the Dey hastened to break abruptly with a Christian nation in order to re-establish, at the expense of the Infidels, his exhausted finances, and also to make himself popular by providing for his turbulent and rapacious subjects the means of satisfying their instincts for plunder.'[3] None the less, the existence of so many treaties had greatly reduced the scale and scope of the activities of the Barbary corsairs by the middle of the eighteenth century.

Operating on this smaller scale the Barbary corsairs were to survive as an institution for another eighty years. The main reason for their long life was the failure of the European powers to combine against them. Such combinations were often mooted, but always fell down before the selfishness of individual nations. Each country felt that as long as their ships and their nationals were protected from the depredations of the corsairs, then the fact that the ships and nationals of other countries were captured could only be to their advantage, in that it hindered the development of rival merchant marines.* And so the eighteenth century is punctuated by the despatch of naval forces by one or other of the European nations in order to restore their treaty relationships *vis-à-vis* the corsairs, but there was never any combined action against them, nor indeed any action by an individual nation to try to eradicate the institution. Corsair ships continued to be fitted out in Tunis, Tripoli, and Algiers, and though their numbers were much less than in earlier times, they continued to make a considerable number of prizes. Nor was the period all decline. During the long period of general warfare between 1789 and 1815 the corsairs took advantage of the confusion at sea and expanded their fleets considerably, as we have seen when discussing the career of Rais Hamidou.

However, attitudes in Europe were changing by the beginning of the nineteenth century. New views on such institutions as slavery were being propounded and accepted. A more constructive approach to the problem of the Barbary corsairs was suggested at the Congress of Vienna in 1814. The British Admiral Sir Sidney Smith, referring to the discussions about ending

* Such reasoning is obviously akin to the protectionist policies of eighteenth-century mercantile powers. The view that the total of trade is constant or grows only slowly and thus it is to any nation's advantage to grab as much of it as possible at the expense of its rivals was to be challenged in the eighteenth century by writers such as Adam Smith.

negro slavery and the slave trade, drew the attention of the delegates to the continued existence of Christian slavery in North Africa and the continued depredations by the Barbary corsairs. He suggested a combination of naval forces to wipe out such institutions. His suggestions were heard with approval, but in fact, once again, no such combinations ever took place. The nearest to combined action was Lord Exmouth's Anglo-Dutch fleet of 1816 which, although it did considerable damage to Algiers, only caused a temporary lull in the activities of the Algerians.

Nevertheless the hardening of European attitudes and the greater intensity of actions by individual European states against the Barbary corsairs had their effect. Very few corsairs ventured to sea in the years following 1816, although all three Regencies continued to prevaricate and no firm promise of the abolition of either slavery or the *corso* could be extracted from them. In truth such institutions were so firmly entrenched in Barbary that only the firmest action could completely eradicate them. As the French consul-general in Algiers wrote in 1819: 'I think that one must pull out the evil by the roots, by besieging the city of Algiers, the soul of the piracy. Once fallen into the hands of Europeans, it would drag down in its wake the whole system of Algerian piracy, and would become a brake to the other Barbary states that still refuse to respect the rights of man.'[4] His prediction was correct. It was the French occupation of Algiers in 1830 that finally brought the three centuries of raiding by the Barbary corsairs to an end. Confronted with the *fait accompli* in Algiers, Tunis and Tripoli very quickly came to heel, and thus managed to retain their independence for a further fifty and eighty years respectively.

The history of the last years of the Maltese *corso* is rather different. By the eighteenth century there was no Moslem power strong enough to bombard Valletta and demand the signature of the Grand Master to a treaty. Indeed, as we have seen, it was Christians and not Moslems who imposed limitations on the Maltese corsairs. By the mid 1740s these limitations were such that it might well have come as a surprise to an observer to learn that the corsairs were still active fifty years later. The corsairs had been banned from their profitable cruising areas in the Levant, and their licences confined them to the waters of Barbary. They were unable to demand the right of inspection on either French or British ships, the two most important carriers in this area. Furthermore, a third common carrier, the Greeks, was protected by Papal insistence on the corsairs' use of the flag of the Order.

At first these limitations seem to have been honoured. In 1747 the Grand Master declared a corsair who had gone east in contravention of the new rules to be a free pirate, and the corsair was in fact executed in Dalmatia the same year.[5] The example seems to have had some effect, and from 1749 to 1751 no licences for the *corso* were issued at all, presumably because there was no demand for them.[6] A memorandum to the Maltese Inquisitor during these years regrets the ending of the Maltese *corso*.[7] Now, it says, the Turks have lost all their fear and have taken up commerce again to the great loss of the French shipping industry. Furthermore, in the absence of Maltese opposition, the Barbary corsairs had expanded their fleet to the detriment of Christian commerce. Although a few privateering licences were issued in the years 1752–4, there are only two for the next seven years. In 1756 Pinto, the Grand Master, assured the Pope that there were no corsairs in the Levant and had been none for ten years.[8] The Maltese *corso* appeared to be virtually dead.

Such indeed was the appearance, but not the reality. In the early 1750s the Maltese corsairs had thought up a new trick – to fly the flag of the Prince of Monaco.[9] At the very time that Pinto was making his assurance to the Pope he must have known that he was lying. At least five corsairs, all with fairly large ships, were at that date operating in the Levant with the flag of Monaco. All were financed with Maltese money, and two of the ships were commanded by the same corsairs who had been flying the flag of the Religion in the early 1740s.[10] Virtually pirates, they had caused considerable damage in the Levant. A letter from the French consul in Cyprus describes their behaviour, and accuses the English of trying to damage French interests in the Levant by telling the Turks that the corsairs were under the orders of the French.[11] How long the corsairs used the flag of Monaco is not known, but the scope for using different flags was considerable. One corsair in the middle of the eighteenth century was licensed in turn by the King of

Spain, the Order of St John, the King of Sardinia, and the Prince of Monaco – every time to attack the enemies of the Christian faith, and every time financed from Malta. The scope was indeed even wider than this. A Greek corsair who had once flown the Maltese flag is later on found flying the Venetian flag, not only against the Turks, but also against the French in the Levant.[12] Maltese corsairs were numbered among the notorious *angligrecs*, corsairs flying the English flag in the wars against France,[13] and later in the century a great harvest of prizes was to be taken by corsairs commissioned by Catherine the Great.[14] Amongst the latter was at least one Maltese corsair, Guglielmo Lorenzi, who commanded a squadron composed of his own ship, *La Fama*, and three other vessels financed by the Russian government.[15]

In Malta itself there was a considerable recovery in the number of privateering licences issued from the 1760s onwards. At first these were issued for the flag of the Order only, as agreed with the Pope in 1733, but from the late sixties there was once more an increasing use of the flag of the Grand Master. It will be remembered that the main significance of this flag was that appeals against depredations could not be taken to the Pope. From the eighties onwards, during the reigns of the last two grand Masters of the Order in Malta, nearly all licences to sail as a corsair were issued for the Magisterial flag. One of the main limitations imposed on the corsairs had thus been unilaterally ignored. But the other remained. All licences were quite specific that the activity of the corsairs was to be confined to the 'waters of Barbary from Cape Misurata up to the Kingdom of Morocco'. In other words the rich waters of the Levant were still a forbidden area.

In fact this provision was systematically ignored. The best evidence for this comes from the years 1778–80 when the reports made by eight corsairs on their return to Malta have survived.[16] All eight of these corsairs had licences which restricted them to the waters of Barbary, but six of them spent most of their time and took most of their prizes in the Levant. A formula had been evolved to salve their consciences as they broke their oath. 'We wished to pursue our cruise in Barbary', reported one corsair, 'but the wind, which was north-west, gale-force, did not permit it, so that we were forced to go to the Levant'.[17] 'On account of contrary and gale-force winds I was not able to reach Barbary and found myself in the Archipelago', wrote another.[18] Since the nearest island of the Greek Archipelago is some 500 miles from the defined limits of Barbary, the repetition of such statements in the reports of the corsairs hardly commands belief!

Indeed, the institution of the *corso* was, in Malta as in Barbary, too deeply entrenched to be destroyed by a few letters written from Paris or Rome. Although most of the ships involved were only felluccas or galleots with crews of forty or fifty men, the Maltese *corso* continued right up to the French occupation of the island in 1798. In 1797 nine corsairs were granted licences, all to fly the Grand Master's flag and all to operate in Barbary.[19] That the corsairs had not changed is shown by one of the last cases decided by the *Tribunale degli Armamenti*. Giorgio Fiamengo, captain of a galleot quite clearly licensed for Barbary, was ordered to return a prize to the Countess of Hochepied. The illegal seizure had taken place in late 1797 in the 'seas of the Levant'.[20]

In 1798 Napoleon, on his way to Egypt, seized Malta, 'an island which sooner or later will belong to Britain if we are stupid enough not to forestall them'.[21] He freed the 2,000 Turkish and North African slaves still held in Malta, and abolished the *corso*.[22] Despite his attack on the Ottoman province of Egypt, Napoleon wished to retain the friendship of Barbary if possible, and so was unwilling to encourage an institution whose whole justification was hostility to all Moslems. Not that the end of the Maltese *corso* meant the end of privateering in Malta. A few years later Malta was British, and in 1807 we can find the Vice Admiralty courts of Malta making a decision on the legality of the prize captured by the tactfully named *La Gran Bretagna*, commander Ignazio Sacchetti![23] There was little new to be learned in the transition from Maltese corsair to British privateer.

Nor did the end of the *corso* mean the end of the Holy War. It was the end of a long episode, certainly. But Mahomet and Christ were still not prepared to clink glasses and drink raki together. The venue of their next engagement was to be right back in the eastern Mediterranean, where they had had their first clashes a thousand years before. The last years of the war of the corsairs led straight into the first years of the long struggle for Greek Independence, a struggle which has always had as much, if not more, religious motivation as the activities of these Maltese and Barbary corsairs.

Bibliography and Notes

LIST OF ABBREVIATIONS

AIM	Archives of the Inquisition in Malta
Annales	*Annales: économies, societés, civilisations*
AOM	Archives of the Order in Malta
ASCJ	Archives of the Superior Courts of Justice
C. de T.	*Cahiers de Tunisie*
Lawsuits	*Tribunal Armamentorum. Acta Originalia**
LCS	*Liber Conciliorum Status*
Lib. Bull.	*Liber Bullarum*
NAV	*Notarial Archives, Valletta*
R.A.	*Revue Africaine*
Reg. Suppl. et Sentent	*Register Supplementorum et Sententiarum*
Revue d'Istanbul	*Revue de la Faculté des Sciences Economiques de l'Université d'Istanbul*
RML	Royal Malta Library
R.T.	*Revue Tunisienne*
TAAO	*Tribunal Armamentorum Actorum Originalium**
Trib. Arm.	*Tribunal Armamentorum*

*N.B. These are two different series.

Chapter 1

BIBLIOGRAPHY

No general study of the Mediterranean in the seventeenth and eighteenth centuries exists. Nor, indeed are there anything like as many monographs as for the fifteenth and sixteenth centuries. The seventeenth and eighteenth centuries were a time of relative decline for Mediterranean countries, and since historians tend to be nationalistic and like to write about success, this period has been relatively ignored by local historians.

I have found the following general books most useful:

BRAUDEL, Fernand: *La Méditerranée et le monde méditerranéen à l'époque de Philippe II* (2nd edition. Paris, 1966). This great work remains the best introduction to the area as a whole. Although written about the second half of the sixteenth century, much of Braudel's work remains relevant to the later period.

BRAUDEL, Fernand: *L'économie de la Méditerranée au XVIIe siècle, C. de T.*, **iv** (1956). A supplement to the above.

AUPHAN, P.: *Histoire de la Méditerranée* (Paris, 1962). A good summary of Mediterranean political history.

ANDERSON, R. C.: *Naval Wars in the Levant, 1559–1853* (Liverpool, 1952). A dry but useful study of naval warfare.

GIBB, H. A. R. and BOWEN, Harold: *Islamic Society and the West*, vol. i, *Islamic Society in the Eighteenth Century*, pt. i (1950). A very useful study of Ottoman society.

MCNEILL, W. H.: *Europe's Steppe Frontier* (Chicago, 1964). A very good introduction to Ottoman political history in its relationship with general themes of European history.

Studies helping to give an understanding of Turkish commerce and economy are:

STAVRIANOS, L.: *The Balkans since 1453* (New York, 1958).

STOIANOVICH, T.: 'The Conquering Balkan Orthodox Merchant', *Journal of Economic History*, **xx** (1960).

GÜÇER, L.: 'Le commerce intérieur des ceréales dans l'Empire Ottoman pendant la seconde moitié du XVIe siècle', *Revue d'Istanbul* (1949–50).

SVORONOS, N.: *Le commerce de Salonique au XVIIIe siècle* (Paris, 1956).

MANTRAN, R.: *Istanbul dans la seconde moitié du XVIIe siècle* (Paris, 1962).

Much has been written on the development of French commerce in the Mediterranean, but the work of Paul Masson written at the beginning of this century still remains important. See in particular:

Histoire du commerce français dans le Levant au XVIIe siècle (Paris, 1896).
Histoire du commerce français dans le Levant au XVIIIe siècle (Paris, 1911).

Histoire des Establissements et du commerce français dans l'Afrique barbaresque, 1560–1793 (Paris, 1903).

BERGASSE, Louis and RAMBERT, Gaston: *Histoire du Commerce de Marseilles*, **iv**. *De 1599 à 1789* (Paris, 1954).

PARIS, Robert: ibid., **v**. *De 1660 à 1789: Le Levant* (Paris 1957). These two volumes of the massive *Histoire du Commerce de Marseilles* bring Masson up to date.

The following works tell of the rise and decline of English naval power and commerce in the Levant during the period:

CORBETT, Sir Julian: *England and the Mediterranean*, 2 vols. (1904). Describes the growth of English naval power in the area.

WOOD, A.: *History of the Levant Company* (Oxford, 1935).

DAVIS, Ralph: 'England and the Mediterranean, 1570–1670', FISHER, F.J. (ed.): *Essays in the Economic and Social History of Tudor and Stuart England* (Cambridge, 1961).

DAVIS, Ralph: *Aleppo and Devonshire Square* (1967).

Works showing the effect of privateering:

TENENTI, A.: *Piracy and The Decline of Venice, 1580–1615* (Eng. trans 1957); the best analysis of the effect of piracy and privateering on a particular area.

MATHIEX, Jean: 'Traffic et prix de l'homme en Méditerranée aux XVIIe et XVIIIe siècles', *Annales*, **ix** (1954) and 'Sur la marine marchande barbaresque au XVIIIe siècle', *Annales*, **xiii** (1958). These works show the effect of religious privateering on the Mediterranean as a whole during this period.

Bibliography on the Barbary and Maltese corsairs will be given in their relevant sections.

NOTES

1   Sir William Stirling-Maxwell, *Don John of Austria* (1883), p. 86.

2   W. H. Lewis, *Levantine Adventurer, the travels and missions of the Chevalier d'Arvieux, 1652–1697* (1962), p. 114.

3   T. Stoianovich, op. cit.; Peter Earle, 'The commercial development of Ancona, 1479–1551', *Economic History Review*, 2nd. ser., **xxii** (1969), pp. 40–4; and E. Rivkin, 'Marrano-Jewish Entrepreneurship and the Ottoman Mercantilist Probe in the Sixteenth Century', paper read at the Third International Conference of Economic Historians held at Munich, 1965.

4   Quoted in Rouse Ball, *Mathematical Recreations and Essays* (1911).

5   R. G. Marsden, *Documents relating to the Law and Custom of the Sea* (1915), **i**, p. xxvii.

6   On the subject of the French galleys see Paul Bamford, 'Slaves for the Galleys of France, 1665–1700' in John Parker (ed.), *Merchants and Scholars* (Minneapolis, 1965) and ibid. 'The Procurement of Oarsmen for French Galleys, 1660–1748', *American Historical Review*, **lxv** (1959).

7   R. Davis, 'England and the Mediterranean', op. cit.; M. S. Anderson, 'Great Britain and the Barbary States in the Eighteenth Century', *Bull. of the Inst. of Hist. Res.* **xxix** (1956).

8   J. Mathiex, 'Sur la marine', op. cit. p. 89.

9   For the Preziosi see below, p. 182; for the Djellouli see Lucette Valensi, 'Esclaves chrétiens et esclaves noirs à Tunis au XVIIe siècle', *Annales*, **xxii**, (1967).

10 Cf. K. H. Andrews, *Elizabethan Privateering* (Cambridge, 1964), pp. 61–123.

Chapter 2

BIBLIOGRAPHY
The Barbary corsairs have, until recently, been poorly served by western historians, most of whom have a clear anti-Moslem, anti-Turkish bias in their writing. This situation is now being slowly remedied, and three modern books have a more objective slant on the subject.

BONO, S.: *I corsari barbareschi* (Turin, 1964). This is the most thorough and contains an excellent bibliography.

FISHER, Sir Godfrey: *Barbary Legend: War, Trade and Piracy in North Africa, 1415–1830* (Oxford, 1957). The author overstates his case in trying to demonstrate the bias of earlier writers.

HUBAC, Pierre: *Les Barbaresques* (Paris, 1949) is very pro-corsair, and tends to glamorize the corsairs more than they deserve.

Of the older books and contemporary accounts of Barbary the ones that I have found most useful are as follows:

D'ARVIEUX, Chevalier Laurent: *Mémoires* (Paris, 1735).

D'ARANDA, E.: *Relation de la captivité et liberté du sieur Emanuel d'Aranda, jadis esclave à Alger* (Brussels, 1662).

DU CHASTELET DES BOYS, R.: *L'Odysée* (La Flèche, 1665), reprinted in *R.A.* **x–xiv** (1866–70).

DAN, Pierre: *Histoire de Barbarie et de ses corsaires* (Paris, 1637).

DE GRAMMONT, H. D.: 'Etudes Algériennes: La course, l'esclavage et la rédemption à Alger', *Revue Historique*, **xxv–xxvi** (1884–5).

GRANDCHAMP, Pierre: *La France en Tunisie au XVIIe siècle*, 10 vols. (Tunis, 1920–33); ibid. 'Une mission délicate en Barbarie au XVIIe siècle: J. B. Salvago, drogman vénitien, à Alger et à Tunis', *R.T.* **xxx** (1937).

DE HAEDO, Diego: 'Topographie et Histoire Générale d'Alger', trans. Dr Monnereau and A. Berbrugger, *R.A.* **xiv–xv** (1870–1).

LANE-POOLE, S.: *The Barbary Corsairs* (1890).

DE PARADIS, Venture, *Alger au XVIIIe siècle* (Algiers, 1898).

SACERDOTI, A.: 'L'esclavage chrétien en Barbarie au XVIIIe siècle', *R.A.*, **xciii** (1949).
Other references will be found in the notes.

NOTES
1 For the political history of Barbary I have relied mainly on Bono, Fisher, Hubac and Lane-Poole, op. cit.; R. Mantran, 'L'évolution des relations entre la Tunisie et l'Empire Ottoman du XVIe au XIXe siècle', *C. de T.*

vii (1959) and E. Rossi, 'Storia della Libia dalla conquista araba al 1911', *Libia*, **ii** (1954).

2 P. Grandchamp, 'Une mission délicate', op. cit. p. 488. For a development of this theme see W. H. McNeill, *Europe's Steppe Frontier* (Chicago, 1964), pp. 111–23.

3 H. D. de Grammont, 'La course', op. cit. p. 14.

4 A. Devoulx, *Le rais Hamidou* (Algiers, 1858), pp, 36–47.

5 J. Pignon, 'La milice des janissaires de Tunis au temps des Deys, 1590–1650', *C. de T.* **iv** (1956), is the most comprehensive study of janissaries in North Africa that I have seen.

6 Venture de Paradis, op. cit. p. 57.

7 Quoted by Pignon, op. cit. p. 307.

8 d'Arvieux, op. cit. v. 251–2.

9 P. Grandchamp, 'Une mission délicate', p. 314.

10 Pignon, p. 307 quoting Salvago.

11 Ibid. p. 325.

12 D'Arvieux, **iv.** 3–4.

13 W. H. Lewis, *Levantine Adventurer, the travels and missions of the Chevalier d' Arvieux, 1653–1697* (1962), p. 25.

14 Mordecai M. Noah, *Travels in England, France, Spain and the Barbary States in the years 1813–14 and 15* (New York, London 1819), p. 372.

15 Devoulx, op. cit. p. 11.

16 Fisher, op. cit. p. 156.

17 Loc. cit.

18 McNeill, op. cit. pp. 31, 137.

19 For introduction of ship-of-war see below pp. 50–52.

20 Dan, op. cit. p. 110.

21 See d'Arvieux, **v.** 246.

22 Quoted by Fisher, op. cit. p. 219.

23 E. Broughton, *Six Years Residence in Algiers* (1839), p. 112.

24 D'Arvieux, **iv.** 21–22. See also J. Pignon, 'Un document inédit sur la Tunisie au début du XVIIe siècle', *C. de T.* **ix** (1961). 124–39.

25 P. Grandchamp, *La Correspondance des Consuls d'Alger, 1690–1742* (Algiers, 1890), p. 71.

26 J. Mathiex, 'Trafic et prix', op. cit. p. 158.

27 D'Arvieux, **iv.** 57. See also Lucette Valensi, 'Les relations commerciales entre la Régence de Tunis et Malte au XVIIIe siècle', *C. de T.* **xi** (1963).

28 G. Cerbella, 'Mare e marinai in Libia', *Libia*, **iii** (1955). 32.

29 For this change of trend see, for Algiers, A. Devoulx, 'La marine de la Regence d'Alger', *R.A.* **xiii** (1869), and for Tunis, Lucette Valensi, 'Enclaves chrétiens et esclaves noirs à Tunis au XVIIIe siècle', *Annales*, **xxii** (1967), pp. 1268, 1287–8.

30 P. Grandchamp, 'Une mission délicate', p. 485.

31 For instance the frigate of Rais Hamidou; see below p. 254. Also d'Arvieux, **v.** 264.

32 See d'Aranda's story of 'The Prudent Corsair', op. cit. pp. 263–66.

33 P. Grandchamp, 'La course', p. 11.

34 Dan, op. cit. p. 262.

35 Dan, p. 258; d'Arvieux, **v.** 266.

36 Fisher, op. cit. p. 155.

37 CSPV, **xxxii.** 233.

38 CSPV, **xxxii.** 308–9; **xxxiii.** 8–9, 13–14, 17.

39 D'Arvieux, **iv.** 105–6.

40 CSPV, **xxxvii**. 88–9.
41 R. G. Marsden, ed. *Documents relating to the Law and Custom of the Sea* (1915), **i**, pp. xxiii, xxvii; **ii**, p. 239.
42 Fisher, op. cit. pp. 215–6.
43 H. D. de Grammont, 'Un Académicien captif à Alger, 1674–1675', *R.A.* **xxvi** (1882). 313–20, 391.
44 Sir Julian Corbett, *England in the Mediterranean* (1904, **i**, 52).
45 Fisher, op. cit. p. 326; A. Devoulx, 'La marine', op. cit. pp. 384–5.
46 Devoulx, loc. cit.
47 De Grammont, *Correspondance*, p. 65, fn. 1; M. S. Anderson, 'Great Britain and the Barbary States in the Eighteenth Century', *Bulletin of the Inst. of Hist. Research*, **xxix** (1956). 99–102.
48 Anderson, op. cit. p. 100.
49 For Christians see Alberto Tenenti, *Piracy and the Decline of Venice, 1580–1615* (1967), p. 38, and see treatment of Greeks below, pp. 112–20. 145–67. For Moslems see d'Arvieux, **v**. 134–5.
50 D'Arvieux, op. cit; de Grammont, *Correspondance*, pp. 63, 130.
51 P. Grandchamp, 'Une mission délicate', pp. 299–322. The anomalous position of Venice in the Mediterranean of the late sixteenth and early seventeenth centuries is well brought out in Tenenti's book cited above. She alone of the nations who fought on the Christian side at Lepanto tried to abide by the peace which followed. But her neutrality made her the victim of all. Moslems stopped and attacked her ships to search for Christian goods. Christians attacked her ships to search for Moslem goods. Slowly her share of Mediterranean trade declined in favour of the new nations from the west with their big and heavily armed ships.
52 De Grammont, *Correspondance*, pp. 80, 132.
53 Ibid. 'La course', p. 36.
54 T. Shaw, *Travels and Observations relating to several parts of Barbary and the Levant*, 2nd ed. (1757), p. 256.
55 For these treaties see Bono, op. cit. pp. 56–66 and his bibliography.
56 Anderson, op. cit. p. 90.
57 Marsden, op. cit. **ii**, p. 239.
58 Grandchamp, 'Une mission délicate', pp. 473–76, 495.
59 For a general discussion of the size of fleets see Bono, pp. 85–91. For Algiers from 1737 to 1827 see Devoulx, 'La marine', *passim*.

Chapter 3

NOTES

1   F. Braudel. *La Méditerranée et le monde méditerranéen* (Paris, 1949), pp. 661–718, especially 715–6, discusses the change in the nature of maritime warfare at this time.

2   See R. C. Anderson, *Naval Wars in the Levant, 1559–1853* (Liverpool, 1952) for an account of these wars.

3   A. Guglielmotti, *Storia della marina pontificia* (Rome, 1886–93), iii, 49 quoted by S. Bono, op. cit. p. 12.

4   For descriptions of the galley and the life of galley slaves see Jurien de la Gravière, *Les derniers jours de la marine à rames* (Paris, 1885); Pantero Pantera, *L'armata navale* (Rome, 1614) and Jean Marteilhe, *The Memoirs of a Protestant condemned to the Galleys of France for his Religion*, trs. Oliver Goldsmith (1895).

5   A classification of galleys can be found in Pantera, op. cit. bk. 1, ch. 4.

6   For an analysis of the time spent under sail or in rowing by Venetian galleys see E. Fasano-Guarini, 'Au XVIe siècle: comment naviguent les galères', *Annales*, **xvi**, (1961).

7   De la Gravière, op. cit. p. 185.

8   See Baron Johann Hermann von Riedesel, *Voyage en Sicile et dans la Grande Grèce* (Lausanne, 1773), p. 63.

9   P. Grandchamp, 'Une mission délicate', op. cit. p. 485.

10 P. W. Bamford, 'The Procurement of Oarsmen for French Galleys, 1660–1748', *American Historical Review*, **lxv** (1959), p. 32.

11 Most writers mention the arrival of the English and Dutch. Detailed references can be found in Jean Pignon, 'Un document inédit sur la Tunisie au début du XVIIe siècle', *C. de T.* **ix** (1961). 191–209.

12 *Relation des voyages*. p. 307 quoted by Pignon, op. cit. p. 208.

13 For the introduction of the ship-of-war (round ship) at Tripoli by a Greek renegade see P. Dan, op. cit. p. 280.

14 Haedo, op. cit. *R.A.* **xv** (1871). p. 45.

15 Albert Devoulx, 'La marine de la Régence d'Alger', *R.A.* **xiii** (1869), pp. 384–420.

16 Dan, op. cit. p. 269; Grandchamp, 'Une mission délicate', op. cit. p. 471.

17 G. B. Salvago, *Africa overo Barbaria* (Padua, 1937), p. 77, quoted by Bono, op. cit. p. 105.

18 Op. cit. p. 41.

19 Grandchamp, 'Une mission délicate', op. cit. pp. 471–3.

20 Sir William Stirling-Maxwell, *Don John of Austria*, (1883), p. 85.

21 ASCJ, *Consolato di Mare*, Manifesti, vol. i.

22 For insurance rates see contemporary notarial records. Volumes contemporary with the register described above are NAV R/55/10 and R/266/13.

23 Voyages to the Atlantic or the Levant might be longer.

24 Op. cit. p. 47. See d'Arvieux, op. cit. **v.** 263 for similar estimates.
25 Op. cit. p. 73, quoted by Bono, op. cit. p. 104.
26 See below pp. 166, 240.
27 Haedo, op. cit. p. 46.
28 See below pp. 144–5.
29 D'Arvieux, op. cit. **v.** 413–4; Grandchamp, 'Une mission délicate', p. 476.
30 Grandchamp, op. cit. p. 477.
31 E. d'Aranda, op. cit. p. 28.
32 For the growth of armed convoys to protect merchant shipping see G. Zeller, 'Le "Convoi" des vaisseaux marchands aux XVIe et XVIIe siècles', *Revue d'Hist. Mod. et Contemp.* **iii** (1956). 67–87, and F. Braudel, 'L'économie de la Méditerranée au XVIIe siècle', *C. de T.* **iv** (1956). 183–7.
33 D'Arvieux, op. cit. **iii.** 375.
34 H. D. de Grammont, 'La Course', op. cit. pp. 28–29. But see Sir Godfrey Fisher, op. cit. pp. 322–3, where he throws some doubt on the extent of the corsairs' raids on the British Isles.
35 See below p. 258.
36 Originally published at La Flèche. The part concerning Algiers was republished as a serial in *R.A.* **x–xiv** (1866–70). The account of his capture appears in **x.** 91–99 and 257–266.
37 J. Foss, *A Journal of the Captivity and Sufferings of John Foss: several years a prisoner at Algiers* (Newburyport, 1798), p. 9.
38 H. D. de Grammont, *Correspondance des Consuls d'Alger, 1690–1742* (Algiers, 1890), p. 26. See also d'Arvieux, **v.** 126–7. French passengers embarked on a ship of Leghorn for fear of falling prisoner to the Spanish with whom France was at war. They met a corsair flying the Dutch flag. The master of the Leghorn ship thought he would deliver his French passengers to their enemies, the Dutch, and share the spoils. In the end the Leghorn crew were enslaved, and their French passengers (technically friends of the Algerians) were released!
39 D'Aranda, op. cit. p. 8.
40 F. Pananti, *Narrative of a Residence in Algiers* (1818), p. 32.
41 D'Aranda, p. 8.
42 Gino Cerbella, 'Mare e marinai in Libia', *Libia,* **iii** (1955). 29.
43 Quoted by Bono, p. 80.
44 H. D. de Grammont, 'Un Académicien captif à Alger, 1674–1675', *R.A.* **xxvi** (1882). 389. This particular story was drawn from *Éloge de M. Vaillant* delivered before the Académie des Inscriptions et Belles-Lettres by M. de Boze, Nov. 1706.
45 Bono, pp. 106–7.
46 D'Arvieux, **iv.** 8.
47 D'Aranda, p. 13.
48 Dan, p. 379.
49 See below for Maltese corsairs; G. Guarnieri, *Origine e sviluppo del porto di Livorno durante il governo di Ferdinando Primo dei Medici* (Leghorn, 1911), pp. 107–11 for Tuscan corsairs; R. G. Marsden, *Law and Custom of the Sea* (1916), **ii.** 51 for English privateers.
50 Op. cit. **v.** 269.
51 See below pp. 128, 153 and K. R. Andrews, *Elizabethan Privateering* (Cambridge, 1964), pp. 40–3.
52 Op. cit. **v.** 262–3.
53 See the experience of the American sailor, John Foss, op. cit. pp. 13–15.
54 Dan, p. 262.
55 Grandchamp, 'Une mission délicate', p. 473.

56 F. Pananti, op. cit. p. 355.

57 Ibid. p. 43.

58 Foss, op. cit. p. 11.

59 G. Loth, 'Le pillage de Saint-Pierre . . . en 1798', *R.T.* **xii** (1905). 9–10.

60 Bono, pp. 131–92 has brought together most of the recorded evidence of the corsairs' raids.

61 See R. Coindreau, *Les corsaires de Salé* (Paris, 1948).

62 Bono, pp. xv, 159–60, disusses this interesting feature of the corsairs' raids, and quotes Italian marxist historians who see in it an example of the struggle against the stranglehold of feudal society. Raffaele Corso, 'Echi leggendari delle incursioni barbareschi sopra Nicotera', *Libia*, **iii** (1953). 38–41, writes about a raid of 1638 by 16 galleys and 2 galleots, which was led by a renegade whose daughter had been seduced by a local nobleman.

63 Bono, chapter v gives an account of the defences against the corsairs.

64 Vincenzo d'Amato, *Memorie historiche . . . di Catanzaro* (Naples, 1670). pp. 229–30.

65 See S. Bono, op. cit. pp. 171–182. One feature of corsair raids which throws little credit on the male sex is the normally high proportion of women and children taken. This is in sharp contrast to the sex ratio of slaves taken from trading vessels.

66 For the Papal navy see Guglielmotti, op. cit. vols. vii–ix. For the Knights of St Stephen see G. Guarnieri, *I Cavalieri di Santo Stefano nella storia della marina italiana, 1562–1859* (Pisa, 1960).

67 For the Maltese navy see below pp. 104–7.

68 Des Boys, op. cit. **x.** 266.

Chapter 4

NOTES

1 Op. cit. **x**. 98.
2 Op. cit. p. 49.
3 H. D. de Grammont, 'Etudes Algériennes: la course', *Revue Historique*, **xxv** (1884). 16.
4 Albert Devoulx, 'Le registre des prises maritimes', *R.A.* **xv** (1871). 74.
5 Ibid. pp. 74–5.
6 This system of division was the commonest practised, though there were some variants. See P. Grandchamp, 'Une mission délicate', op. cit. pp. 742–3. It was also similar to the systems of division in both Malta and Leghorn; for Malta see below pp. 118–22, and for Leghorn, G. G. Guarnieri, *Origine* op. cit. pp. 107–11.
7 Bono, op. cit. pp. 115.
8 Venture de Paradis, op. cit. p. 48.
9 Devoulx, op. cit. p. 75.
10 Venture de Paradis, op. cit. p. 49. For shares in prizes in general see Devoulx, op. cit. *passim*.
11 Pananti, op. cit. p. 349.
12 D'Arvieux, op. cit. **v**. 262–3.
13 Ibid. **iv**. 17.
14 De Grammont, 'La course', pp. 24–5, refers to the habit of destroying ships. Other writers are split between those who say ships went to the State, to the owners, or into the general share-out. See Haedo, op. cit. **xv**. 48; Devoulx, op. cit. p. 72; Venture de Paradis. op. cit. p. 49.
15 P. Grandchamp, *La France en Tunisie*, op. cit. **vi**. 20.
16 Ibid. **viii**. 252.
17 D'Arvieux, **v**. 269–70.
18 See Gino Cerbella, 'Mare e marinai in Libia', *Libia*, **iii** (1955). 26.
19 Haedo, **xv**. 91.
20 De Grammont, *Correspondance*, op. cit. p. 137. For an analysis of many different estimates of the Jewish population in Algiers and Tunis see M. Eisenbeth, 'Les Juifs en Algérie et en Tunisie à l'époque turque, 1516–1830'. *R.A.* **xcvi** (1952). 150–4.
21 Eisenbeth, op. cit. pp. 156–60, 348–50.
22 CSPV, 15 May 1627.
23 De Grammont, *Correspondance*, p. 170. For the normal range of prize cargoes see Devoulx, op. cit. For some exceptional cargoes see de Grammont, 'La course', op. cit. p. 29.
24 Bono, op. cit. pp. 221–222.
25 R. Mantran, *Istanbul dans la seconde moitié du XVIIe siècle* (Paris, 1962), p. 507.

26 N. R. Bennet, 'Christian and Negro Slavery in Eighteenth-Century North Africa', *J. of African History*, **i** (1960). 77 quoting Thomas Nicholson, *An Affecting Narrative of the Captivity* . . . (Boston, n.d.), p. 7.

27 Bono, op. cit. pp. 222–3.

28 D'Aranda, pp. 13–15.

29 A. Sacerdoti, 'L'esclavage chrétien en Barbarie au XVIIIe siècle', *R.A.* **xciii** (1949). 134–5.

30 Ibid. p. 138.

31 D'Arvieux, **iii**. 458.

32 Sir Godfrey Fisher, op. cit. p. 103.

33 Lucette Valensi, 'Esclaves chrétiens et esclaves noirs à Tunis au XVIIIe siècle', *Annales*, **xxii** (1967). 1273–81.

34 Anon, 'Un corsaire algérien au XVIIe siècle', *R.A.* **xxxvi** (1892). 11–17.

35 Bennet, op. cit. p. 70; Foss, op. cit. pp. 20–23.

36 D'Arvieux, **iii**. 499.

37 Bono, op. cit. pp. 220–221 discusses the number of slaves held in Barbary at various times.

38 Haedo, **xv**. 394–5.

39 W. H. Lewis, *Levantine Adventurer, the travels and missions of the Chevalier d'Arvieux, 1653–1697* (1962), p. 125.

40 D'Arvieux, **iv**. 3–5.

41 Ibid. **v**. 228–229.

42 Foss, p. 28.

43 Bono, pp. 225–49, discusses the life of the slaves.

44 D'Aranda, p. 238, quoted by de Grammont, 'L'esclavage', op. cit. p. 25.

45 Bono, pp. 336–49.

46 On ransom organizations see Bono, pp. 283–322.

47 Sacerdoti, op. cit. p. 137.

48 P. Desfeuilles, 'Scandinaves et Barbaresques à la fin de L'Ancien Régime', *C. de T.* **iv**. (1956). 333.

49 Bennet, op. cit. p. 79.

50 See, for instance, d'Arvieux, **iii**. 461.

51 P. Grandchamp, 'Une mission délicate', p. 497.

52 Ibid. *La France en Tunisie.*

53 NAV, R/191/2, fo. 97v.

54 Grandchamp, *Tunisie*, **vi**. 2.

55 Sacerdoti, op. cit. pp. 135–6.

56 Eisenbeth, op. cit. p. 358.

57 De Grammont, 'L'esclavage', p. 15.

58 Grandchamp, *Tunisie*, **iv**. 132–3 quoted by Bono, pp. 218–9.

59 Jean Mathiex, 'Trafic et prix', op. cit. pp. 161–4.

60 Grandchamp, *Tunisie*, **ii**. 43–4 quoted by Bono, p. 335.

61 AOM 462, fo. 305r.

62 Ibid, fo.297v.

63 Haedo uses this expression, 'les turcs de profession', op. cit. **xiv**. 496–7.

64 Loc. cit.

65 Bono, pp. 252–3.

66 For the business engaged in by the brothers see Grandchamp, *Tunisie*, **vi**. 175, 190, 207, 211, etc. For the renegade's flight p. xii.

67 AOM 479, fo.262.

68 Quoted by Marcel Emerit, 'L'essai d'une marine marchande barbaresque au XVIIIe siècle', *C. de T.* **iii** (1955). 363.

69 Grandchamp, *Tunisie*, **vii**. p. x.

Chapter 5

BIBLIOGRAPHY

Although Malta under the Knights of St John has attracted many historians, very few have considered the social and economic history of the island.

I have found the following general works most useful:

BLOUET, Brian: *The Story of Malta* (1967). This is the best summary.

SCHERMAHORN, Elizabeth: *Malta of the Knights* (1929). A popular and useful book.

DEL POZZO, B.: *Historia della sacra religione militare di S. Giovanni Gerosolimitano, detta di Malta* (Verona, 1703). This and the following work are two old books on the history of the Order in Malta which are still very useful.

DE BOISGELIN, Louis: *Ancient and Modern Malta*, 2 vols. (1805).

CAVALIERO, Roderick: *The Last of the Crusaders* (1960) is an admirable study of Malta in the eighteenth century.

ROSSI, E.: *Storia della marina dell'Ordine di S. Giovanni di Gerusaleme, di Rodi e di Malta* (Rome, 1926). The best book on the history of the navy of the Order.

ENGEL, C. E.: *L'Ordre de Malta en la Méditerannée, 1530–1798* (Monaco, 1957). Another useful book on the history of the navy of the Order.

The Maltese corsairs have been discussed by:

CASSAR, Paul: 'The Maltese Corsairs and the Order of St John of Jerusalem', *Catholic Historical Review*, **xlvi** (1960).

CAVALIERO, R. E.: 'The Decline of the Maltese Corso in the XVIIIth Century', *Melita Historica*, **ii** (1959).

MATHIEX, Paul: In the two articles cited in Chapter I. Mathiex coined the phrase used as the title to this chapter.

NOTES

1 On the fortifications of Malta see J. Quentin Hughes, *The Building of Malta* (1967), pp. 20–38.

2 G. E. Mainwaring (ed.), *The Diary of Henry Teonge, 1675–1679* (1927), p. 58.

3 Dal Pozzo, op. cit. **i.** 590.

4 Blouet, op. cit. p. 122. G. F. Abela, *Della descrittione di Malta* (Malta, 1647), p. 64 describes the western part of the island as 'inabitata'.

5 Blouet, op. cit. pp. 91–2.

6 Sir William Young, *A Journal of a Summer's Excursion . . . in the year 1772* (1777) pp. 85–86.

7 RML 23, 'Breve relazione . . . del Cardinale Federico Borromeo', fo. 239r.

8 Louis de Boisgelin, op. cit. p. 10.

9   J. Godechot, 'La France et Malte au XVIIIe siècle', *Revue Historique*, **ccvi** (1951). p. 67.

10 R. Cavaliero, *The Last of the Crusaders* (1960), p. 85.

11 Ibid. p. 11.

12 Ibid. pp. 28–29.

13 Rossi, op. cit. p. 78.

14 For these wars see R. C. Anderson. op. cit.

15 Cavaliero, *The Last of the Crusaders*, pp. 105–110.

16 Rossi, p. 57.

17 Cavaliero, pp. 15–16.

18 G. Wettinger, 'The Galley-Convicts and Buonavoglie in Malta during the rule of the Order', *Jnl. of the Faculty of Arts*, **iii** (1965).

19 Tenenti, op. cit. p. 39.

20 Op. cit. p. 231.

21 Paul Cassar, op. cit. p. 142.

22 Dal Pozzo, op. cit. pp. 493–4. The rules governing the *corso* are in RML, MS 152.

23 Many examples of the oaths sworn by corsair captains can be found. See for example ASCJ, *TAAO*, **ii**, fos. 1–3.

24 AIM, *Memorie* di Mons Ludovico Gualtieri, fos. 193–8.

25 AOM 258, *LCS* 1647.

26 AOM 264, *LCS* 1699.

27 AOM 1214, fo. 13. Letter from the Bailli de Souvré, Ambassador of the Order in Paris to the Grand Master, dated 20.11.1663.

28 AOM 1214 contains letters from de Souvré to the Grand Master, 1662–9. AOM 1558 contains letters in French from the Grand Masters to the Ambassador, King Louis and Colbert.

29 AOM 261, *LCS* 1665, fos. 19–20.

30 AOM 1558, fo. 75, GM to Colbert, 7.3.1666.

31 AOM 1558, fo. 60, GM to de Souvré, February 1666.

32 AOM 261, fos. 19–20.

33 AOM 262, *LCS*, fo. 12v. 26.5.1673.

34 Dal Pozzo, op. cit. **i**. 276, 310, 313, 352, 356.

35 AOM 1465, Perellos to Sacchetti, 20.2.1704.

36 AIM, *Memorie*, di Mons. Ludovico Gualtieri, fo. 193.

37 RML, MS 392, 'Costituzioni del Consolato di Mare'.

38 For a discussion of this see R. Cavaliero, 'The Decline . . .', op. cit.

39 See ASCJ, *Trib. Arm.* Memoriali, vols. i and 11.

40 Cavaliero, op. cit. p. 234.

41 Ibid. p. 235.

42 NAV R/394/11, fo. 417.

43 AIM, *Memorie* di Mons Fabrizio Serbelloni, fos. 322–327.

44 AIM, *Memorie* di Gualtieri, fo. 200.

45 AIM, *Memorie* di Mons. Gio. F. Stoppani, fo. 139r.

46 Ibid. fos. 155–62.

47 Ibid. fos. 149–67. See also NAV, R/394/11; R/374/5–7; R/182/25–29 for notaries who registered contracts relating to corsairs flying the Tuscan and Spanish flags.

48 AIM, *Memorie* di Serbelloni, fo. 350.

49 For the oaths of Tuscan corsairs see the volumes of notaries referred to above, e.g. NAV R/374/5 fos. 231–4.

40 Cavaliero, op. cit. p. 235.

51 NAV, R/394/11 fo. 28v.

52 AOM 1566, fo. 1832. GM Vilhena to the Bailo Desmesnes, Ambassador in Paris, 16.4.1732. The use of the Spanish flag by Maltese corsairs caused diplomatic problems with England, when it was found that two corsairs were capturing English ships and selling them in Malta during the War of 1718–20. M. S. Anderson, 'Great Britain and Malta before 1798', *Mariner's Mirror*, **xl** (1954), p. 131.

53 AIM, *Memorie* di Stoppani fos. 168–72; di C. F. Durini fo. 179; di Gualtieri fo. 202.

54 AIM, *Memorie* di Durini fo. 202.

55 Cavaliero, op. cit. p. 236.

56 AIM, *Memorie* di Stoppani fos. 197–216.

57 AOM 544, fo. 175. 28.5.1740.

58 Records can be found in AOM, *Libri Bullarum*; RML 429, *Bandi e prammatiche della Gran Corte della Castellania* and ASCJ, *Trib. Arm.* Memoriali.

59 ASCJ, *Trib. Arm.* Reg. Suppl. et Sentent. vol. i, fos. 130–133.

60 Taking an average of 450 men for each of the seven galleys then in commission, 200 slaves, 180 soldiers, 30–40 sailors plus 30–40 reserves.

61 ASCJ, *Consolato di Mare*, Manifesti, vol. i.

62 S. Bono, *I corsari barbareschi* (Turin, 1964), p. 88.

63 Albert Devoulx, 'La marine de la Régence d'Alger', *Revue Africaine*, **xiii** (1869), pp. 391–2.

Chapter 6

NOTES

1   See above pp. 107–8.
2   These applications and the Commissioners' reports can be found in ASCJ, *Trib. Arm.* Memoriali, vols. 1 and 2, 1704–34.
3   Ibid. vol. i, fo. 87r.
4   Ibid, vol. i, fo. 3v.
5   Letters patent in AOM, *Libri Bullarum.*
6   ASCJ, *Trib. Arm.* Memoriali, vol. ii, fo. 8.
7   RML MS 152, Rubrics 36–42.
8   Ibid. Rubric 49.
9   Loc. cit.
10 ASCJ, *TAAO*, vol. ii, fo. 100v.
11 ASCJ, *Lawsuits*, 2nd. ser., Filza 12, No. 8, fo. 17.
12 Ibid. 2nd. ser. Filza 12, No. 15, fos. 2–5.
13 Loc. cit.
14 ASCJ, *Lawsuits*, 2nd. ser., Filza 12, No. 13, fo. 27r.
15 For an example of a bottomry bond see ASCJ, *TAAO*, vol. ii, fo. 3.
16 ASCJ, *TAAO*, vol. 8.
17 This can be done by examining contemporary notarial records.
18 For an example of a *conserva* agreement see ASCJ, *Trib. Arm.* Verbal Vendita Schiavi, vol. i, fo. 393r.
19 ASCJ, *Trib. Arm.* Reg. Suppl. et Sentent. vol. i, fos. 130–133.
20 For an example of a *scrivano*'s oath see ASCJ, *TAAO*, vol. ii, fos. 7–8.
21 For receipts and disbursements of the *Cassa* see ASCJ, *TAAO*, vols. iii, viii, etc.
22 ASCJ, *TAAO*, vol. 3, fo. 94v.
23 Ibid. fo. 135r.
24 Ibid. fo. 179r.
25 Ibid. vol. 9, fo. 30v.
26 For commercial bottomry and insurance contracts see contemporary notarial records. E.g. NAV R/125/10; R/191/2; R/230/18.
27 ASCJ, *TAAO*, vol. 6, fos. 50, 53, 85.
28 ASCJ, *Lawsuits*, 1st. ser., Filza 5, No. 1, fo. 3.
29 Ibid. fos. 3–8.

Chapter 7

NOTES

1 For Barbary ships see above pp. 48–53.
2 Sir Julian Corbett, *England in the Mediterranean* (1904), **i**. 36.
3 AOM 461, fo. 292v.
4 Several eighteenth-century log-books survive in the collections ASCJ, *Trib. Arm.* Giornali and Verbal Vendita Schiavi.
5 ASCJ, *Trib. Arm.* Memoriali, vol. i, fo. 130v.
6 AOM, 453, fo. 314r.
7 G. E. Mainwaring (ed.), *The Diary of Henry Teonge, 1675-1679* (1927), p. 128.
8 See Louis Bergasse and Gaston Rambert, *Histoire du commerce de Marseille,* **iv** (Paris, 1952), pp. 430–57, for a discussion of French shipping.
9 AIM, *Memorie* di Mons. G. F. Stoppani, fos. 149–53.
10 NAV, R/374/6 fos. 302–11.
11 ASCJ, *Trib. Arm.* Reg. Suppl. et Sentent. vol. i, fos. 131–133.
12 Ibid. Memoriali, vol. i, fo. 8r.
13 Ibid. vol. i, fo. 71r.
14 Ibid. vol. i, fos. 123–6.
15 Ibid. vol. ii, fo. 185.
16 Dal Pozzo, op. cit. **i**. 800.
17 Ibid. **ii**. 329–30.
18 H. A. R. Gibb and Harold Bowen, *Islamic Society and the West*, vol. i, *Islamic Society in the Eighteenth Century*, pt. i (1950), pp. 96–98.
19 Ibid. p. 105.
20 R. C. Anderson, *Naval Wars in the Levant, 1559–1853* (Liverpool, 1952) pp. 221–234.
21 See pp. 53–54.
22 A. Boppe (ed.), *Journal et Correspondance de Gédoyn 'Le Turc', consul de France à Alep, 1623–1625* (Paris, 1909), p. 106 uses this expression to describe the guns in the Straits of Gallipoli, but later (p. 141) Gédoyn notes: 'I saw the cannon in disorder without wheels ... and they told me freely that they had only three gunners to serve 200 mouths of fire, which make a show and a parade outside.'
23 ASCJ, *Trib. Arm.* Reg. Suppl. et Sentent. vol. i, fos. 130–133. Dal Pozzo, **ii**. 383.
24 See below pp. 241–2.
25 ASCJ, *Lawsuits*, 1st. ser., Filza 5, No. 7.
26 J. Mathiex, 'Trafic et prix', op. cit. p. 157, attributes the decline of the Turkish and North African marine almost entirely to the activities of Christian corsairs, but he is probably going too far.
27 ASCJ, *Lawsuits*, 1st. ser., Filza 1, No. 11, fo. 2.
28 ASCJ, *TAAO*, vol. iii, fos. 37–38.
29 ASCJ, *Trib. Arm.* Giornali, No. 7, fos. 3–4.

30 ASCJ, *Lawsuits*, 2nd. ser., Filza 12, No. 11, fos. 173–4. Captain Preziosi engaged two land pilots with rights to 10 per cent of the value of all slaves captured ashore while they acted as guides.

31 François Billacois (ed.), *L'Empire du Grand Turc vu par un sujet de Louis XIV, Jean Thévenot* (Paris, 1965), pp. 279–85. My translation.

32 Ibid. p. 274.

33 ASCJ, *Lawsuits*, 1st. ser., Filza 1, No. 11, fo. 3.

34 Ibid. 2nd. ser., Filza 12, No. 11, fo. 139.

35 ASCJ, *Trib. Arm.* Memoriali, vol i, fo. 71.

36 See ASCJ, *Lawsuits*, 1st. ser., Filza 4, No. 7. The barber of a corsair ship is sued for the price of some slaves who died because of his negligence.

37 AOM, 262, *LCS* 1679, fo. 84r.

38 ASCJ, *Lawsuits*, 2nd. ser., Filza 12, No. 11, fos. 142–3.

39 Ibid. fo. 173.

40 ASCJ, *Lawsuits*, 1st. ser., Filza 4, No. 10, fo. 3.

41 Ibid. 1st. ser., Filza 5, No. 7, fo. 2.

42 Loc. cit. fos. 9–10.

43 See below chapter 11.

44 AIM, *Memorie* di Stoppani, fos. 149–153.

Chapter 8

NOTES

1 For more detail on the selling and ransoming of prizes in the Levant and Barbary see pp. 158–61, 240–1.
2 ASCJ, *Trib. Arm.* Registrum Prese (Armamenti).
3 For the activities of these men and several others who engaged in similar business see ASCJ, *TAAO*, vol. ii; NAV R230/18 and AOM 738, *Treasury Contracts (1645–62)*.
4 Registrum Prese, op. cit. fos. 33–34.
5 Godfrey Wettinger, 'The Galley-Convicts and Buonavoglie in Malta during the rule of the Order', *Journal of the Faculty of Arts of the Royal University of Malta*, **iii** (1965), p. 29.
6 Ibid. 'Coron Captives in Malta', *Melita Historica*, **ii** (1959), p. 220.
7 P. W. Bamford, 'The Procurement of Oarsmen for French Galleys, 1660–1748', *American Historical Review*, **lxv** (1959), p. 33.
8 Ibid. p. 47.
9 Registrum Prese, op. cit. fo. 13v.
10 Ibid. fo. 15v.
11 Jean Dumont, Baron de Carlscroon [Le Sieur du Mont], *A New Voyage to the Levant*, Eng. trans. (1696), p. 138.
12 The best source for this sort of information are notarial records.
13 Wettinger, 'Coron . . . ', op. cit.
14 AOM 646, p. 14.
15 Ibid. p. 126.
16 Ibid. p. 215.
17 Ibid. p. 83.
18 Ibid. pp. 181–2.
19 See above p. 91.
20 AOM 469 c277v.
21 AOM 465 c307v.
22 AOM 464 c381v.
23 NAV R191/2 c300.
24 NAV R412/26 cc201–3.
25 Pierre Grandchamp, *La France en Tunisie au XVIIe siècle* (Paris, 1920). **viii**. 140.
26 J. Mathiex, 'Trafic et prix de l'homme en Méditerranée aux XVIIe et XVIIIe siècles', *Annales*, **ix** (1954). pp. 160–4.
27 RML MS429, vol. ii. fo. 48r. An order by the Gran Corte della Castellania, made in 1738, condemned corsair captains who ransomed renegades to the galleys for life, so perhaps they discontinued the practice!
28 P. Grandchamp, op. cit. **vii**, p. xii.
29 For these and other regulations regarding slaves see AOM 1759, section 46 and AOM 270, *LCS* 23.6.1749.

30 RML MS 1146(1), pp. 695–6.
31 AOM 1759, fos. 409–11.
32 D'Arvieux, op. cit. **iv**. 317.
33 See R. Cavaliero, *The Last of the Crusaders*, p. 78.
34 See applications for such payment, e.g. AOM 646, fos. 105–6, 139.
35 AOM 646, fos. 39–40.
36 AOM 650, fo. 132.
37 For accounts of the rebellion of the slaves see RML 436; AIM, *Memorie* di Mons. Passionei, fos. 66ff.
38 The new rules are in AOM 270, fos. 105–110.
39 Patrick Brydone, *A Tour through Sicily and Malta* (1773), **i**. 321.
40 J. Mathiex, op. cit. p. 159, fn. 3.

Chapter 9

NOTES

1 AIM, *Lettere*, Cyprus.
2 ASCJ, *Trib. Arm.* Memoriali, vol. i, fo. 120.
3 AOM, 261, fos. 19–20.
4 Paul de Saumur. Information on his career from the *Bibliographie Universelle*.
5 Some of these can be found in Dal Pozzo, op. cit. E.g. **i.** 545, 761–3, 800, 806, 826; **ii.** 41, 291, 328–30, 348, 356–8, 383–5.
6 ASCJ, *Trib. Arm.* Memoriali. Capt. Napulon was the captain killed in action, vol. i, fo. 30.
7 AOM, 478, fos. 473–5.
8 AOM, 1933, fo. 253v.
9 ASCJ, *Lawsuits*, 1st. ser., Filza 6, No. 11, fo. 19.
10 Ibid. Filza 5, No. 7, fo. 11r.
11 Ibid. Filza 6, No. 6, fo. 20r.
12 Ibid. Filza 5, No. 7, fos. 2–3.
13 Loc. cit. fos. 9–10.
14 D'Arvieux, op cit. **iv.** 312–313. Cf. the mutiny in Ch. XII below, pp. 222–5.
15 ASCJ, *Lawsuits*, 1st. ser., Filza 6, No. 12.
16 Ibid. 2nd. ser., Filza 12, No. 8, fo. 19.
17 AIM, *Memorie* di Mons. F. Serbelloni, fo. 349.
18 Paul Cassar, 'The Maltese Corsairs and the Order of St John of Jerusalem', *Catholic Historical Review*, **xlvi**, (1960), p. 147.
19 Dumont, op. cit. p. 342.
20 AOM 262, fo. 84r.
21 ASCJ, *Lawsuits*, 1st. ser., Filza 6, No. 6, fo. 21v.
22 *The Life of Captain Alonso de Contreras*, trans. C. A. Phillips (1926), p. 40.
23 ASCJ, *Lawsuits*, 1st. ser., Filza 4, No. 14, fo. 2. Chaplain's contract.
24 Ibid. Filza 6, No. 6, fo. 16v.
25 ASCJ, *Trib. Arm. Reg. Suppl. et Sentent.* vol. ii, fos. 31–33. The chaplain was suing the heirs of the Captain, who had died. The Court awarded him his coat.
26 ASCJ, *Trib. Arm.* Memoriali, vol. i, fo. 6.
27 ASCJ, *Lawsuits*, 1st. ser., Filza 6, No. 6, fo. 22.
28 Louis Deshayes, baron de Courmenin, *Le voyage de Levant fait par le commandement du roi l'année 1621*, 3rd. ed. (Paris, 1645), pp. 455–6.
29 Le Sieur du Loir, *Les Voyages* (Paris, 1654), pp. 288–94.
30 ASCJ, *Trib. Arm.* Giornali, No. 4.

Chapter 10

1   The original manuscript of Alonso de Contreras' autobiography is in Madrid. Several modern editions and translations have been published. I have relied mainly on the English translation by C. A. Phillips published in 1926, but have also used the edition by M. Serrano y Sanz, *Boletin de la Real Academia de la Historia*, vols. 36–37 (1900) and the French translation by Marcel Lami and Léo Rouanet, *Mémoires du Capitan Alonso de Contreras* (Paris, 1911).

Chapter 11

NOTES

1 ASCJ, *Lawsuits*, 1st. ser., Filza 5, No. 7: Gio Paulo Gimac et altri *v.* Captain Aloisio Gamarra.
2 Ibid. fo. 10r.
3 Ibid. fos. 29–30. Evidence of Enrico Mancuso.
4 RML 477, fo. 202r, 16.5.1659.
5 Ibid. fo. 213v. 5.7.1660.
6 Information on the business activities of merchants can be found in notarial records of the same date. See in particular NAV: R125/10; R230/19; R230/18; R412/26; R213/11 *passim*.
7 *Lawsuits*, vol. cit. fo. 4.
8 Ibid. fos. 2–3.
9 Loc. cit.
10 Ibid. fo. 19v.
11 Ibid. fos. 9–10.
12 e.g. ibid. fo. 20. Evidence of Angelo Casciera.
13 Ibid. fos. 22–23. Evidence of Guillaume Giran.
14 Ibid. fos. 22–32. Evidence of Giran et al. Fos. 35–36. Evidence of purser.
15 Ibid. fo. 2v.
16 *Lawsuits*, vol. cit. fos. 11–16. Evidence of Morello and Grech.
17 ASCJ, *Trib. Arm.* Registrum Prese (Armamenti).
18 Ibid. fo. 2v.
19 Ibid. fo. 9.
20 Ibid. fo. 11. Evidence of Morello.
21 Ibid. fos. 35–36. Evidence of purser, Antitio Grigi.
22 Ibid. fo. 11.
23 ASCJ, *Trib. Arm.* Reg. Suppl. et Sentent. vol. 1, fo. 11.
24 *Lawsuits*, vol. cit. fo. 2v.
25 Ibid. fo. 9r.
26 Ibid. fo. 3r.
27 Ibid. fo. 10r.
28 Ibid. fos. 13–15. Evidence of Giran.
29 Ibid. fo. 2v.
30 Ibid. fo. 9v.
31 Ibid. fos. 13–15. Evidence of Grech.
32 Ibid. fo. 3r.
33 Ibid. fo. 11.
34 Ibid. loc. cit.
35 ASCJ, *Trib. Arm.* Reg. Suppl. et Sentent. vol. 1, fos. 9–10.
36 ASCJ, *TAAO*, vol. 3, fos. 136–7.
37 ASCJ, *Trib. Arm.* Reg. Suppl. et Sentent. vol. 1, fo. 11.

Chapter 12

NOTES

1 The original manuscript of this letter is in Istanbul. A fine German translation was made by Andreas Tietze, 'Die Geschichte von Kerkermeister-Kapitan', *Acta Orientalia*, **xix** (1942). The English translation, which is the basis of this chapter, was done for me by my colleague, John Gillingham, from Tietze's German.

Chapter 13

NOTES

1 RML MS 1213. *Processo de' pirati.*
2 AOM 543 fo. 197r.
3 From references in the log-book and in the court cases referring to the voyage.
4 *Lawsuits.* 2nd. ser., Filza 12/13 fos. 28–32.
5 Ibid. Filza 12/8.
6 The log-books are in the collection ASCJ, *Trib. Arm.* Giornali (Corsari) and are numbers 4 and 10.
7 For these events and the rest of the paragraph see *Lawsuits*, 2nd. ser., Filza 11/15 and Filza 12/14.
8 Ibid. Filza 11/15.
9 ASCJ, *Trib. Arm.* Reg. Suppl. et Sentent. vol. ii, fo. 268r.
10 *Lawsuits.* 2nd. ser., Filza 12/13.
11 Ibid. Filza 12/8.
12 Ibid. Filza 12/8 fo. 17. These three captains with a total of 59 years' experience as corsairs between them gave their professional opinion on a point in Natale *v.* Rossi.
13 ASCJ, *Trib. Arm.* Reg. Suppl. et Sentent. vol. ii.
14 Ibid. fos. 191–5.
15 *Lawsuits.* 2nd. ser., Filza 12/11.
16 The next section is based on log-book 4.
17 RML MS 429 fo. 158v.
18 AOM 548 fo. 149r.
19 *Lawsuits.* 2nd. ser., Filza 13/13.
20 RML 689. See also below pp. 268–9.

Chapter 14

NOTES

1 Translated from the Arabic by Albert Devoulx in his book *Le raïs Hamidou* (Algiers, 1858). Most of this chapter is based on this book.
2 Ibid. pp. 27–28.
3 Elizabeth Broughton, *Six Years Residence in Algiers* (1839), p. 200.
4 Ibid. p. 19.
5 Devoulx, op. cit., p. 55.
6 Broughton, p. 200.
7 Filippo Pananti, *Narrative of a Residence in Algiers* (1818), pp. 25–66.
8 Broughton, p. 199.
9 Mordecai M. Noah, *Travels in England, France, Spain and the Barbary States in the years 1813–14 and 15* (New York, London, 1819), pp. 371–3. See also E. Dupuy, *Americains et Barbaresques, 1776–1824* (Paris, 1910), pp. 303–5.

Chapter 15

NOTES

1   For Malta see pp. 108–20; for Barbary pp. 40–1.
2   For detail on treaties see S. Bono, op. cit. pp. 56–65.
3   Albert Devoulx, 'Le registre des prises maritimes', *R.A.* **xv** (1871). 71.
4   Quoted by Bono, p. 75.
5   For the Grand Master's declaration see R. Cavaliero. 'The Decline . . .', op. cit. p. 232. For the corsair's execution AIM, *Lettere*, 'Smyrna', 20.3.1747.
6   References to licences are based on AOM, *Libri Bullarum* and RML, 429.
7   AIM, *Memorie di Mons. Paulo Passionei*, fos. 88–91.
8   Cavaliero, op. cit. p. 233.
9   For the accounts of Maltese corsairs flying the flag of Monaco see RML 689.
10 Girolamo Preziosi and Giovan Francesco di Natale. See Chapter 13.
11 AIM, *Lettere*, 'Cyprus', n.p.
12 N. Svoronos, *Le commerce de Salonique au XVIII siècle* (Paris, 1956), p. 128.
13 Ibid. pp. 128–31.
14 Ibid. pp. 131–33.
15 M. S. Anderson, 'Russia in the Mediterranean, 1788–1791: a little-known chapter in the history of naval warfare and privateering', *The Mariner's Mirror*, **xlv** (1959), p. 31.
16 ASCJ, *Trib. Arm.* Verbal Vendita Schiavi. For the period 1763–92 see also J. Godechot, 'La course maltaise le long des côtes barbaresques à la fin du XVIIIe siècle', *R.A.* **xcvi** (1952).
17 Verbal Vendita Schiavi, op. cit. fo. 202v.
18 Ibid. fo. 40.
19 AOM, 623, fos. 74–121.
20 ASCJ, *Trib. Arm.* Reg. Sententiarum, vol. iii, fos. 232–35.
21 Quoted by Victor Denaro, 'The French in Malta', *Scientia*, **xxix** (1963).
22 H. P. Scicluna, *Actes et documents pour servir à l'histoire de l'occupation française de Malte, 1798–1800* (Malta, 1923), p. 145.
23 ASCJ, *Vice Admiralty Courts of Malta*, 'Oster Risoer'. See also 'Il Centauro' captured by the 'Corvo', Giuseppe Debono, commander.

Index